AF078422

JFK An American Coup D'etat

The Truth Behind The Kennedy Assassination

Colonel John Hughes-Wilson

16pt

Copyright Page from the Original Book

Published by John Blake Publishing Ltd,
3 Bramber Court, 2 Bramber Road,
London W14 9PB, England

www.johnblakepublishing.co.uk

www.facebook.com/Johnblakepub facebook
twitter.com/johnblakepub twitter

ISBN: 978-1-78219-478-1

All rights reserved. No part of this publication may be reproduced, stored in a retrieval system, or in any form or by any means, without the prior permission in writing of the publisher, nor be otherwise circulated in any form of binding or cover other than that in which it is published and without a similar condition including this condition being imposed on the subsequent publisher.

British Library Cataloguing-in-Publication Data:

A catalogue record for this book is available from the British Library.

Design by www.envydesign.co.uk

Printed in Great Britain by CPI Group (UK) Ltd

1 3 5 7 9 10 8 6 4 2

Copyright © John Hughes-Wilson 2013

The right of John Hughes-Wilson to be identified as the Author of this Work has been asserted by him in accordance with the Copyright, Designs and Patents Act, 1988.

Papers used by John Blake Publishing are natural, recyclable products made from wood grown in sustainable forests. The manufacturing processes conform to the environmental regulations of the country of origin.

Every attempt has been made to contact the relevant copyright-holders, but some were unobtainable. We would be grateful if the appropriate people could contact us.

TABLE OF CONTENTS

A NOTE ON THE SOURCES ... iv
INTRODUCTION ... vi
   1 : PROLOGUE: WASHINGTON DC, 21 JANUARY 1961 ... 1
   2 : THE FLAWED PRESIDENT ... 5

PART 1 : JFK'S PROBLEMS ... 13
   3: CROOKS AND CUBA ... 13
   4: THE BAY OF PIGS AND OTHER CRISES ... 20
   5 : ALL THE PRESIDENT'S WOMEN ... 36
   6 : MARILYN MONROE – ANATOMY OF A COVER-UP ... 54

PART 2 : KENNEDY'S ENEMIES ... 73
   7 : BROTHERS IN ARMS – THE CUBAN EXILES AND THE CIA ... 73
   8 : JFK VERSUS THE MAFIA ... 89
   9 : JFK VERSUS BIG OIL ... 101
   10 : JFK VERSUS THE GOVERNMENT OF MONEY ... 107
   11 : THE PROBLEM OF LBJ ... 126
   12 : ISRAEL AND HER FRIENDS ... 141

PART 3 : THE PLOT IS HATCHED ... 163
   13 : THE ANTI-KENNEDY COALITION ... 163
   14 : THE WIDENING CIRCLE ... 180
   15 : PLANNING THE AMBUSH ... 196
   16 : THE KENNEDYS' COUP IN CUBA ... 206

PART 4 : TO KILL A PRESIDENT ... 219
   17: THE ROAD TO DALLAS ... 219
   18 : DALLAS ON THE DAY ... 249
   19: AFTERSHOCKS ... 266
   20: SILENT WITNESSES – THE WOUNDS ... 293
   21 : THE VOICE OF THE GUNS ... 307
   21: THE CAMERA CANNOT LIE – CAN IT? ... 320
   23: ANOTHER 'SHOT HEARD ROUND THE WORLD' ... 337
   24 : OFFICER TIPPIT ... 344

25 : DEAD MEN TELL NO TALES – LEE HARVEY OSWALD	362
26 : THE SPY WHO CAME IN FROM THE COLD – THE CURIOUS CAREER OF LEE HARVEY OSWALD	377
27 : FROM A VIEW TO A KILL – JACK RUBY AND OSWALD'S MURDER	401
PART 5 : THE GREAT COVER-UP	419
28 : COVERING THE TRACKS	419
29 : WARREN – AND A WHITEWASH	446
30: DEAD SILENT?	470
31 : THE STORY UNRAVELS AND THE TRUTH EMERGES	492
32 : WHO KILLED JFK?	503
33: HOW THE DEED WAS DONE	529
34 : CONCLUSION	550
APPENDIX	559
BIBLIOGRAPHY	569
FRONT COVER FLAP	584
BACK COVER FLAP	587
Index	589

Fifty Years On, A Former British Intelligence Officer Reveals The Truth Behind The Greatest Conspiracy Of All Time

BY THE SAME AUTHOR:

Military Intelligence Blunders and Cover-Ups

The Puppet Masters: Spies, Traitors and the Real Forces Behind World Events

Blindfold and Alone: Military Executions in the Great War (with Cathryn Corns)

A Brief History of the Cold War: From the Bolshevik Revolution to the Fall of the Wall

A History of the First World War in 100 Objects (Imperial War Museum)

This book is dedicated to:
Andy Hayward
Anna Jordan-Veltrop
and my wife Lynn,
all of whom helped to make it possible.

***

Who will rid me of this turbulent priest?
King Henry II of England, speaking of Thomas à Becket

Oh! what a tangled web we weave,
When first we practise to deceive!
Sir Walter Scott, Marmion

A NOTE ON THE SOURCES

Because many of the topics I have written about in this book are not only highly contentious but will undoubtedly provoke indignant challenges, I am compelled to weary the reader with extensive indications of my sources, so that the reader may rest assured that even what appears to be the least credible part of the narrative is securely rooted in contemporary records, archived documentation, or secondary sources which have been broadly accepted as fact. The full notes are available online at www.jfkcoupdetat.wordpress.com.

Where the jigsaw of evidence lacks the occasional piece, I have followed the logic of 'Ockham's razor', which says that the simplest and most obvious explanation of events is usually the correct one.

This is a book written as an intelligence assessment of the best evidence available to us, not as some prosecuting attorney's wearisome legal argument 'beyond all *possible* doubt.' That is impossible given the fact that so much evidence remains locked away – still.

If the narrative therefore sometimes lacks lawyers' 'courtroom evidence' it is because the people and organisations who shot and killed Jack Kennedy went to extraordinary lengths to keep their tracks well covered from lawyers, courts and nosy journalists. There are – unsurprisingly – few signed confessions to the murder of the President of the USA and the criminal knowledge of the deed. Assassins don't leave tidy paper trails for academic researchers.

What we have instead is the first full assembly of the pieces of the great jigsaw puzzle of information and intelligence that we know about the assassination of JFK. There are, inevitably, some gaps.

But we can make shrewd assessments of these few missing pieces. From that evidence there can only be one logical conclusion, *beyond reasonable doubt.*

INTRODUCTION

The assassination of John Kennedy was a world-shattering event.

The world was a very different place in 1963 and the idea that the President of the United States could be gunned down in broad daylight was almost unbelievable. In America men and women wept openly in the streets for their dead leader. But the police and the FBI seemed to be in control and so the murder of the assassin soon afterwards seemed at the time no more than natural justice. The Warren Commission's report explained what had happened. Vietnam, the Beatles, rioting on the streets and the whole roaring tide of the 1960s soon made the Kennedy story fade to a distant memory, and then one of those curious benchmarks of history as 'a day everyone could remember where they were'.

But events soon began to unpick the original version of events. It turned out that official report was little more than a crude government whitewash designed to hide the real truth. Even American presidents admitted as much. President Nixon memorably confessed in private that 'The Warren Report was the biggest hoax ever perpetrated'on the American public. It began to emerge that maybe Lee Harvey Oswald, the original 'lone nut gunman', may not have acted on his own; others were involved, too. That meant no lone gunman, but a conspiracy.

However, dark theories of conspiracy are nowadays beneath the dignity of serious metropolitan intellectuals and *bien pensants.* The conspiracies behind the stories of Julius Caesar, Mary Queen of Scots, the French and American Revolutions and the July bomb plot to kill Hitler are accepted as part of the historical record – but, for some strange reason, never a conspiracy to murder John F. Kennedy. This dismissive and prejudiced attitude to facts as they emerge only serves to help those who want to suppress the truth for their own dark reasons.

***

The sheer weight of evidence and the minutiae surrounding the murder of President Kennedy has been trawled over – sometimes with great effort – by many dedicated individuals over half a century. They have done an immense amount of research and their theories are fascinating, if often conflicting. However, the big question has always been, what does it all mean? It is as if all the pieces of a giant jigsaw have been laid on the table but no one seems to have assembled the puzzle into a coherent picture.

This book attempts to put that jigsaw together and to answer the big question: who really shot JFK? And, more important still, exactly *why* was he shot?

In the Kennedy case this is not easy. Someone has been laying a smokescreen of disinformation; a lot of smokescreens in fact, and over a long period of time. False evidence and false documents have been planted and every new research discovery has been swiftly greeted by what looks suspiciously like a rapid rebuttal unit hard at work behind the scenes. The result is that it is sometimes hard to separate fact from myth, and truth from fiction, in a wilderness of mirrors and deliberate diversions, worthy of a stage illusion. But one thing has become clear over the years: there was some secret agenda behind the assassination of John F. Kennedy, and someone has gone to great lengths to cover it up. We can however take comfort from the reaction of President Charles de Gaulle of France. When he was told about the official American explanation of the assassination, he roared with laughter, '*Vous me blaguez!* [You're kidding me!] Cowboys and Indians in Texas?!'

At some time in the future, when a new US President considers it safe for the million documents on the Kennedy assassination still squirreled away in the Archives to be declassified and shown to the taxpayers who actually paid for them, we may learn even more of the hidden stories behind what was rightly called 'The Crime of the Century' by the American media.

Until then my money is on the independent judgement of Jack Kennedy's cynical but very well-informed contemporary, President de Gaulle. Someone has been trying to kid a lot of people for a very long time.

We need to get at the truth.

PROLOGUE: WASHINGTON DC, 21 JANUARY 1961

WHAT DANGERS THREATEN A GREAT REPUTATION!
PLUTARCH

The group of worthies that gathered in the freezing cold on Capitol Hill on 21 January 1961 was arguably one of the biggest public assemblies of crooks seen in years. Even by Washington DC's standards.

From highest to lowest, the huddled cluster of black suits marshalled to inaugurate the new President reeked not just of intrigue and double-dealing but of deep criminal corruption. Hardly a man among them had clean hands. The new Vice President was deeply implicated in ballot-rigging, theft, bribery and misappropriation of federal funds, and employed his own tame murderer to eliminate political foes and embarrassing family members. He was also in the pay of big business and the Mafia.

The head of the FBI had openly misused federal funds for his own private purposes and had been secretly bugging and blackmailing politicians for years. In his turn, he was being blackmailed by the Mafia and simultaneously receiving payment for keeping his mouth shut about their very existence.

The Chief Justice of the Supreme Court, the man who would administer the oath, was effectively in the pockets of both the Leader of the Senate and the head of the FBI. They knew all the judge's dark and dirty secrets.

Even the crestfallen leader of the opposition, the man who was supposed to win the election, was bank-rolled by the Mafia, who had been paying his political campaign contributions for years, as well as providing him with free holidays and paying off their man's gambling debts.

And finally, there was the new President himself, elected by the smallest margin in American political history. Even some of those final winning votes had been paid for and rigged by the Chicago Mafia, delighted at last to see the son of one of their own criminal associates now elevated to the highest office in the land. For the rich and dangerous fat cats of organised crime, federal protection and rich pickings beckoned under the new President's regime.

As the TV cameras and the crowd inspected their new young president, now uttering the usual pious political promises of peace, hope, and prosperity, little did they realise that they had sold their birth right to a desperately ill, womanising drug taker and a man who had relied on the Mafia to place him in power. Despite the cosy TV images, the admiring PR puffs and the spin, Camelot it most certainly was not.

The stench of corruption hovered over the marshalled American power elite that cold January day, competing with the whiff of their mothballed morning suits and tailcoats. All were in hock one way or another to big business, crooks, organised crime, or blackmailers. Most had committed some kind of illegal act: from bribery to stealing the taxpayers' money; from taking money from the Mob to outright murder. But then, for Washington DC it was business as usual.

President John F. Kennedy raised his right hand.

2

THE FLAWED PRESIDENT

BEHIND EVERY GREAT FORTUNE IS A GREAT CRIME.
HONORÉ DE BALZAC

In the end it was the Chicago Mafia who effectively bought the 1960 presidential election of the United States for the Kennedy clan. The crucial votes of the Districts of Illinois and Chicago were bought by the Mafia bribes paid out by Sam Giancana and Santos Trafficante's mobsters at the direct request of the new President's father, ex-Mafia associate and one-time criminal, Joseph Kennedy. Out of a record-breaking 69 million voters who went to the polls, fewer than 12,000 people actually determined which man won the presidency. If only 4,500 voters in Illinois and 24,000 voters in Texas had changed their minds, Richard

Milhouse Nixon would have been president.

Thanks to the Mob's help with the votes, a margin of 0.01 per cent – the smallest margin in American history – won JFK and his family their seat in the White House. The Mafia expected the new President to be suitably grateful.

***

The Kennedys' links with the Mafia were both deep and old. Old Joe Kennedy was a crook. He had made a fortune out of smuggling illegal liquor to the Mafia gangs to supply their 'speakeasy' drinking dens during Prohibition back in the 1920s. The Volstead Act, barring the sale of alcohol from 1919 until its repeal in 1933, had the effect of spreading and consolidating the Mafia's networks of Italian-style family criminal gangs across America. Prohibition reinforced the iron rule of economics: demand will always find a supply. A thriving trade in banned bootleg liquor grew and flourished in the 1920s and suppliers of illegal alcohol flourished and prospered along with it.

None prospered more than Joseph Kennedy.

A third generation Irish Catholic immigrant, 'Old Joe' Kennedy had done well for himself. He was obsessed by money. 'If you want to make money, then go where the money is,' was one of his favourite sayings. Like Al Capone, Bugsy Siegel, Meyer Lansky and thousands of other crooks, 'Old Joe' Kennedy joined the highly profitable world of the bootlegging gangsters and the Mafia.

Joe Kennedy already understood the business. His father had originally made his money from a string of legal liquor outlets, shops and bars in Massachusetts. Joe Kennedy now turned to the lucrative underground market spawned by Prohibition and offered his expertise – for a price. By the end of the 1920s Joe Kennedy was deeply involved with the big names of the criminal fraternity of the day: Lansky, Siegel and Frank Costello were all either customers, business rivals or – literally – his partners in crime. A notorious mobster, Sam Giancana, later recalled the heady days of Prohibition by saying:

'Joe Kennedy was the biggest crook I ever met.' Coming from the Chicago Don who had spent a lifetime in organised crime, this was a remarkable tribute to a man who would one day be appointed US ambassador to the United Kingdom.

Kennedy Senior's genius lay in his ability to link business and crime seamlessly in pursuit of profit. Sometimes his business methods were straight out of a gangster movie. As the 'talkies' swept American cinemas, the new movie business offered rich pickings for those with money to invest. Swiftly spotting the potential of the rapidly expanding market for cinema and films, Joe Kennedy bought up undervalued movie companies to form RKO Pictures.

His criminal business methods were exposed by the Pantages affair. In 1929 Kennedy bid for a string of West Coast cinemas owned by a Greek called Alexander Pantages. To Old Joe's astonishment and fury, Pantages refused to sell. Kennedy Sr was outraged. *No one refused Joe Kennedy.* He resorted to tried and trusted Mafia methods: he framed him. A young Vaudeville dancer called Eunice Pringle was hired to visit Pantages' office, hide in a cupboard, rip off her underwear and rush into the street shouting 'Rape!' to the first passing cop. Loudly protesting his innocence, Pantages was hauled off to the County jail.

Pantages got 50 years for rape; Eunice Pringle got her movie contract and Joe Kennedy got his way. Although the rape conviction was later dismissed on appeal (he hired an army of private detectives who uncovered the true story of greed, amateur prostitution and string of sexual partners behind his 'sweet little' accuser), Pantages' reputation and finances suffered and when he died in 1936 of a heart attack, Kennedy bought his business at a knock down price. The final confirmation came years later when Eunice Pringle made a death-bed confession admitting that she had been hired for $10,000.

By 1932 everyone knew that the 'noble experiment' of banning alcohol was doomed. It had served only to criminalise normal folk and to encourage a new army of well-heeled and increasingly powerful crooks. Kennedy began to stockpile whisky and gin secretly against the day that it could legally be released onto the market. He even bribed a Sheriff of Palm Beach to open a secret warehouse *inside* his Florida jailhouse in order to hide part of the illegal hoard.

The rewards were spectacular. By 1935 Joe Kennedy had effectively cornered a new market in legal whisky and made another fortune. By 1936 he was a multi-millionaire and turned his acquisitive eye on Wall Street, where the real money was, while at the same time raising vast sums for Franklin D. Roosevelt and the New Dealers of the Democratic Party in an open attempt to buy political influence in Washington.

This, then, was the business tycoon whom Roosevelt appointed as the first Head of Wall Street's Securities and Exchange Commission in 1934. Wall Street's new overseer and first regulator of US financial probity was an insider dealer; an associate and partner of Mafia members; a trader in illegal goods; a tax fraudster; a ruthless crook and a greedy millionaire of stunning ambition. The effect was to make John Fitzgerald Kennedy's father believe he was untouchable and above the law. It was a set of values that he would bequeath to his large and close-knit Catholic family.

To such an individual, founding a dynasty was secondary to his ultimate ambition, which he touted quite openly: getting the Kennedys to actually run the country. For Joe Kennedy even high political office and influence was regarded as just another commodity.

Old Joe's downfall came, ironically, at the hands of the British. Roosevelt's appointment of his fund-raising tycoon as Ambassador to the UK in 1938 surprised many. In the end it was old Joe's dislike of 'the English', his inability to recognise Britain's determination to fight Hitler, and his pessimistic – and poorly judged – reporting on Britain's prospects in the war against Nazi Germany that forced FDR to recall him at the end of 1940.

This was the family background that nurtured the sprawling Catholic Kennedy family and especially the boys, Joe Jr, John, Robert and Edward. It was an amoral world of big money, a place where anything – and anyone – could be bought, and where crime, crooks and big business openly rubbed shoulders with the world of Wall Street, politics and power. All you needed was money, ambition and the right contacts. Old Joe – now insisting on being addressed as 'Mr Ambassador' – made it quite clear that the presidency was his family's ultimate goal.

So when his heir, Joe Jr, was blown up and killed in a bomber over the English Channel in 1944, second son John automatically moved up to take his place. Old Joe Kennedy had a dream, and his sons were going to fulfil it for him. He had powerful friends, no shortage of money, and was owed many favours. He would effectively buy the presidency for his boy. From the moment the Chicago Mafia bought the Illinois vote for the Senator from Massachusetts in 1960, sleaze and the taint of the Mob would haunt John F. Kennedy to the end of his days.

The truth was that from its very birth, Camelot was built on a landfill of crime, corruption and conspiracy.

PART 1

JFK'S PROBLEMS

3

CROOKS AND CUBA

IF EVER THERE WAS IN THE HISTORY OF HUMANITY AN ENEMY WHO WAS TRULY UNIVERSAL ... THAT ENEMY IS YANKEE IMPERIALISM.
FIDEL CASTRO

Even as he sat down for the first time in the Oval Office, the flawed President had other problems besides the usual domestic political sleaze and the paybacks expected by his backers, criminal or otherwise. A fearful American public, raised on Cold War notions of anti-Communism and the Red Menace, watched for any sign of weakness from their new young President, as did the hard-line generals in the Pentagon.

For American big business too, the Cold War arms race was an important source of profit and thus a major preoccupation. Preparing for Armageddon might be frightening, but the fear of the 'Red Threat' provided a lucrative – and guaranteed – source of steady sales and huge profits for US Corporations and their shareholders.

The experienced and world-weary Dwight Eisenhower had seen the dangers of power being concentrated in a group dedicated to, and with a vested interest in, continued spending on arms. The 1961 speech is remembered mainly for the phrase 'US militaryindustrial complex', but Ike said much more than just that.

> Until the latest of our world conflicts, the United States had no armaments industry. American makers of plowshares could, with time and as required, make swords as well. But now we ... have been compelled to create a permanent armaments industry of vast proportions ... This conjunction of an immense military establishment and a large arms industry is new

in the American experience ... In the councils of government, we must guard against the acquisition of unwarranted influence, whether sought or unsought, by the military-industrial complex.

Although Eisenhower had been advised not to link members of Congress with this 'military-industrial complex' when he made his famous speech, he believed that certain members of Congress and the Administration had been bought and were being paid by the armaments industry to maintain high levels of defence spending. For cigar-chomping generals like the hawkish Curtis LeMay, late of Strategic Air Command, this was entirely proper. (LeMay was mercilessly parodied by Peter Sellers as 'General Jack D. Ripper' in Stanley Kubrick's film, *Dr Strangelove.*) For LeMay, fighting – and winning – a nuclear war seemed a genuinely viable strategic option. As far as LeMay was concerned, US Strategic Air Command was ready to do just that and the President's main job was to keep the cash flowing to arm the US Air Force and the US arms manufacturers who built the airplanes for them.

During Kennedy's first year in power General Lyman Lemnitzer and the other Joint Chiefs bombarded their new President with crazy schemes to attack Fidel Castro's Cuba, and in the 1962 plan for 'Operation Northwoods' Lemnitzer even approved a memo suggesting that an American ship be blown up off Cuba so that the list of US casualties would get public opinion on the Government's side. Kennedy is on record as thinking that his Pentagon advisers were 'mad'.

From the other side of the Iron Curtain, America's communist opponents had moved swiftly to test the mettle of their young and untried adversary. Kennedy himself wanted to establish personal links with Khrushchev, the Soviet leader. An east-west dialogue was a priority for both sides. Unfortunately, for the first and not the last time, the problem of Cuba derailed Kennedy's plans almost before he had settled in the presidential chair. Cuba would come to haunt – and ultimately help end – his term of office.

***

In 1959 a young Cuban lawyer called Fidel Castro had led a popular army of 'Revolutionary Socialists' into Havana. The corrupt President Batista and his fellow racketeers fled, leaving Castro to clean up an island that had effectively been run as a very profitable business by organised American criminal gangs. Among the groups to be eventually eased out of Havana were the fat cats of the Mafia. Men like Meyer Lansky and Santo Trafficante saw their casinos closed down as their rich pickings from drugs, girls and gambling ended for good.

The disgruntled Mafia families retired to New York and Florida to mourn their lost cash cows and to try and build a new criminal capital in the desert at Las Vegas. But there was also a strong desire for revenge.

The problem was that the Mafia were not the only group determined to get their revenge on Castro. From the day Castro took over in 1959, the American government had been obsessed by the notion of a Communist safe haven only 90 miles from Florida's shores. The anti-Communist crusaders of the CIA were given strict instructions to bring the revolutionary Communist regime down, by fair means or foul. The result was that Cuba brought together a deadly conjunction of the Mafia and American governmental agencies, both united in their determination to get rid of Castro.

The result would be to cement an unholy alliance between theoretically natural adversaries, between law-makers and lawbreakers. To add to the dangerous cocktail, a third factor intruded into the political equation. The Cuban exiles who had fled the Castro regime, and who were now clustering in Florida, wanted rid of Castro too. One of the very first plans that Jack Kennedy inherited on entering the Oval Office was a long-standing scheme to get rid of Castro by a full-scale invasion. A rebel army of Cuban exiles, secretly armed and trained by the USA, would invade Cuba and seize it back for the Free World, the Mafia, and US business. The landing place selected for the freedom fighters of *Brigada* 2506 to storm ashore and liberate the island would be at Cuba's narrowest point: the Bay of Pigs.

4

THE BAY OF PIGS AND OTHER CRISES

ANY DAMNED FOOL CAN WRITE A PLAN ... IT'S THE EXECUTION THAT GETS YOU SCREWED UP.
GENERAL JAMES F. HOLLINGWORTH

In 1960 the Eisenhower presidency had decided to destabilise and attack Castro's new Communist Cuba, a plan approved by President Kennedy upon taking office. Cuban intelligence officer Fabian Escalante recorded:

> Tracy Barnes ... called a meeting on January 18, 1960. Those who gathered there included E. Howard Hunt ... The team responsible for the plans to overthrow the government of Guatemala in 1954 was reconstituted, and ... this would be a rerun of the same plan. Vice-President Richard Nixon was the Cuban 'case officer', and had

assembled an important group of businessmen headed by George Bush [Snr.] and Jack Crichton, both Texas oilmen, to gather the necessary funds for Operation 40.

The Cuban adventure turned out to be a complete and bloody disaster. The Kennedy Presidency started with a military defeat and a political debacle.

The plan was put together by a shadowy group called the '5412 Group', a subcommittee of the National Security Council. Thus was born the CIA's notorious 'Operation 40', later memorably described by Lyndon Johnson as 'a goddamn "Murder Inc" in the Caribbean' and whose associates included men like Sam Giancana, front man for the Chicago Mafia. The highly secret deal offered by the US government to the Mafia Don was simple: you help Washington get rid of Castro and you'll get your 'businesses' back in Havana.

The CIA's operations to get rid of Castro fell mainly into two quite distinct areas. There was a top-secret assassination squad codenamed ZR/RIFLE, plus a completely separate army of Cuban exiles trained and equipped by the CIA. These included a highly secret group tucked away deep inside the CIA's 'Operation 40'.

This was a band of exile volunteers equipped with Cuban army uniforms and weapons who would be put ashore on Cuba and would launch a fake assault on the US Guantanamo naval base to coincide with the main invasion. The CIA believed that if the new President could be convinced that there was a direct Cuban attack on the US base on Cuba's eastern tip, then he would have no option but to send in the Marines to defend it and support the small exiles brigade.

From mid-1960 on, the Cuban exiles brigade began to form and train in secret bases in Nicaragua, Guatemala and Florida. By the time Kennedy took office in January 1961 the secret plan to depose Castro and his regime was well in place. Strict security was enforced, initially at least. Although there is no suggestion that he knew anything about the Mafia's clandestine role, there is considerable evidence that the landing plan was supported by the young George Bush's Zapata offshore oil drilling corporation.

William Corson of the CIA agreed, and recorded that Bush was officially considered a CIA asset. 'Dulles convinced him that he could contribute to his country as well as get help from the CIA for his overseas business activities.'

The whole complicated invasion operation was to be controlled and run out of the CIA's Miami station. By the March of 1961 it was obvious that any security had been lost. Castro himself brought his forces to alert and warned of an impending *Yanqui* invasion.

In the view of many observers, although Kennedy inherited the problem of Cuba, the Cuban exiles and the CIA, he managed to make it much worse by his own decisions. The key meeting where he intervened took place on 11 March 1961 when CIA Director Allen Dulles gave a briefing to the new President.

Kennedy insisted on moving the attack from the Escambray area further south to the Bay of Pigs. He also refused to allow any badged US forces to participate. This policy went back to an Eisenhower Administration NSC Directive of 1954, which declared that no active duty US Military personnel were to be involved in covert operations. Legally, this was to be a CIA operation – period. The President went on to direct that if the planners were unable to obey him, then the operation would have to be cancelled.

Months of planning and training the exile brigade 2506 looked like being thrown out of the window. Alan Dulles pointed out that even cancellation was a dangerous option now, as the disappointed and furious members of the exiles brigade would disperse to the US. They would talk and the whole story was bound come out anyway. The CIA duly altered the plan and, after receiving a personal assurance from Allen Dulles that Operation Zapata's chances of success were 'even higher that the successful CIA coup against Guatemala in 1954', Kennedy authorised the attack for 5 April. In what would become became a characteristic JFK dither, he postponed it first until 12 April and then finally 17 April. With those presidential delays, any faint hope of operational security disappeared out of the window.

The CIA's secret political scheme to drag the President and American troops into a shooting war with Cuba was invested in a boat called the *Santa Anna.* Her role was to sail to a point near Guantanamo naval base under cover of darkness and drop off 168 Cuban exile troops to stage their fake attack on the US facility. However, the recce party that went ashore in the dark came back spooked by sights of cigarettes glowing in the night, strange lights and unusual vehicle traffic. The Cubans' leader decided not to take a risk and ordered the *Santa Anna* back out to sea.

The operation's success now depended on a preliminary surprise airstrike by the exiles' bombers to catch Castro's tiny air force on the ground. This first strike was vital to knock out Cuban's four T-33 jets and ten old but dangerous Sea Fury fighters. A successful strike would guarantee air superiority over the beaches. The Exiles' other problem was that they had to fly all the way back to Nicaragua, over 500 miles away, to refuel and reload.

The dawn airstrike was a complete failure. At the last moment, Richard Bissell, head of the CIA's Covert Operations Division, ordered the force to be cut back to only six of the sixteen B-26 bombers. Castro foiled the attack by planting dummy aeroplanes as targets, which came as a complete surprise to the exiles' supposedly professional USAF air warfare advisers.

This was the crucial moment. National Security Advisor McGeorge Bundy telephoned the CIA's air force liaison officer, General Charles Cabell, directing him to cancel the Cuban exile force follow-up B-26 attack. It was a fatal mistake by the politicians and the CIA high command alike, and the moment when the plan began to unravel.

By the time Cabell had asked the Secretary of State, and then consulted the President on what to do next it was far too late. Castro's tiny air force had homed in on the little cluster of ships off the beach. The invaders were already in trouble. The men who struggled ashore saw their vital equipment being destroyed before their eyes by Castro's planes.

First to go was the *Houston.* She was struck repeatedly and began to sink with her precious cargo of ammunition. The *Rio Escondido* erupted in a fireball taking with her the Brigade's medical stores, spare ammunition and all the fuel. The command ship *Marsopa* was the next casualty, losing all the exiles' radios and communications gear. The surviving ships upped anchor and sped for the safety of international waters, abandoning the soldiers ashore in the mangrove swamps of the Bay of Pigs.

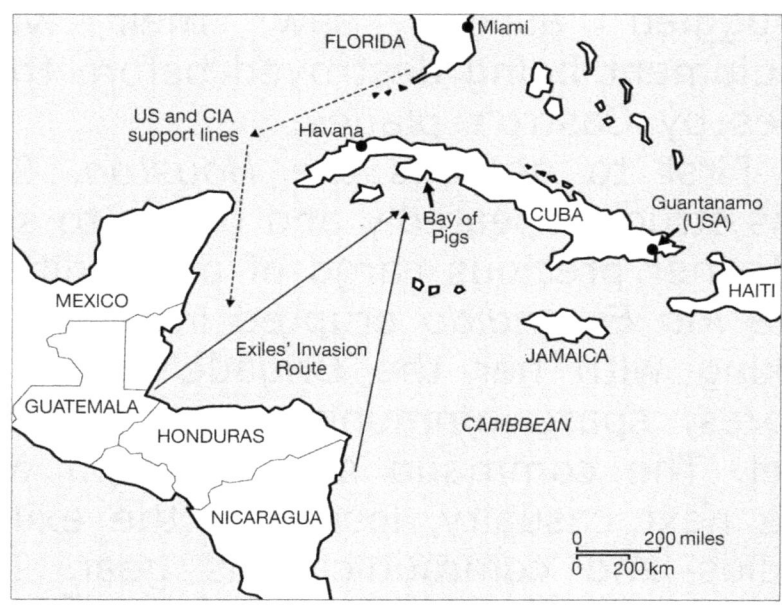

The Bay of Pigs posed serious logistical problems for any invader.

On the horizon a US Marine battalion landing team watched impotently as the trap closed. There was no report of any attack on the Americans in the Guantanamo Base. The CIA advisers ashore watched in horror later as the follow-up C-47s flew in with their 170 paratroopers. A C-47 went down in flames. The rest scattered and fled.

By the next day Castro had surrounded the 900 men still alive and ashore with 20,000 well-armed soldiers. As the situation in the shrinking beachhead deteriorated, the CIA and Joint Chiefs of Staff turned to the President asking for direct US aid and re-supply. JFK reminded the Pentagon and the CIA that the Eisenhower NSC policy was still in effect. The exiles were on their own and tried to reinforce by air one last time. Once again, Castro's fighters were waiting. Five planes went down. Outnumbered, outgunned and without support the *Mercenarios* surrendered. They had suffered nearly 40 per cent casualties. They were out of ammunition, out of luck and had nowhere to run.

At 14.00 on the afternoon of the 19 April, San Roman cursed the CIA, shot his radio to pieces and surrendered. CIA man Grayston Lynch later said, 'For the first time in 37 years ... I was ashamed of my country.'

It had all been futile. The Bay of Pigs operation had turned out to be a catastrophe.

JFK and his cocky younger brother were both furious and unrepentant. They blamed Eisenhower, the Pentagon, but most of all the Covert Ops Division of the CIA for the disaster. They argued that the operation had been a hare-brained scheme, doomed from the start and the CIA had made a complete hash of it. The CIA in their turn claimed that the fiasco was the result of presidential weakness; JFK should have sent in the Marines.

***

Kennedy had barely recovered from the disasters of spring 1961 when the Cold War began to rear its head once again in the longrunning dispute over Berlin. In the words of one cynical observer, a general on the US Chiefs of Staff, 'for once the great John Fitzgerald Kennedy charm didn't work' (see William Taubman, *Khrushchev: The Man and His Era,* Norton 2003). The hardnosed Soviet leader saw off the naïve and inexperienced Kennedy, whom he likened to 'a rich mummy's boy,' with threats of a nuclear war. The humiliated President returned home, as Russian tanks at Checkpoint Charlie in Berlin forced a frightened Kennedy, despite his tough rhetoric, to beg for an excuse behind the scenes to back down and save face. Khrushchev did just that and noted the interesting Kennedy formula for dealing with confrontation ('Back Down but Talk Big') for future reference.

In October 1962 the Kremlin put the squeeze on Kennedy once again. If the Berlin crisis of 1961 had worried the world, the Cuban missile crisis terrified it. Armed, in his own words, 'with a nuclear missile under each arm,' Khrushchev secretly ordered Soviet rocket troops and nuclear missiles to move into Castro's Cuba, only 90 miles off America's Florida coast, and waited to see what the Americans would do. It was a quite deliberate provocation.

Khrushchev's motives were clear. The Kremlin were only too well aware that they were at a serious disadvantage in the strategic nuclear confrontation with the Americans. While the Soviets' shorter-range missiles could devastate Western Europe, their long-range missiles could only strike the continental United States with less than 20 per cent of the long-range capability of the United States. The Soviet leaders were also mindful of the fact that the Jupiter missiles that the Americans had based in Turkey could strike the Soviet Union in 10 minutes – and without warning. Moreover, watching US manoeuvres and exercises, from Moscow's paranoiac view, the Americans seemed to be preparing for a nuclear first strike.

The resolution of the Cuban crisis came late one night after a tearful Bobby went to Anatoly Dobrynin, the Soviet ambassador to Washington, and begged for a face-saving formula. A startled Dobrynin duly obliged this secret plea for help from the US President's brother. The Kennedy brothers agreed to end their naval blockade of Cuba and remove the American missiles from Turkey, provided the Soviets promised to take back their offending rockets from Cuba. Chairman Khrushchev complied. The Soviet leader had achieved his aim, effectively blackmailed Kennedy into backing down and given the Yankees a taste of their own medicine.

There was, however, a typical Kennedy twist: the US climbdown had to be spun in the public eye to look like a glorious triumph for the Kennedy boys. The press trumpeted JFK's 'diplomatic triumph' and the world breathed again.

But not everyone was fooled. One Admiral commented, 'we've all been had ... and not just by the Russkis either.' Behind the scenes, many agreed. It was Kennedy who had backed down, not the Kremlin – whatever the papers said.

To make matters worse, it turned out that even Khrushchev couldn't enforce the alleged deal with Kennedy. His stubborn client Castro flatly refused to allow UN, let alone American, observers into Cuba to confirm the Soviet withdrawal. A Soviet garrison stayed on in Cuba. By the beginning of 1963, it slowly became clear to those in the know, as well as an increasingly suspicious American press, that Cuba was still a Soviet-controlled outpost off the coast of Florida. And 1964 was an election year. The Republican opposition sharpened their knives and began to voice the suspicion – felt by many – that the Kennedy boys were fooling everybody.

Cuba became the catalyst for JFK's problems, and the rallying point for his enemies. The Pentagon was still planning an invasion; the CIA was plotting to assassinate Castro; and Kennedy's political rivals were demanding to know 'what was really going on in Cuba?' To make matters worse Khrushchev openly warned Kennedy that any US invasion of Cuba would mean war. The Kennedys were becoming increasingly desperate. They then made their fatal mistake. If an open assault by the US on Cuba was going to be too dangerous, they reasoned, why not get the Cubans to get rid of Castro themselves?

Behind the scenes, in the spring of 1963 the Kennedy brothers set up their own private, very secret and totally illegal plan for a *coup d'état* in Cuba. It was called 'Plan Amworld' and controlled directly from the White House by Bobby Kennedy. Castro was to be assassinated by a hired 'Cuban' assassin from within his own cabinet; then a 'reliable' Cuban revolutionary leader – now secretly negotiating with CIA agents – would take his place. Once in charge, Cuba's new leader would invite US troops to move in 'to help restore order'.

There was a problem, however. In order to carry out this audacious scheme, the White House needed help, and help from men who knew their way around Cuba. So Bobby Kennedy turned to the men who really knew Cuba. On his brother's orders, the senior Law Officer of the United States approached the Mafia for help.

What the Kennedy boys hadn't realised was that the CIA had already *officially* hired Sam Giancana and the Mob to help get rid of the Cuban leader. The CIA and the Mafia were already deeply intertwined in American efforts to rid Cuba of Castro.

It was a dangerous combination.

5

ALL THE PRESIDENT'S WOMEN

CHERCHEZ LA FEMME!
ALEXANDRE DUMAS

Jack Kennedy had two other serious complications in his life: first, he was a very sick man, and second, he couldn't keep his fly zipped up.

By the time he entered the White House, Kennedy was already seriously unwell. According to Dr Jeffrey Kelman, Kennedy had been ill on and off from his early teens. He suffered from a variety of ailments: a chronic irritable bowel; a series of compression fractures in the lower back caused by a degenerative bone disease; and worst of all, Addison's disease, a serious adrenal hormone deficiency that causes blood pressure to go haywire and effectively disables the patient for limited periods.

This was the man who took over the reins of power as President of the US at the height of the Cold War in 1960. Only his family and physicians knew that he was on powerful steroids. Sometimes he needed 10 different medications a day just to function. At one point the new President was taking Cortisone and Testosterone as steroids, anti-spasmodics, painkillers and the muscle relaxants Phenobarbitone and Librium. In 1954 a close friend said, 'That metal plate they put into his spine after the war had never healed over. You could look into an open hole in his back and see it.'

The new President of the United States couldn't tie his own left shoe, and could hardly walk down the stairs first thing in the morning; a man who had to wear a back brace and corset to keep him straight. This was a man who couldn't put his own socks on because he couldn't bend or bear the pain.

Nowadays we know that long-term use of steroids can have seriously damaging side effects. Kennedy's face – and personality – altered under the influence of his medical regime and the steroids brought on a series of respiratory and skin infections over the years, all of which required antibiotics. Worst of all, his overzealous sexual activities caused him to suffer semi-permanent urinary tract infections. The truth was that the American people had voted in a very sick man as their new leader. Given his crippling list of ailments it is surprising therefore that Kennedy could find the time and inclination to have a string of affairs both before and after marriage. If there is anything heroic in Jack Kennedy it was his overcoming the physical odds to spend a lifetime chasing women. For the truth was that Jack Kennedy was an inveterate sex addict.

JFK's list of sexual conquests was impressive and included some fairly startling names: Marilyn Monroe; actresses Angie Dickinson and Gloria Swanson; socialite Mary Meyer; gangster's moll Judith Exner; an alleged East German spy, Ellen Rometsch; his wife's Press Secretary; White House aides nick-named 'Fiddle' and 'Faddle' by the President's aides and literally dozens – if not hundreds – of others.

Even on the night of his inauguration, Kennedy actually enjoyed a 'quickie' with *two* of his guests in the White House. During the lull after dinner he nipped upstairs and bedded the girls while the new First Lady sat downstairs entertaining Washington's political elite.

This incident highlights the probable motives behind Jack Kennedy's relentless womanising. He was a lousy lover who didn't believe in foreplay, forcing Jackie Kennedy to admit to her doctor that Jack was sexually no great shakes and asking the doctor for advice. Actress Angie Dickinson even commented dryly that sex with Jack Kennedy was the 'best 20 seconds' of her life.

The problem was that he was also a risk taker who enjoyed the thrill of the clandestine chase. Old Joseph Kennedy had openly flaunted his adulteries, even bringing some mistresses home to eat at the family dining table. Remarkably, one of his long-term amours, Gloria Swanson, was bedded by both father and son. For the Kennedy menfolk, as long as you had enough money, you could do what the hell you liked.

John Fitzgerald Kennedy's sexual proclivities were well known in Washington circles long before he was elected president. As early as 1942, J. Edgar Hoover, that snuffer-up of political dirt and sexual secrets, had taken careful note of the young Kennedy's amorous activities. As a young lieutenant in Naval Intelligence, Kennedy began a passionate affair with Inga Arvad, a beautiful Danish journalist and known Nazi sympathiser. When the lovers talked of marriage, Hoover tipped off Old Joe Kennedy and the Navy packed Jack off to the Pacific and command of a torpedo boat, PT 109. For decades afterwards the head of the FBI kept a beady eye on John Kennedy's progress in both politics and the bedroom. In one 1950s FBI memo Hoover noted that Senator Kennedy had participated in 'immoral activity'. Hoover wanted to be able to blackmail him and control him as he did with so many other prominent Americans.

Therein lay the risk for Kennedy. His womanising left him intensely vulnerable for a prominent figure in public life. Five of his conquests posed particular danger to both his reputation and his career.

As early as 1960, rumours began surfacing that Jack Kennedy had been married before. Obscure Republican magazines trailed their coats, alleging that in 1947 John Kennedy had married a Florida hostess called Durie Malcolm. The wily Hoover then did his usual trick. He leaked the story to one of his own secret mouthpieces in the Press, a United Features journalist called Henry Taylor. Taylor's story exposing the marriage was shown to the White House for comment, as normal, throwing Kennedy's Press Secretary into a panic.

Having secretly primed and set the political booby trap, the helpful Hoover now offered to come to the rescue and defuse it. More FBI papers allegedly refuting the allegations appeared from Hoover's hoard of 'official and confidential' files and were conveniently loaned to *Newsweek* magazine, which squashed the rumours in a high-minded scoop debunking the story. Not for the first time, to his intense frustration, Jack Kennedy's skin had been saved by J. Edgar Hoover's long arm and inside knowledge. The suspicion that the FBI Director set the whole thing up by briefing his tame journalists about the story in the first place placed the President firmly in Hoover's debt.

Being indebted to J. Edgar Hoover was a dangerous place in which to find oneself, especially for a president with some nasty skeletons in the cupboard. The knowledge that the FBI Director, a man whom he detested, now had him writhing like a worm on a pin must have been painful. Jack Kennedy had wanted to get rid of the old man as the Director of the FBI once and for all. Now he dare not. Hoover knew too much. He was stuck with the ageing and spiteful Hoover as FBI Chief.

But worse was to follow. Adulterers should never forget the dangers of an angry spouse thirsting for revenge. When Jack Kennedy bedded the beautiful and artistic socialite Mary Meyer and carried on a very public affair with her in 1959, he was cuckolding Cord Meyer, the head of one of the CIA's Special Operations divisions; the organisation responsible for political propaganda and dirty tricks.

In one of the curious – and unexplained – twists in the Kennedy story, Mary Meyer later became one of the large group of people associated with the Kennedy assassination who died in curious circumstances soon after the events in Dallas. On 12 October 1964 she was shot and killed on a canal bank in Georgetown. The police claimed that it was a mugging, although Mary Meyer's purse had not been stolen. She had been executed by two softnosed bullets in the back of the head and another shot to the heart at point blank range. A CIA officer (reputed to be no less than James Jesus Angleton, the Head of CIA Counterintelligence himself) was discovered by one of Mary Meyer's friends rifling the bureau in her house and looking for her diary, which reputedly contained details of her trysts with Kennedy. Although a man named Raymond Crump was arrested and tried for Mary Meyer's murder, he was acquitted.

Even more dangerous was Kennedy's astonishing affair with a Mafia Don's mistress. The woman was Judith Campbell – later known as Judith Exner. She was introduced to JFK on 7 February 1960 at the Sands Hotel in Vegas and ended up in his bed. Known among show business circles as a 'star-fucker' – a woman overawed by the celebrities of the day, whether from films, business, politics or the Mafia – Judith Campbell was sexually available to the rich or famous. The Don was Sam Giancana, who now headed up the Chicago Families, one of the biggest crime syndicates in the country.

The FBI's ubiquitous FBI wiretaps had once again exposed the secrets of Kennedy's sex life to one of his arch-enemies in Washington. In the case of the Kennedy/Judith Campbell/Sam Giancana sex triangle, the implications were potentially explosive. Giancana had already been approached by the CIA in 1960 to help assassinate Castro on behalf of the US government. Not only was the President carrying on a sexual relationship with a known girlfriend of a gangster who was one of the FBI's principal targets in Bobby Kennedy's 'war on crime', he was also using her to pass secret messages to the Mafia as Judith Campbell's claims to have carried sealed envelopes from the White House to her Mafia lover turned out to be true.

Given the circumstances, the indiscretion is breathtaking. Jack Kennedy's uncontrolled libido had led him into an extraordinarily compromising position – the vulnerability to blackmail is obvious. When therefore J. Edgar Hoover was summoned to the White House on 22 March 1962 to be formally dismissed from his cherished post as FBI Director by the President, the cunning old man actually came away after a four-hour lunch, with his job security *enhanced.*

Once again J. Edgar Hoover was the man who knew too much. Both the Kennedy brothers were now in the palm of his hand. Thanks to his sexual shenanigans with a Mafia leader's girlfriend, the President now found himself being blackmailed by his own Chief of Secret Police. Ironically, Hoover was in his turn being blackmailed by the Mob, who knew the FBI's boss man was a closet homosexual.

Behind the sexual dimension, however, lurked a much more dangerous factor. Sam Giancana felt that the Kennedys were now guilty of 'speaking out of both sides of their mouth,' in the Mafia's telling phrase. Giancana and the Mafia had been instrumental in buying votes for Kennedy in Chicago during the 1960 election. Now the Feds – in the person of the President's brother, Robert Kennedy – were publicly hounding him as a mobster and threatening to put him and his friends in jail. From Sam Giancana's point of view, the Kennedys had double-crossed the Chicago Mafia men.

Perhaps the most astonishing claim about the President's indiscretions was not that he was sleeping with a gangster's moll but that he was using 'recreational drugs' in the White House. The claim came from JFK's favourite girlfriend, Mary Meyer herself. She told her friends that not only did the President bed her in the White House, but they also used drugs there.

Frank Sinatra's valet is our witness to that. George Jacobs worked for Frank Sinatra in the 50s and 60s and saw all Sinatra's guests at close hand when they came to stay at the star's mansion. In his 2003 article in *Playboy* magazine, Jacobs revealed details of Senator Jack Kennedy's life in the late 1950s and his obsession with women. Jacobs said that when he expected them to be talking politics they were in fact having an animated discussion about Juliet Prowse's shaved *mons veneris* or trying to find some celebrity *'poontang'*. The other thing that startled Jacobs was Senator Kennedy's open drug use. Sinatra wouldn't tolerate drugs in the house. To be caught would mean the end of his career. Jacobs was startled therefore one day to catch Jack Kennedy snorting lines of cocaine with his brother-inlaw, actor and fellow Rat Pack member Peter Lawford, in Lawford's room.

Corroboration of this astonishing claim comes from two other sources. After Meyer's death, Deborah Davis wrote a book about Katherine Graham, the grandee socialite owner of the

Washington Post. When interviewed, Davis confirmed some explicit references to the Kennedy/Meyer affair, which Graham knew all about:

> Mary Pinchot Meyer was the principal lover of John F. Kennedy when he was President of the United States ... A lot of them got their marijuana and LSD from Timothy Leary ... she was involved with Kennedy and together they supposedly used to smoke marijuana together in Kennedy's bedroom, and I think Leary said she also gave him LSD.

Timothy Leary, drugs guru of the wild 1960s, confirms the story in his book *Flashback.* Mary Meyer told Jim Truitt that Kennedy had remarked to Meyer: 'This (LSD) isn't like cocaine. I'll get you some of that.' Unbelievably, not only was the President of the United States screwing any woman who would let him, he was also using drugs in the White House.

If this combination of sex, Mafia, drugs and blackmail were not enough, Jack Kennedy's penis led him even deeper into the clutches of Hoover and the FBI. Disastrously, one of his women was alleged to be an East German spy.

Ellen Rometsch, a beautiful dark-eyed Elizabeth Taylor lookalike, was born in Kleinitz, East Germany in 1936. She arrived in Washington in 1961 and soon became a *habitué* of the Quorum Club, a select watering hole on Capitol Hill. The Q Club was a high class 'gentlemen's club' and was run by Bobby Baker, Senator Lyndon Baines Johnson's right-hand man and political fixer.

Rometsch's dark good looks and easy manner caught the eyes of the men of power. According to Baker, Rometsch and the President were soon skinny-dipping in the White House pool.

The affair then exploded in Kennedy's face, because in July 1963 the notorious Profumo sex scandal in Britain was at its height. It appeared that *Frau* Rometsch had been a little too free with her favours. In the Cold War the security implications of the married President of the United States – the Commander in Chief himself – sleeping with a woman who had emigrated from Communist East Germany were enormous.

The hints of sexual scandal went deeper still. Rumours were circulating in Washington that President Kennedy had also bedded Mariella Novotny, a member of the Christine Keeler/Stephen Ward/Ivanov ring of London vice girls. This was political dynamite. Newspapers began dropping hints, among them:

HIGH AMERICAN OFFICIALS LINKED TO PROFUMO SCANDAL, WASHINGTON VICE GIRL CLAIMS

This time, Kennedy faced a real political crisis over his sexual indiscretions.

The President escaped disgrace only thanks, once again, to the suspiciously obliging J. Edgar Hoover, whom many suspect of leaking the 'vice girl' story in the first place. Hoover passed 'incriminating' (but never fully disclosed) FBI files to Bobby Kennedy.

Within a month the unfortunate Rometsch had been quietly deported at the request of the State Department as an alleged security risk, victim of nothing more than being caught bedding the President. Later FBI reports show clearly that there was never any evidence of espionage against her and her deportation was obviously designed to remove a political embarrassment to the President of the USA. Nonetheless, it was a narrow squeak for the President and, ominously, he was now even deeper in debt to the detested Hoover, who now had the dirt on both John and Bobby Kennedy and was virtually invulnerable.

With hindsight, we can see that Kennedy could well have been impeached or forced to resign as president – if he had lived. The possibility of explosive sexual revelations losing him the 1964 election were suddenly very real. Only Hoover stood between him and ruin.

Why, then, did Kennedy do it?

***

John Kennedy's 'Casanova Complex' may well have been inherited from his father. But other factors influenced his priapic behaviour. As the second, weakling son, Jack had always competed, even over girls, with his elder brother Joe Jr (who was killed during the war in 1944 while flying a B-17 bomber packed with explosives).

Brought up in the American social elite of money, power and politics, Kennedy enjoyed the freedoms that a 10 million dollar trust fund bestows upon its fortunate beneficiaries. In the world of the Anglo-American aristocracy, mistresses and bed-hopping were just an accepted way of life. The result was that Kennedy's White House, far from being the 'golden Camelot' of legend, sometimes seems to have had more in common with the Papal excesses of the Borgias.

And yet, nothing quite explains the sheer irresponsibility and relentless risk taking of John Kennedy's sexual exploits. Power only seemed to increase his appetites. In June 1961 he confided to an astonished British Prime Minister Harold Macmillan that he 'got headaches' if he went three days without sex. (The urbane MacMillan supposedly replied that he felt the same about being unable to read Jane Austen.) The President's aides thereafter began to refer to Kennedy's women as 'his aspirins'.

The key to Jack Kennedy's behaviour seems to have been the sheer love of risk. Kennedy was always a gambler. With his casual attitude towards women, a strong desire for sexual gratification and an aristocratic disdain for the rules of the common herd, it seems that Kennedy's reckless tomcatting was just a form of harmless diversion and thrill seeking on his part. When it came to sex, he thought he could get away with anything. For one of his conquests, however, Jack Kennedy's harmless bit of fun would end in scandal and tragedy.

Her name was Marilyn Monroe...

6

MARILYN MONROE – ANATOMY OF A COVER-UP

HOLLYWOOD IS THE PLACE WHERE THEY PAY YOU $1,000 FOR A KISS AND 50 CENTS FOR YOUR SOUL...
MARILYN MONROE

The death of Marilyn Monroe on the night of 4/5 August 1962 proved that the old lines of the anti-conspiracy brigade, *You could never cover up something as big as that,* and *Someone would have talked* ... are demonstrably untrue. Marilyn Monroe was murdered. The real story of Marilyn Monroe's fatal love affairs with Jack Kennedy and his brother offers us a very clear model of how the events in Dallas just over a year later were covered up by America's power elite.

By 1960 Marilyn Monroe had become the most photographed and sought-after woman in the world. Her image adorned several million locker rooms and dens. The blonde film star was simply regarded as the most beautiful and most famous woman on the planet.

Born Norma Jean Mortensen in Los Angeles, she never knew her father and had a broken childhood. Before she was married off at 16, she had been in a succession of foster homes after her mother was admitted to a mental hospital. In 1943, as she had fun in the endless California sunshine while her first husband, Jim Dougherty, was away in the Pacific with the Merchant Marine, the busty brunette was discovered by an Army photographer looking for Forces' Sweethearts.

Within two years she was transformed. She had her teeth fixed, dyed her hair and became a fixture as a pin-up girl on magazine covers. Screen tests and the inevitable rites of passage on the Hollywood casting couch followed. Then in 1949, infatuated 53year-old agent Johnny Hyde left his wife to make her a film star. Soon the insecure young woman, with no real sense of her own identity, had become a blonde bombshell called 'Marilyn Monroe'. When Hyde died in 1950 she tried to commit suicide, because 'Marilyn Monroe' was a very disturbed young woman.

The next 10 years made her an international superstar and took her into the President's bed. But they also destroyed her grip on reality. To Jack Kennedy, Marilyn Monroe was, in the words of one of his aides, 'just another lay'. But to the disturbed Norma Jean, after three husbands, three divorces and dozens of lovers, bedding the President betokened bigger things to come.

In early 1961, out of the blue, Marilyn confided to a friend that 'she had a date' with Jack Kennedy, who had just been elected the next President of the United States. The new President's brother-in-law, Peter Lawford, had virtually procured Marilyn for Kennedy after the Los Angeles Democratic convention the previous July. The FBI's J. Edgar Hoover recorded an affair between the film star and the future president.

The problem was that it continued after Kennedy moved into the White

House. The couple were spotted in New York City at the Carlyle Hotel; on one occasion Marilyn was seen in a brunette wig and dark glasses. The confused film star really believed she was in love with JFK and fantasised about a divorce and moving into the White House as 'Mrs Kennedy'. These were dangerous daydreams, because the interest wasn't mutual: to the President, Monroe was just another notch on the bedpost.

By 1961 Marilyn's complicated life was beset with drama and breakdown on every side. Her reputation in the film industry was plummeting as a result of her bad timekeeping and lack of commitment. Sir Laurence Olivier, who played opposite her in *The Prince and the Showgirl,* was scathing: 'She is the stupidest, most self-indulgent tart I have ever come across.' In particular, the end of her third marriage to Arthur Miller in 1961 had brought about a complete breakdown.

On 5 February 1961, Marilyn checked in to a New York hospital for some rest under medical supervision as 'Faye Miller'. However, she found herself being locked in a padded cell where she screamed hysterically until the nurses came and threatened to put her in a straitjacket. Eventually second husband Joe DiMaggio rescued her – but the damage was done.

Matters were complicated even further when Bobby Kennedy was sent down to California to tell Marilyn that the President didn't want to hear from her again; to pay her off in the usual Kennedy family style. But Bobby fell under her spell too; he spent the night with Marilyn in Peter Lawford's house as a new Monroe-Kennedy relationship began. By the summer of 1962 their supposedly discreet affair was far from secret. On one occasion Marilyn even jumped stark naked out of the bath to greet Bobby when he turned up unannounced at the door of her LA apartment. The evidence is strong that by September 1961, Marilyn had stopped sleeping with the President but was now the occasional mistress of his brother, the Attorney General of the United States. She was also sharing her bed at the time with Frank Sinatra, a close friend of known Mafia men and gangsters. Marilyn Monroe was risking compromising the President and the Attorney General with the Mafia.

The Mob was only too well aware of Marilyn's dalliances. The Mafia took a close and unhealthy interest in the lives of Hollywood stars, primarily so they could blackmail them. Sam Giancana, the Chicago Don, even encouraged his mistress Judith Campbell to hop into JFK's bed to compromise the President.

But the Mob wasn't after blackmailing Monroe: they wanted to use her to get at Kennedy, in order to blackmail *him.* When Giancana was deliberately harassed by the FBI agents at Chicago airport on 12 July 1961, he burst out in a rage, 'I know all about the goddamn Kennedys ... you tell your boss that one of these days we're going to tell all!'

The next move was inevitable. Marilyn Monroe's house was bugged by Bernie Spindel, 'King of the Wiretappers', to find out just what she was up to, and with whom. The bugs had been commissioned by Jimmy Hoffa, the Teamsters Union leader and close colleague of Mafia boss Giancana. The purpose of the bugs was to record

Marilyn's bedroom trysts with the younger Kennedy so that Hoffa and his Mafia friends could discredit and blackmail the Attorney General. Hoffa and his Mafia connections were high priority for the Feds. In turn that made the Kennedys a high priority for entrapment and blackmail by the Mafia.

Marilyn Monroe was the unwitting link between the two. By the spring of 1962 that link was very weak indeed. The star was under psychiatric care, was overdosing on a variety of drugs (including an LSD trip with Timothy Leary), had had at least two abortions and had been sacked by her studio for her erratic behaviour on set.

Something's Got to Give, her aptly named final film for Twentieth Century Fox, was the last straw. She had been ill on the first day of shooting. The hard-nosed lawyers who owned Fox sent their own studio doctor, who reported that she had a viral sinus infection that might take weeks to cure. Marilyn tried to film the next day but collapsed. The production slid behind schedule. Every day cost the studio money – a lot of money.

Marilyn then made a fatal mistake. Despite being warned by Fox's lawyers that if she quit the set early she would be deemed to have broken her contract, she flew to New York to attend John Kennedy's birthday gala. This was the final straw for Fox. The Burton-Taylor *Cleopatra* was way over budget in Europe and Zanuck's epic, *The Longest Day,* was running up equally epic bills. They couldn't afford any more delays on *Something's Got to Give.*

On 19 May 1962 she made a stunning appearance at Madison Square Garden, singing a breathless 'Happy Birthday, Mr President', while wearing a $6,000 dress so sheer that it had to be stitched on. Five days later, the Director of the FBI had a personal interview with President Kennedy 'on an urgent matter of national security.'

Behind closed doors Hoover laid out a damning series of presidential indiscretions, ranging from sleeping with Judith Exner, a Mafia mobster's girlfriend, to skinny dipping in the White House with Ellen Rometsch, whom the FBI were investigating as a possible East German spy. On top of that the

President had been conducting a very public affair with Marilyn Monroe. If it all became public knowledge, it could bring down the presidency, Hoover warned. We do not know the precise wording of what was said that afternoon; the files remain long sealed.

What we do know is what the Kennedys did next. Both the Kennedy boys moved fast to dump Marilyn Monroe. The record shows that the next day, the White House switchboard was instructed not to accept any of her calls. It was the President's brother-in-law, Peter Lawford, who broke the bad news to her, with brutal directness: 'Look Marilyn, you're just another one of Jack's fucks.'

But Marilyn couldn't handle this harsh truth. She fell to pieces – again. The flat mood continued throughout July 1962 and was not improved by constant visits to her doctor and her psychiatrist. Even when she accompanied the Lawfords on a trip to the Cal-Neva Hotel on the California-Nevada border to see Frank Sinatra perform in late July, the event did not improve the fading star's morale. Lawford might have been using the weekend to 'talk some sense into Marilyn'. Instead she became hysterical and overdosed in a drunken stupor and had to be walked around by her hosts until she recovered.

Another clue to the cause of her depression may be found in her last interview with journalist George Barris: 'When a man leaves a woman, when she tells him that she's going to have his baby, when he doesn't marry her, that must hurt a woman very much...'

Her friends said that Marilyn had been 'going on about babies' for the previous month, but the fact is no one knows whether she was pregnant or not. The psychiatrically disturbed star was prone to fantasising and making up stories. (She had even claimed that Clark Gable, her co-star in *The Misfits,* was her long-lost father.)

But if she really was pregnant by Bobby Kennedy and had an abortion, only to be abandoned by the Attorney General, then any chances of Jack getting re-elected in 1964 would go out of the window if word got out that both the Catholic Kennedys had been sharing the bed of Hollywood's screen goddess and then dumped her. And to make matters worse, Marilyn had kept a diary of her relationship with the Kennedys.

Late in June 1962, a tearful and angry Marilyn called old flame Robert Slatzer. She showed him a little red notebook, which she called 'her diary', plus a bundle of handwritten notes on US Justice Department stationery. Slatzer realised that Marilyn was brandishing political dynamite: evidence that she had slept with and talked delicate political matters with both the President and his brother the Attorney General. If it got out, it could bring the Kennedys crashing down.

If the Kennedys had been aware of the whole story they would have been even more worried: because both the Mafia and J. Edgar Hoover at the FBI knew all about the Kennedy brothers' sexual exploits through Hoffa's excellent little wiretaps. Marilyn spelled trouble – or opportunity – for all. To the Mafia, Marilyn had ensnared the Kennedys into deeper indiscretion; to J. Edgar Hoover she was now a real risk to national security; and to the President and his brother she spelled mortal political danger.

On the night of 4/5 August 1962, Marilyn Monroe was murdered. During the afternoon of Saturday 4 August, Bobby flew to Los Angeles and, accompanied by Peter Lawford, went to see Marilyn at her house. Neighbours witnessed his arrival. There was a quarrel and a scene during which Marilyn threatened to call a press conference on Monday and expose the Kennedys. Bobby Kennedy demanded the notes she had taken; Monroe refused, even when he offered her a million dollars for the papers. They fought and he walked out, making threats. Later that evening neighbours saw two men go to the house, one carrying what looked like 'a big briefcase'. They ordered the domestic staff to leave and emerged about half an hour later. Shortly afterwards Marilyn was picked up by ambulance from Schaefer's Ambulance Service and driven to Santa Monica Hospital.

Either in the ambulance or on arrival at the hospital Marilyn Monroe expired and was taken back to her house. The body was replaced face down on the bed and, at about midnight, Bobby Kennedy was driven by Peter Lawford to take off in a hastily-hired helicopter from nearby Culver Airfield. He was flown to Los Angeles International Airport to rejoin his family in northern California. When Mrs Murray, Marilyn's housekeeper, 'discovered' the body later, Marilyn had in fact been dead for hours. By the time the doctors and the police arrived at the scene of an apparent suicide (timed at around 4.45a.m.), the house had been carefully sanitised of all traces of Bobby Kennedy's visit. Even as the investigating officer arrived, Mrs Murray was calmly washing clothes and tidying up. Sgt. Clemmons of the LAPD saw her loading boxes into her car.

Jack Clemmons was an experienced cop and, taking in the scene at the house, he became suspicious. Why were there two doctors already at the house? Why had the housekeeper called her son-inlaw to repair the broken window in Marilyn's room *before* calling the police? Why was the washing machine on its third load? Why was there no glass or cup? Clemmons knew that swallowing up to 50 tablets needed water or some other liquid. 'It looked' said Clemmons, 'as if the whole thing had been staged.'

It had. Bernie Spindel, the wire tap expert hired by Jimmy Hoffa to spy on Marilyn, had recorded the sound of a slap, followed by a body hitting the ground and a man's voice asking, 'What shall we do with the body?' Sgt. Clemmons reported his suspicions of murder to the DA and was told to back off. As far as the LAPD was concerned Marilyn Monroe had committed suicide by means of an overdose.

The Coroner's office agreed. The pathologist's report stated that the level of barbiturates in the deceased's blood and liver samples was consistent with between 40 and 50 Nembutal capsules. Even the Coroner's assistant later admitted that he was unhappy about the circumstances (there were some odd bruises on the body) but was pressured by his superiors into signing a certificate that said the death was suicide. The key question was, how had that overdose got into her system?

There was no trace of barbiturates in the stomach or intestines. Massive doses of barbiturates taken by mouth leave a chemical trail in the human body. Marilyn had allegedly taken nearly 50 'yellow jackets', yet there was no sign of any coloured residue in her stomach. The only other way such a massive dose of barbiturates can be taken is either by a powerful injection or by suppository. Dr Noguchi, the pathologist, did record Marilyn's curiously bruised lower intestine and the beginnings of *rigor mortis* by the time the police arrived, putting the verdict of suicide at odds with the evidence.

The key question is not just how the murder may have been committed but *cui bono?* Who stood to benefit from Marilyn's untimely death? The Kennedys faced certain political ruin had she lived to carry out her threat to tell all at a press conference on Monday morning. The swift and well-organised cover-up that followed her death lends further weight to such a conclusion. It could only have been ordered from a very high level indeed.

First, Arthur Jacobs, the Public Relations Consultant, had actually been summoned from a concert at the Hollywood Bowl at 22.45 *the previous evening.* The two doctors were on the scene from the start, to be swiftly followed by private detective Fred Otash. The 'private detective to the stars' had been hired by an agitated Peter Lawford at 5a.m. to 'screen' Monroe's house and check for any evidence incriminating the President or his brother. The fees on offer were astronomical.

At the City and State level the Police were given orders direct from Washington. Responsibility for the enquiry was transferred exclusively to the Chief of Police's office. The Chief of Homicide was ordered to hand the case over to Captain James Hamilton, a personal friend of Bobby Kennedy. He in turn reported directly and personally to the LAPD Chief of Police, James Parker. Chief Parker kept all the files on the Monroe case in his personal safe. All the typing was done by his private secretary and all reports were sent to Washington. Chief Parker held a 'very big' file on the investigation that he took to Washington – 'and it never returned'. Marilyn's explosive 'Red Diary' was seen by a young man called Lionel Grandison, one of the Coroner's Assistants. Grandison claims that he had even flicked idly through the pages out of curiosity, noting some references to the Kennedys and the words 'Cuba' and 'Mafia'. Once the effects were passed to the LAPD the notebook disappeared without trace.

There was also clear evidence of federal interference. Within 12 hours all Monroe's telephone records had been removed from the Bell Telephone Company. Only the FBI or the Secret Service had that authority in rules-conscious America. Local FBI agents were surprised to find senior out-of-town agents suddenly appearing on their patch within one day of the Monroe death and carrying out 'some kind of hush-hush investigation'. In 1982 Peter Lawford's former wife Deborah Gould admitted the truth: Marilyn had died well before midnight.

The assembled facts point to a death that happened sometime late on the evening of 4 August and which was either a straightforward murder, or an attempted suicide by Marilyn that was 'helped along'. The evidence points to the latter and to murder, probably by lethal suppository. The Mafia would undoubtedly have preferred a live, angry and vengeful Marilyn to denounce and discredit the Kennedys come Monday morning. But if she had already taken an overdose on her own and left an explosive suicide note blaming the Kennedys, then a dead Monroe with a suicide note would do just as well to bring the Kennedy dynasty down and get the Feds off the back of the Mobsters. And if Marilyn was not killed by the Kennedys but by the Mafia after Robert Kennedy left, then her murder would still implicate the Kennedy brothers in a messy celebrity suicide or even murder.

These are the only conclusions consistent with the known facts. What they hadn't bargained for was Lawford discovering this and rushing round to clean up the scene and destroy any suicide note that named the Kennedys. In later life when he had fallen from favour, Lawford always claimed that the Kennedys had used the FBI to stop any proper investigation into the doomed star's death. His deathbed confession in 1984 confirmed this.

The sad, tragic end of Marilyn Monroe proves not only that a major cover-up operation orchestrated by the Federal government was possible, but that the cover-up of the events in Dallas 15 months later had a clear precedent.

PART 2

KENNEDY'S ENEMIES

7

BROTHERS IN ARMS – THE CUBAN EXILES AND THE CIA

SO LONG AS WE GAIN SUCCESS, THE INTERFERENCE OF POLITICIANS IN MILITARY MATTERS CAN BE RESISTED. BUT, ON THE FIRST DISASTER...
MAJOR-GENERAL HENRY HALLECK, 1863

Kennedy began making enemies the moment he won the presidential election. Conventional thinking in 1960 had been that the election would be close but Richard M. Nixon, the Republican leader already deeply in hock to big business, the Mafia and Wall Street, would win.

Kennedy's arrival therefore upset a lot of pre-planned defence contracts and business deals. For example, the final contract $6.5 billion for the F-111 fighter-bomber had been deliberately kept on hold to await the arrival of the new President. Now, unexpectedly, it would all have to be renegotiated. The bitter losers counted their financial loss. Not all Americans were happy with America's charismatic new young President's victory.

One group regarded Jack Kennedy as a liar and a traitor from the start. When the Cuban Exiles brigade came ashore at the Bay of Pigs in April 1961 to be ambushed by Castro's soldiers, they had expected American help. Despite the promises of their CIA masters, it never came. The only thing that could have saved the exiles was direct American support. But Jack Kennedy had turned his back on them. The sullen survivors were marched off into captivity, cursing the new President of the United States who had refused American air cover over the invasion beaches – or so the Cuban survivors believed.

Even when Kennedy ransomed the exile prisoners from Castro in December 1962 in return for $62 million it did little to appease their grievances. For many of the hot-headed Latin hardliners who had endured the hell of Castro's jails, John Fitzgerald Kennedy was a liar, a traitor. They wanted revenge for their betrayal and the death of their friends.

While the anger of the Cuban Exiles and the Mafia could – just possibly – be ignored or contained, the enmity of the CIA could not, especially in the early 1960s. The Agency was anxious to shift the blame for its own operational incompetence over the Cuban debacle and claimed that it was all the fault of the inexperienced President. The CIA leaked that the real reason their plan had failed was that Kennedy had lost his nerve.

The Central Intelligence Agency had grown out of the post Second World War Office of Strategic Services (OSS) into a power in its own right. It was a self-governing state within a state, confronting Communism everywhere with a limitless supply of tax dollars to fund its Cold War task. Under its Director, the legendary Allen Dulles, the CIA controlled private armies, spied on whomsoever it liked, ran its own printing companies, banks and airlines, ran drugs for cash and was virtually unaccountable.

With hindsight it is clear that the success of the whole CIA adventure to attack Cuba had always relied for success on the commitment of US forces. The *Santa Anna's* 168 fake 'Cuban soldiers' were concrete proof of that. The CIA planners had always bargained on the exiles getting into trouble on the beach and then relied on the President coming to their rescue nudged along by the pretext of an 'unprovoked attack' by the 'Cuban army' on a US base. But the *Santa Anna's* fake army and their fake attack never materialised. As a result Kennedy failed to play his CIA-appointed role as a pawn of their planners, much to the dismay of the Agency and the fury of the Cuban Exiles. As far as the majority of the CIA's officers were concerned, Jack Kennedy had failed their Agency and their country, and let them down.

The CIA's brothers in arms, '*Their Cubans*', had been betrayed.

***

While the Cuban Exiles could be discounted and bought off with fresh promises of support, the CIA, on the other hand, could not. Many senior figures in the CIA felt that they served 'the cause of freedom' in their own right. Now, their new president had effectively abandoned them as well as their loyal Cuban clients. One day, the disaffected CIA men swore, there would be a reckoning. As proof of the strength of feeling against Jack Kennedy within the CIA, in 1963 when hardliners heard the news that the President had been assassinated 'there was joy in the CIA's Tokyo Station'. The CIA officers cheered and 'brought out the bottles' to toast Oswald amid shouts of 'This is for the Bay of Pigs!'

The problem was that by the time Kennedy took over, the CIA was almost completely out of control. What Truman had started originally as a simple intelligence reporting and briefing agency had under Alan Dulles swelled into a bloated and self-tasking undercover action organisation. Intelligence had been sidelined. The Agency was dominated by its secret undercover warriors, the Covert Actions Division. This emphasis on dirty tricks at the expense of intelligence reporting should have come as no surprise. CIA Director Alan Dulles had first made his name as an undercover OSS man in the Second World War. For him the lure of Special Operations and 'secret agents' far outstripped the more mundane tasks of collecting, collating and interpreting intelligence.

However, there was another reason for Dulles' policy of emphasising Special Operations. It opened the door to vast secret funds and a bigger budget from a credulous Congress and the long-suffering taxpayer. By 1960 nearly 60 per cent of the CIA was engaged in 'dirty tricks' rather than collecting intelligence. More dangerously, very few people knew what the CIA's clandestine services were up to, least of all the elected politicians supposed to be in charge.

Eisenhower had been warned about this problem by his predecessor, Harry S. Truman, who said:

> For some time I have been disturbed by the way the CIA has been diverted from its original assignment. It has become an operational and at times a policy-making arm of the government ... I never had any thought when I set up the CIA that it would be injected into peacetime cloak-and-dagger operations.

Despite this warning from his predecessor, even the intelligence-experienced Eisenhower was unable to grip the Agency during his presidency. Right at the start he had blasted the Agency's analysts when he discovered that they didn't know about Stalin's death. In 1958 the President's Board of Intelligence consultants warned him that the CIA was 'incapable of making objective appraisals of its own intelligence information as well as of its own operations' and begged him to separate Covert Ops from intelligence by taking the former away from the CIA.

The result was that in the early 1960s, even for an elected president, the CIA had grown to become a powerful and dangerous foe. As Richard Starnes reported:

> The CIA's growth was likened to a malignancy which the very high official was not sure that even the White House could control much longer. If the United States ever experiences an attempt at a coup to overthrow the government it will come from the CIA and not the Pentagon. The Agency represents a tremendous power and total unaccountability.

Over Cuba the Agency had even tried to take over control of American foreign policy. It had attempted to force the President to do what *it* wanted, and not the other way round. The CIA had now grown to become a Cold War political force and global powerbroker in its own right. It was effectively a self-tasking, self-governing independent organisation, hiding its mistakes and contemptuous of vacillating presidential direction. By May 1961 the CIA, the most secretive and powerful – and certainly the most out of control – organisation in America, was no friend of Jack Kennedy.

Kennedy returned the compliment. He was furious at the CIA's blatant attempt to drag him and the United States into a shooting war with Cuba behind his back. The last straw was when Alan Dulles turned up at the National Security Council's inquest on the Bay of Pigs on 22 April 1961 with a copy of NSC 5412 (The charter for the CIA's Special Operations) and to the astonishment of the President and the assembled NSC members claimed that the CIA shouldn't really be held responsible for Covert Operations.

John Kennedy decided to clip the wings of the CIA once and for all. In a genuine rage he lashed out at the all-powerful Agency. By the end of the year he sacked its director, the redoubtable Allen Dulles, who had headed America's undercover intelligence efforts since the Second World War, as well as his number two, Richard Bissell, the Director of Covert Operations and the man who had failed over Cuba.

Kennedy even threatened to break up the Agency completely.

CIA 'lifers' were appalled. In New Orleans an ex-CIA asset called David Ferrie openly said that someone should shoot Kennedy. Latin tempers ran hot and threats to 'get Kennedy' were loud and frequent from both the Cubans and their CIA backers. They would be the first of many.

***

The failure of the CIA's Cuban adventure was to set the tone for the Kennedy administration. After the Bay of Pigs it was almost as if the charismatic Kennedys felt that they were being taunted by Castro, the bearded *Jefe Máximo* just across the water. The result was that Cuba became a serious personal problem for both the Kennedys.

But the Cuban leader was never personally a mortal threat to the US. All he had really done was to humiliate the Kennedys and give their political enemies a stick with which to beat them. On 19 January 1962, Bobby Kennedy told the new director, John McCone, that the overthrow of Fidel

Castro was 'the top priority for the US government ... no time, effort or manpower is to be spared.'

Although the President threatened to 'splinter the CIA into a thousand pieces', in reality it seems that he was more interested in getting the CIA to work better. What Jack Kennedy really wanted was to shake things up, put his own trusted man in charge and bring a revitalised and more accountable Agency firmly under his own control, with the Pentagon in charge of military special operations.

He put renewed emphasis on the problem of eliminating Castro. In a sign of the times, Robert F. Kennedy was put in charge of the overall programme by his brother as head of the 'Special Group (Augmented)', a cover name for the Kennedys' private war against Castro's Cuba. (In another sign of the times, the new CIA Director was kept in the dark about this.)

A new independent CIA station was established in Florida to deal specifically with Cuba. It raised a new army of Cuban exiles and soldiers of fortune, which was trained at secret sites in

Guatemala, No-Name Key in Florida and Lake Pontchartrain in Louisiana.

This expanded CIA Florida base, code-named JM/WAVE, now launched a new campaign to destabilise Castro. Operation Mongoose provided the plan for the CIA's secret 'Force W' to launch a series of guerrilla attacks against Castro and Cuba. The exiles and their CIA controllers harassed the Castro regime wherever they could, blowing up bridges, burning cane fields, sabotaging British Leyland buses being shipped to Cuba and, inevitably, devising new and ever more bizarre ways in which they might assassinate the Cuban leader, from poisoned face cream to exploding cigars. The JM/WAVE base grew to of over 300 CIA officers and controlled 3,000 agents. It had a fleet of over 100 staff cars and behind the cover of 'Zenith Technological Service', operated warehouses, printing works, a petroleum depot, an air haulage company, 35 different front corporations and 'the third largest navy in the Western hemisphere'.

JM/WAVE also controlled a new 'International Anti-Communist Brigade'

(IAB) consisting mainly of American soldiers of fortune and the more machismo exiles. Special operations teams such as 'Alpha 66' and 'Operation 40' regularly raided Cuba with secret sabotage and subversion operations. A European assassination expert codenamed 'QJ/WIN' was hired to talent spot and head hunt likely gunmen as part of CIA covert operations chief Bill Harvey's ZR/RIFLE assassination programme.

Despite all this, in November 1961 Bobby Kennedy accused the CIA of 'not doing anything about getting rid of Castro and the Castro regime.' CIA agent Sam Halpern complained that 'Bobby (Kennedy) wanted "boom and bang" all over the island ... it was stupid ... the pressure from the White House was very great.' Eventually CIA Special Operations expert William Harvey took over responsibility for the Mafia assassination contracts as well as his own ZR/RIFLE programme and was effectively given *carte blanche* to go after *el Jefe* – no questions asked.

Trouble loomed however because Harvey's anti-Castro empire was now firmly under the theoretical control of Robert Kennedy. In spring 1963 Bobby visited 'his' Cuban Exiles in Florida and got into a memorable public slanging match with Harvey, who combined a long experience of dirty tricks and black operations with a healthy contempt for the Kennedys' weak handling of the Bay of Pigs and a serious dislike of Ivy League New Englanders playing at spies. Harvey was not a man to hold his tongue, particularly after a long liquid lunch, and his views on the 'rich little mummy's boy' (ironically, nearly identical to Khrushchev's own view of Jack Kennedy) made for a lively exchange of views between the CIA man and his political boss when they argued.

Bobby Kennedy returned to Washington in a towering rage and demanded that the CIA move Bill Harvey. The result was that in mid-1963 the CIA's senior expert on special ops against Cuba was abruptly packed off to become station chief in Rome as yet one more senior CIA officer bearing no great love for the Kennedys. Ominously, 'Wild Bill' Harvey and Mafia Boss Johnny

Rosselli went off for a day's quiet fishing together off Miami the day before Harvey departed for his new post, his career in ruins. It would have been interesting to know just what the Mafia's 'liaison officer' to the Cuban Exiles and the CIA's disaffected and sacked chief of secret operations and assassinations against Cuba discussed in the boat that summer day in 1963.

CIA heads continued to roll in the aftermath of the Bay of Pigs. Soon after giving a talk in New Orleans to the Foreign Policy Association on the Bay of Pigs operation, General Charles Cabell of the USAF was removed from his post by order of JFK. As the liaison officer between the CIA and the White House, he had been one of the CIA's chief architects for the Cuban invasion and the man who actually stopped the Cuban Exiles' airstrikes. He was, unsurprisingly, no fan of John F. Kennedy either.

In a curious coincidence Dallas-born Cabell was introduced onto the platform in New Orleans by another ex-CIA man, called Clay Shaw. They were all linked. General Cabell's brother was the mayor of Dallas, Texas, where Kennedy would be murdered two years later. Clay Shaw would later be charged unsuccessfully by the New Orleans D.A., Jim Garrison, with the murder of John Fitzgerald Kennedy.

The tentacles and unseen links behind the CIA's failure at the Bay of Pigs would reach far and wide. In fact, as Richard Nixon was to say much later in an unguarded moment on the notorious Watergate tapes, 'No. We don't want to reopen the whole Bay of Pigs thing all over again...'

At the time he was referring to the assassination of President John F. Kennedy.

8

JFK VERSUS THE MAFIA

EVERY COUNTRY GETS THE TYPE OF CRIMINALS IT DESERVES...
ROBERT F. KENNEDY AS ATTORNEY GENERAL OF THE UNITED STATES

The word 'Mafia' has become a by-word for organised crime. When they arrived in America in the 1870s the Sicilian Mafia brought together two baleful influences: a secret elite, dedicated to protecting its members and its friends from any outside oppression, and secondly, a ruthless tradition of clan vendetta and justice by murder. When combined with ancient Mediterranean concepts of 'blood-honour', plus an oath of *omerta* (silence), this mixture has proved a unique challenge to law-abiding societies and to the State.

Of course there had been organised crime in America before. Jewish and Irish gangs had already carved out criminal empires by preying on their own teeming immigrant populations of New York, Boston and the other great cities of North America. The *Mafiosi,* whatever their faults, did not invent organised crime in the United States.

None of these ethnic criminal enterprises, however, shared the unique Sicilian mixture of secrecy, organisational skills and crime. The Mafia brought with them for the first time a ruthless internal discipline and cohesion that had evolved over the centuries to resist all attempts to bring them to justice, let alone stamp them out. As the new century dawned, the well-entrenched criminal protection rackets preying on Italian immigrants grew fat on the steady supply of new immigrants flooding into the cities of the north east.

Helped by prohibition, by the 1930s the wider infiltration of *la Cosa Nostra* – 'Our Thing' – into American culture was not only obvious to all, but openly celebrated in movies and popular culture. Edward G. Robinson's *Little Caesar* packed the box office. The Mafia and organised crime became part of the

American way. The key to this expansion of the local Mafia gangs into something much more widespread and interlinked was really a Jewish Mafia boss called Meyer Lansky.

Meyer Lansky was born in Poland of Jewish parents and moved to New York City in 1911. In school, Meyer teamed up with a boy named Charles Luciano and between them started up a gang. Meyer was the perfect partner to 'Lucky' Luciano (so called because he survived an attempted murder), providing the brains to go with Luciano's muscle. Their little gang of toughs prospered on the mean streets of New York. They stole booze from gangsters and sold it for 100 per cent profit. When they weren't stealing liquor, they were hired to protect other gangsters' bootlegged liquor shipments.

In 1931, Meyer helped Luciano to kill Lucky's Mafia boss, Joe Masseria, enabling Lucky to become Don of the Masseria Crime Family. Luciano then went on with Lansky's help to form the 'The Commission', a loose grouping of the five New York Mafia families and then a National Crime Syndicate, which acted as a kind of Mafia High Council, allocating territory, resolving disputes and smoothing trouble.

The Commission effectively became a board of directors that included Meyer, who, although not Italian, was regarded as a good man with money and a crook that the other crooks could trust. Throughout the 1930s, Meyer expanded his operations, setting up new gambling casinos in New Orleans, Florida and Cuba. By the time Luciano went to jail on rigged prostitution charges in 1936, Lansky ran the Mafia's secret High Council in his absence.

It was the US invasion of Sicily in the Second World War that really recognised the Mafia as an independent organisation. America's Office of Strategic Services (OSS) found the help of the Mafia irresistible to speed Patton's advancing American troops during the invasion of Sicily.

Lansky exploited his position to the hilt. He had acted as a secret personal emissary from President Roosevelt to President Batista of Cuba in 1944 and advised the Cuban leader to step aside. A well-bribed Batista obligingly did so and Lansky allegedly won a promise that for services rendered, the Feds would never come after him with the IRS as they had with Capone.

After the war the *Mafiosi* saw the real value of these temporary alliances. The Feds owed them a favour and the Dons exploited their advantage to the hilt. They didn't bother the government and, by and large, the government didn't bother them. The socalled 'Five Families', now working in relative harmony, went their own way for over a decade unhampered by the attentions of the FBI. In this the Mafia leaders were greatly helped by the fact that the FBI's boss, J. Edgar Hoover, was actually on their books. Hoover took regular race track bribes from the Mafia bosses and in return staunchly denied that such a thing as the Mafia and 'organised crime' even existed.

Freed from the unwelcome intrusions of Federal law enforcement, for years the Mob went about their routine business of protection rackets, milking union funds and the more traditional services of gambling, loan sharking and prostitution, with entirely predictable results. As the cash poured in, the American Mafia grew hugely rich. The impact of prohibited drugs during the 1950s accelerated the process still further. By 1960 the Mafia's bloody fingers extended into virtually every major money-making enterprise of the USA, from Hollywood films to the New York waterfront, and from bribing policemen to buying politicians.

The Kennedys were not the only politicians to flirt with the Mobsters or yield to the corrupting lure of the Mafia's gold. Richard Nixon's gambling debts in the Mob's Havana casino were paid off by his generous hosts in 1952, and both Barry Goldwater and Lyndon Johnson received sizeable slabs of cash to help fund their election campaigns in the late 1950s. Although Richard Nixon was by no means alone among politicians on the Hill in accepting the Mob's largesse, he was the most blatant. The Secret Service was even warning him about keeping bad company when he eventually became president. The press had been on to him from the start. A *New York Post*

headline of September 1948 could have been from any year for Richard Nixon:
SECRET RICH MAN'S TRUST FUND KEEPS NIXON IN STYLE FAR BEYOND HIS SALARY

The 'rich man' in question was Meyer Lansky and his Mafia friends in Havana.

Whichever side won the elections, the Mafia bosses were taking each way bets to make sure that they would be owed big favours by the victorious politicians who were returned on Capitol Hill. Politicians were not the only group to seek the Mafia's assistance. The CIA and the Mafia had much in common. Both groups were rich, powerful and shared traditional American values, if from different sides of the fence. Both groups operated well outside the restricting clutches of the law, and both sides were not afraid to resort to force when it was needed. They were natural bedfellows and Cold War allies, especially against Castro's Cuba.

As early as August 1960 the Director of the CIA's Office of Security, Col Sheffield Edwards, was proposing that the Agency hire known Mafia assassins to murder the Cuban leader on behalf of the United States government. The Mafia leaders that he recommended for the anti-Castro project were names that would crop up later at the time of President Kennedy's assassination: Sam Giancana; Johnny Rosselli; Jimmy Hoffa; Santo Trafficante and the Boss of Bosses, Carlos Marcello. Ironically, these CIA 'subcontractors' were the very men who would come to hate the Kennedys – and particularly Bobby Kennedy – more than most.

Bobby Kennedy was a difficult figure. The third son of Joe Kennedy's nine children, after graduating from Harvard and the University of Virginia School of Law he had made his name as a thrusting, aggressive young lawyer and politician and the mastermind behind his elder brother's campaigns for office. In 1963 he was, at only 38, the youngest Attorney General in United States history. His appointment surprised Washington's political elite. Suddenly a Kennedy dynasty became a very real possibility. We have clear proof of that from a conversation between Hoover and his number two and boyfriend, Clyde Tolson. 'Goddamn the Kennedys,' Tolson said. 'First there was Jack, now there's Bobby, and then Teddy. We'll have them on our necks until the year 2000.'

No one was in any doubt that the abrasive and ruthless Bobby Kennedy only held his post by virtue of his brother. But Joe Kennedy's third son had ambitions of his own. He knew that when Jack Kennedy stood down, hopefully after two full terms, he could be the prince in waiting. To achieve the Democratic nomination in 1968 he had to make his political name in his own right before that day. The post of Attorney General offered him a headlinegrabbing opportunity for national recognition and a popular political platform. All he needed was a popular cause.

In the thrusting young Attorney General's very public attack on the Mafia and organised crime in general, Bobby Kennedy was shamelessly playing to the gallery. The Mafia had really come to public attention three years before.

At a supposedly secret meeting in Apalachin, upstate New York, the State Police arrested and photographed 62 gangsters. America was astonished by press photographs of smartly dressed hoodlums running through the woods. Vito Genovese was never forgiven by his fellow gangsters for exposing *La Cosa Nostra* to the glare of publicity.

The 'Great Apalachin Mafia Bust' of 1957 left an indelible impression in the popular mind that the time had come for 'something to be done' about the Mafia. Bobby Kennedy seized his opportunity. The new Attorney General was soon harassing the Godfathers as publicly as possible. Congressional hearings on the Hill degenerated into question after question being stonewalled by sweating gangsters in expensive suits and their tight-mouthed attorneys with the answer, 'I'll take the Fifth.' (The Fifth Amendment to the US Constitution guarantees a suspect's right to remain silent and not to incriminate himself.)

The gangsters began to mutter among themselves that something needed to be done about Bobby

Kennedy, never mind organised crime. And none muttered more than Jimmy Hoffa, long-time Mafia associate and the deeply corrupt leader of the Teamsters Union.

If there were two individuals who really detested Bobby Kennedy, J. Edgar Hoover and Jimmy Hoffa led the field. The difference was that while the FBI Director Hoover had all the dirt on Bobby Kennedy and his family, Hoffa was already mixed up in numerous Mafia rackets and was under investigation for bribery and using Union funds to pay off the Mob.

On one occasion in July 1963 he actually assaulted the Attorney General of the United States in his own office. Bobby Kennedy didn't press charges; but from that moment on it was war to the death between the two men.

We now know from released CIA documents that Hoffa had good cause to feel aggrieved. As one part of the US government was publicly hounding him and trying to send him to jail, another part of the US government was secretly begging him to act as their official agent to fix a murder.

No wonder that by the summer of 1963 Hoffa felt that he had had enough of the Kennedys' duplicity. His lawyer, Ragano, heard him say that the time had come for Carlos Marcello and Santo Trafficante to 'get rid of him ... kill that fucking son of a bitch Kennedy', openly calling for the President to be murdered.

Bobby Kennedy's hounding of the Mafia to boost his political ambitions was stirring up a deadly hornets' nest for the Kennedys. By mid-1963 the Kennedy brothers were pursuing two completely contradictory policies: a secret plot begging the Mafia bosses for help them to murder Castro on behalf of the US government; and a public battle in which another part of the government was trying to send those self-same Mafia leaders to jail. From the Mafia leaders' point of view it looked very much as if the Kennedy boys were trying to play both ends against the middle and double-cross the 'Men of Honour'.

It was to prove a deadly error.

9

JFK VERSUS BIG OIL

GOD HATH ANOINTED THEE WITH THE OIL OF GLADNESS ABOVE ALL THY FELLOWS.
PSALM 45

IF YOU CAN COUNT ALL YOUR MONEY THEN YOU ARE NOT REALLY A RICH MAN...
J. PAUL GETTY, OIL BILLIONAIRE

Having made mortal enemies of the Cuban Exiles, and an institutional enemy of the powerful CIA, as well as the Mafia and organised crime, the 'Fighting Irish' then proceeded to take on big business and Wall Street.

In April 1962 the US Steel Corporation announced a sudden increase of $6 a ton in the price of steel. As the price hike was four times the anticipated cost of a new labour agreement, a storm of controversy arose. Jack Kennedy moved rapidly to stamp out this blatant and obviously coordinated attempt to fix prices. He ordered an anti-trust investigation and the Federal Price Commission began a probe into secret price fixing deals which would have added *one billion* dollars to the total US Defence budget overnight.

Faced with an implacable president, a hostile press and a federal enquiry, on oath, into their most secret boardroom machinations, the steel barons capitulated. Wall Street and its rich moguls were not pleased. Had not President Coolidge himself said that the business of America was business?

Unlike Eisenhower, Nixon and Johnson, JFK was not in the pocket of big business. In May 1962 there was a mysterious minicrash on Wall Street. Someone dumped millions of shares overnight and created a panic not seen since 1929. Kennedy rode out the short-lived storm. But it looked like a test of his political will and a demonstration by Wall Street that that even presidents have to heed the marketplace.

In 1962 John Kennedy moved to take on the Texas oil barons. Thanks to oil, Texas had one of the greatest concentrations of millionaires in the world. Following the discovery of vast new oilfields in 1930, a handful of Texas landowners became very rich indeed. Among them were Sid Richardson, Billy Byars, Haroldson L. Hunt and Clint Murchison.

At the heart of the Texans' oil money was the unique tax concession called the 'Oil Depletion Allowance'. First introduced in 1913 as a tax break to encourage oil drilling and keep supply going, it allowed oil drillers to offset 5 per cent of their costs against tax. In 1926 it was increased to 27.5 per cent. This was effectively a licence for the oil men to print money. A three-year well guaranteed a return of nearly three quarters of a million dollars in profit – seven times the original investment. A 10-year well guaranteed a return of no less than 27 times the original investment. A man could afford to drill a lot of dry holes for odds like that.

The Texas oil men loved their Oil Depletion Allowance.

***

This was the cash cow that Kennedy now proposed to lead to the slaughter as part of a general cleaning up of tax loopholes and removal of special privileges.

Although he had pledged support for the Oil Depletion Allowance during the 1960 election campaign, in October 1962 he persuaded Congress to table an act that would end the oil industry's unique tax break and bring it into line with general business tax law. The oil men were appalled. At a stroke the President was promising legislation that would cost them half their profits and take up to $300 million a year out of their pockets ($3 billion at 2013 prices). The hard-nosed men in Dallas and Houston moved quickly to stop this federal interference with the giants of Texas Oil.

At the heart of the oil cartel was an informal, shadowy cabal calling itself the '8F Group' after the suite where it held its meetings at the Lamar Hotel in Houston. The group brought together some of the richest and most powerful men in Texas. In their number by the early 1960s were also representatives from state and federal politics, lawyers, bankers, businessmen and the Mafia.

In 1962/63 the 8F Group included oil barons H.L. Hunt, Billy Byars, Sid Richardson and Clint Murchison; State Governor John Connally and State Attorney General Waggoner Carr; Lyndon Baines Johnson; his personal Mr Fixit, Ed Clark; as well as prominent bankers and businessmen, including selected Mafia Dons who were, after all, local 'businessmen'. The Texas oil moguls had cultivated J. Edgar Hoover over the years; both Billy Byars of Humble Oil and Clint Murchison helped to pay for the FBI Director's annual vacation at a Mafia-owned and run resort in Del Mar, California. And all of them were friends with Vice President Johnson. Texas oil was big and powerful and had bought key individuals in Washington DC.

LBJ held a special position in the 8F Group because he was effectively their spokesman in Washington. LBJ joined that group in the late 1930s and by 1960 he was openly the representative of Texas capitalism. As a Senator and Leader of the House, LBJ represented himself, the business interests of the Texas 8F Group (especially Brown & Root), and his constituents – in that order.

By the autumn of 1962 the 8F Group were becoming collectively concerned about their president in Washington. Not only did they not own and control him, but he was beginning to do things that would reduce their income. For the power brokers, oil billionaires and bankers of Texas, the answer was simple.

Someone was going to have to do something about John F. Kennedy. Up to then the rich Texans had tolerated him. But removing the Oil Depletion Allowance was a step too far. In 1962 $300 million was a lot of money. Around the 8F Group table 'groupthink' was unanimous. John F. Kennedy was dangerous. He would have to be stopped.

Texas said so.

10

JFK VERSUS THE GOVERNMENT OF MONEY

GIVE ME CONTROL OF A NATION'S MONEY SUPPLY, AND I CARE NOT WHO MAKES ITS LAWS.
MAYER AMSCHEL ROTHSCHILD

HE WHO CONTROLS MONEY CONTROLS THE WORLD.
HENRY KISSINGER

Every US dollar bill says 'In God We Trust'. To say that money and the making of money is sacred to America is not blasphemy; it is merely the recognition of a truth that goes back to the American Colonies' war for independence from Great Britain in 1776. The Founding Fathers were never driven primarily by any noble desire for 'Liberty' in the abstract. They wanted to have the freedom to make their own money in their New World, without interference from tiresome outsiders trying to tax them from 3,000 miles away.

Right from the start, the Founding Fathers saw the importance of a sound currency as something to be controlled by the people's representatives, not bankers and moneylenders. Thomas Jefferson wrote: 'The central bank is an institution of the most deadly hostility existing against the Principles and form of our Constitution. I am an Enemy to all banks discounting bills or notes for anything but Coin.'

On 4 June 1963, President Kennedy approved a little-known presidential Executive Order, number 11,110. It effectively stripped some of the US Federal Reserve Bank's power to lend printed money to the government for interest and returned the right to print money to the US Treasury. On that day Kennedy took back for the US government the right to issue its own currency, without going through the Federal Reserve. The order gave the Treasury the power 'to issue silver certificates against any silver bullion, silver, or standard silver dollars in the Treasury.'

The implications were enormous. With the stroke of a pen, Kennedy was on his way to putting the Federal Reserve Bank out of business. If enough of these 'silver certificates' were to come into circulation, they would have eliminated the demand for Federal Reserve banknotes. According to Fletcher Prouty, former CIA insider turned critic:

> Mar. Kennedy challenged the 'government of money' by challenging the two most successful vehicles that have ever been used to drive up debt – war and the creation of money by a privately owned central bank. His efforts to have all troops out of Vietnam by 1965 and Executive Order 11,110 would have severely cut into the profits and control of the New York banking establishment.

Prouty's reference to Vietnam is crucial, because Vietnam was the other issue seen by the business men and bankers as an important source of revenue under threat from John F. Kennedy's meddling.

The idea of the Vietnam War as a source of good business may seem shocking to some, but it is nothing less than the truth. War diverts taxpayers' money into the pockets of arms manufacturers, sub-contractors and their shareholders. War can be very profitable. For example, 4,865 US helicopters were lost during the Vietnam War. At a cost of roughly $250,000 each in the 1960s that comes to a total of nearly $1,300,000,000.

Estimates reckon that the total cost of the war in Vietnam was between $220 and $570 billion during the 20 years of fighting, at 1960s prices. Many US corporations wanted and supported the war in Vietnam because of the financial benefits it brought them. To the secretive international bankers of Wall Street and the rich stockowners of the major corporations a nice little war in some far off country was seen as a positively beneficial financial development – for them.

To take just one example, in early November 1963 LBJ's oil millionaire crony D.H. ('Dry Hole') Byrd bought a major slice of the Texas-based aircraft manufacturer Ling Temco Vought's (LTV) stock. LTV was in deep trouble at the time.

It was Dry Hole Byrd's good friend President Lyndon Johnson's decision in early 1964 to commit more troops and aircraft to Vietnam that brought the company an order for 1,500 new A7 aircraft. By 1968 LTV was worth $3.8 billion. We can be sure that Dry Hole Byrd was suitably grateful to LBJ, his good old buddy from the 8F Group. He was not the only one: Halliburton, Brown & Root and General Dynamics were all based in Texas, and all would make a lot of money out of Lyndon Johnson's decision after the assassination to reverse JFK's policy of withdrawal from the Vietnam War, and instead commit the US to a much bigger effort. One of the results of increasing the American stake in the war was blindingly obvious: it meant that companies could get their hands on more taxpayers' money to line rich men's pockets.

It was as brutally simple as that. The twin policies of trying to cut American dependence on the US 'Central Bank' for money supply and to reduce the costs of war to the taxpayer therefore made Jack Kennedy a very serious threat to the 'invisible government' of Big Business, Big Money and to the New York Stock Exchange.

For these shadowy financiers, by far the more dangerous of the two moves was the President's attempt to seize control of the US money supply. The President was throwing down a direct challenge to the Federal Reserve Group of Banks and its chokehold on the American economy. By doing that, JFK was openly challenging the power of the 'invisible government of money'. That such a shadowy group existed – and still does – is not in doubt. Congressman Wright Patman, a Democrat from Texas and contemporary of JFK, summed it up in the 1960s: 'In the US today we have effectively two governments. We have the duly constituted government. Then we have an independent uncontrolled Federal Reserve System operating the money powers which are reserved to Congress by the Constitution.'

As early as 1913, President Woodrow Wilson – the man who actually signed the Federal Reserve Bank into law – stated:

> The government, which was designed for the people, has got into the hands of the bosses and their employers, the special interests. An invisible empire has been set up above the forms of democracy ... Some of the biggest names in the US in the field of commerce and manufacturing are afraid of somebody, of something. They know that there is a power somewhere so organized, so subtle, so watchful, so interlocked, so pervasive that they had better not speak above their breath when they speak in condemnation of it...

The 28th President was talking about Big Money and the bankers' cartel. He knew better than most what he was talking about, for he had been personally groomed by Bernard Baruch as the 'bankers' representative' and owed his presidential nomination to the backing of the big international bankers. Wilson was genuinely frightened by the power of the money cartel.

Relatively few people are aware that 'the Fed' is emphatically not an arm of the US Government or Treasury. It is a bank for profit, formed of a group of *private* banks, and it maintains a very agreeable monopoly. It holds the legal licence to print and issue US banknotes. The dollar notes in circulation are actually printed for the Federal Reserve by the US Bureau of Engraving and Printing, and then lent by the Fed back to the US government – in return for interest. Astoundingly, the US government uses taxpayers' money to pay a group of private bankers for the privilege of printing and using its own banknotes, which it then borrows from the Fed and pays interest on them.

A sub-committee of the US House Committee on Banking and Currency summed it up neatly in a 1964 report:
> The Federal Reserve is a money-making machine. It can issue money or checks. It never has a problem of making its checks because it can obtain the $5 and

$10 bills necessary to cover its check by asking the Bureau of Engraving to print them.

The US Constitution specifically states that 'only Congress shall coin and regulate money'. How on earth could a group of powerful bankers acquire the legal right to print as much money as they liked?

The answer lies in a curious and highly secret meeting at Jekyll Island on 22 November 1910. Literally sneaking out of New York under cover of darkness, seven men assembled in a private clubhouse on a secluded island off Georgia. They represented the cream of the US banking community: Senator Nelson Aldrich, Chairman of the National Monetary Commission; Abe P. Andrew, Assistant Secretary to the Treasury; Frank Vanderlip, President of the National City Bank of New York and representing the Rockefellers and Kuhn Loeb; Henry Davison of JP Morgan, Inc.; Charles Norton, President of JP Morgan's bank; Benjamin Strong of the Bankers' Trust; Paul M. Warburg, representing the Warburgs and the Rothschilds. They had gathered in the chateaulike rich men's clubhouse on the secluded island to plan a breathtaking banking coup.

The key players were Senator Aldrich, leader of the National Money Commission, who knew little about banking but everything about political manipulation. His daughter was married to a Rockefeller. The other key player was the quiet, bookish German, Paul Warburg. The plump and scholarly Warburg was a European banking specialist and the real drafter of the plan that was finally hashed out over the next week behind closed doors.

It was Warburg who proposed the idea of a 'Federal Reserve System'. The problems were that it was not federal, there were no 'reserves', and it wasn't a system at all. It was instead a new big central bank, with one great difference. It did not belong to the government. It would actually be a consortium of *private* banks, owned by private individuals, all of whom would profit from their ownership of shares in the new big 'national' bank.

It was a breathtaking scheme, and it worked. The final plan was presented to Congress as the 'Aldrich Bill for

Monetary Reform'; and no mention of the Jekyll Island bankers' meeting leaked out for over six years. It was only in the 1930s that the full story began to emerge and the public became aware of the real authors of the 'Aldrich Plan'. But by then it was too late. In 1913, the Federal Reserve Bill became law.

The bill was passed on the sly on 23 December 1913 by a single vote in the Senate. There were only three Senators present as the Senate had supposedly broken up for Christmas. With most of the Senate away for the holidays, a special Congressional Conference Committee meeting attended by only three Senators was called for *half past one in the morning.*

As dawn broke, a prepared version of the Committee report was handed hastily to the printers. On the evening of 23 December, President Woodrow Wilson signed the Federal Reserve Act of 1913 into law. The Act transferred control of the money supply of the United States from Congress to a private group of international bankers. It can be argued that it was the biggest, and boldest, financial ramp in history.

Many saw through the scheme at the time. When the Bill was finally passed, Congressman C.A. Lindbergh, father of the solo Atlantic aviator, said, 'Our financial system is a false one ... This Act establishes the most gigantic Trust on earth'. Senator 'Fighting Bob' La Follette pointed out that 'a Money Trust of less than 50 men now controls the United States'. On hearing this, one of banker JP Morgan's close banking associates is reported to have said, 'That's nonsense! Why, there are only eight...'

The Fed however did more than print money to enrich its members. It soon had serious form as a manipulator of the whole US economy. According to Milton Friedman, the Nobel Prizewinning economist, the Federal Reserve bankers deliberately caused the Great Depression by contracting the amount of money in circulation by one third between 1929 and 1933. Friedman unhesitatingly points the finger at the bankers' cartel as the architects of the crash.

The economic boom of the Roaring Twenties had encouraged millions to invest and speculate heavily in the stock market, fuelled by a surge in the supply of printed bank notes. Many had borrowed money from their local banks to buy shares. Rising share prices encouraged more and more people to invest; people hoped the share prices would rise still further. Having pumped money into the US economy throughout the 1920s, the Fed now cold-bloodedly turned off the money tap.

The plan went into action when trading began on the morning of 24 October 1929. The Fed suddenly refused to lend short-term money to small banks. Everything that followed about the Great Wall Street Crash stemmed from that deliberate and cynical manipulation of the money supply. Congressman Louis McFadden, Chairman of the House Banking and Currency Committee, later commented that the depression '...was not accidental. It was a carefully contrived occurrence ... The international bankers sought to bring about a condition of despair here so that they might emerge as the rulers of us all.'

***

For 50 years the Fed and its shadowy owners had enjoyed this monopoly of total control of a scarce commodity that everyone needed and wanted – money. The Fed controlled all major American finances. It printed and issued money; it set interest rates across the country; it loaned money to the US Treasury at interest and was handsomely rewarded in return by American taxpayers. The power of the Federal Reserve and its regional banks was colossal. A small group of very rich men had grown fat on the power to create their own money.

JFK now decided to try and bring this over mighty cabal of bankers to heel. In common with Presidents Jackson and Lincoln, JFK was keenly aware that any privately owned US Central Bank was not only greedy and inefficient but it was also theoretically unconstitutional. The US Constitution clearly states that 'only the Congress shall coin and regulate money.' By trying to wrest back control of the US money supply Kennedy was returning the power to print money to its legal home. It was a brave – if not a downright dangerous – move. Presidents who had crossed the big international bankers in the past had traditionally had a very rough ride. The murdered Presidents Garfield and Lincoln had both been staunch and highly vocal opponents of the bankers' cartel. Lincoln had paid for it with his life.

The other assassinated president, Garfield, had been a hard currency man too, insisting that paper banknotes must be backed by real value. He warned against the bankers and their friends in Congress who opposed him: 'Whoever controls the volume of money in our country is absolute master of all industry and commerce ... and when you realize that the entire system is very easily controlled, one way or another, by a few powerful men at the top...'

There was another grisly warning for Kennedy of what could happen to people who spoke out against the big bankers and the Fed in particular, this time a little nearer to home. Thirty years before, Louis T. McFadden, who had been the chairman of the House Banking and Currency Committee, and who was an experienced banker himself, launched a vitriolic attack on the Fed. On June 10 1932 the House was debating a bill that would expand the types of securities the Federal Reserve could trade. McFadden said:

> We have in this country one of the most corrupt institutions the world has ever known. I refer to the Federal Reserve Board and the Federal Reserve banks. The Federal Reserve Board, a Government board, has cheated the Government of the United States out of enough money to pay the national debt ... It has done this through defects of the law under which it operates ... and through the corrupt practices of the moneyed vultures who control it.

Shortly afterwards McFadden was poisoned.

It was clear from the start, therefore, that Kennedy's decision to challenge the big names of banking and the owners of the Federal Reserve was always going to be a long, drawn-out fight, even for the President of the United States, because for the Rothschilds and their plutocrat banking friends, there was just too much at stake.

Kennedy promptly used the new powers of Executive Order 11,110 to issue new banknotes. As a result of the President's order, over four billion dollars' worth of new low denomination banknotes were printed and issued by the US Treasury. These were 'United States' banknotes (and not 'Federal Reserve') and they were printed as new 'silver certificates'. Unlike the Federal Reserve Notes, the new $2 and $5 'Silver Certificate' dollar notes were backed by silver; Federal Reserve Notes are backed by nothing.

One of the immediate effects of Kennedy's decision was to wipe out $120 million off the Fed's balance sheet, because the Fed would have charged 3 per cent for the privilege of lending the US government $4 billion of its own banknotes. This was no mean sum in 1963 – or today – and was a clear threat to the bankers that backed the Fed. In signing EO 11,110 Kennedy was striking at the very heart of the international bankers and their monopoly.

To go up against the cartel of international bankers who ran the Federal Reserve and attack their profit base was a brave thing to do, even for a president. It was unthinkable that such a group of rich, well-connected men who owned and controlled fortunes across the globe would permit half a century of fat profits and total control of the US money supply and its gold reserves to be snatched from their grasp without a fight. Whatever else he lacked, John Kennedy did not lack balls.

The bankers of the Federal Reserve decided to strike back. *Their* mighty dollar was more important than mere presidents and their whims of policy. Something would have to be done about Kennedy to stop his meddling with America's most sacred commodity – money. Much worse: he was challenging the private cartel of international bankers behind 'the secret government of money'. The President was daring to meddle with 'their' money. Who did he think he was?

If anyone had a motive to see President Kennedy and his policies stopped dead in his tracks, it was the secretive group of bankers and their friends who owned and ran the US 'Federal Reserve Bank.'

Significantly, soon after Kennedy was murdered, the order to print new US Treasury banknotes was rescinded and the Federal Reserve's monopoly was reinstated.

11

THE PROBLEM OF LBJ

ON N'EST JAMAIS TRAHI QUE PAR SES SIENS. ('ONE IS NEVER BETRAYED EXCEPT BY ONE'S FRIENDS.')
OLD FRENCH PROVERB

Lyndon Baines Johnson's problems were simple: he was a deeply corrupt politician on the take, and a murderous crook as well.

So the announcement that Lyndon Baines Johnson was going to be John Kennedy's running mate as Vice President on the Democratic ticket in 1960 took many by surprise. A more ill-matched pair would have been hard to find even in the bizarre world of American politics. Kennedy was a sophisticated, liberal, well-educated aristocrat, heir to a New England dynasty. Johnson was seen as a crude 'Good Ol' Boy' from Texas, rough and tough, with the manners of the oil rig and with decidedly conservative political views.

The reason for this unusual union was, as is so often the case, political expediency. LBJ had stood against Kennedy for the presidential nomination in the 1960 Democratic Convention. But JFK was the golden boy and won the Democratic nomination for President on the first ballot.

As part of the usual stitch up that follows political parties' internal struggles for power, Kennedy then offered the vice presidency to his rival. In many ways it made sense: LBJ could not only deliver the second biggest state of the Union but also bring a lot of the South along too. Kennedy also calculated that by offering the powerful Senate Majority Leader the post of Vice President he could curb LBJ's considerable power and influence in the Senate.

***

The new Vice President had much to hide: and he fully intended to keep it that way. If he were to stand for President in 1968 not a breath of scandal must appear against him. This was a problem as LBJ had been a crook all his political life and realised he was vulnerable in a number of key areas. LBJ could be indicted – should anyone care to look – on five serious charges, any one of which could ruin him:

- He had rigged the ballot in his 1948 election to the Senate.
- He had received hundreds of corrupt pay offs from corporations, organised crime and individuals over the years.
- He had illegally procured government contracts for his friends and backers in big business – particularly Texan big business.
- He had ordered the murder of at least five individuals using a gunman called Mac Wallace.
- He was heavily implicated in the corruption scandals surrounding Bobby Baker and Billy Sol Estes.

The 1948 ballot-rigging is now a matter of record. It involved a simple fixing of illegal votes to win election to the US Senate. It reflected LBJ's whole political career. LBJ, the man who had first come to prominence as a Roosevelt 'New Dealer' in 1935, had always been a ruthless fixer and user of other people's money to buy power for himself.

By 1937 he was in Congress and backed by Brown & Root, builders of the $10 million Marshall Dam in Texas. Brown & Root needed a paid mouthpiece on Capitol Hill. In return for their cash, LBJ obliged. No sooner had he taken his seat, than the young Congressman managed to get Federal funds for the boys back home. Although he was not particularly popular with many ordinary voters in Texas, LBJ was respected by businessmen as the local politician who delivered fat federal contracts and tax dollars to 'his' folk. He also benefited from coming under the protection of the Texas political machine in Washington, led by Sam Rayburn.

In 1948 he stood for Senate. The race was a very close one and there was a run-off ballot between LBJ and the Texas Governor, Coke Stevenson. In the far-flung rural counties of the biggest state in the Union, votes came in slowly. Five days after the election Wells County held a recount and found

202 more votes in favour of Johnson, giving LBJ a victory margin of just 87 votes. Despite taunts of 'Landslide Lyndon', LBJ claimed his seat as Senator for Texas amid a storm of protests and recrimination.

In 1977 the truth finally came out. Johnson had bribed Duke Parr, the local Democrat boss, and a judge later admitted that he had rigged the ballot for Johnson. A journalist investigating the case was murdered and all LBJ's IRS and legal documents were destroyed by a mysterious fire in a hut where the records were stored. LBJ's tame enforcer, Mac Wallace, had burned the hut to destroy the evidence; and to make it look like arson he had burned down a couple of other huts and barns in the neighbourhood too. Once again LBJ had escaped unscathed, mainly thanks to his good friend and lawyer, Ed Clark, and his other criminal partner, Cliff Carter. From 1948 onwards LBJ, Ed Clark and Cliff Carter were inseparable as they worked to consolidate LBJ's position and his power.

The team worked as a straightforward business arrangement.

Johnson did the politics, found the money and worked tirelessly for the Texas oil barons and big business. Meanwhile behind the scenes, lawyer Clark stood guard for his powerful front man, fending off trouble, paying off friends, bribing enemies and acting as LBJ's 'office manager'. And Cliff Carter collected the contributions from rich folk who wanted to buy Johnson's political services and power. Mac Wallace provided the muscle when needed.

A major test of their operating procedures blew up in the early 1950s. Lyndon had a wayward younger sister called Josefa. By early 1950 she had divorced two husbands and moved into the twilight zone of 'escorting' minor political figures and lobbyists in Austin. She was broke, she was bisexual and she was an exhibitionist. Josefa Johnson was in fact exactly the kind of younger sister an aspiring national politician didn't need.

Among Josefa's group of friends were Doug Kinser and Mac Wallace. Mac's wife, Mary André Wallace, was attracted to Doug Kinser. In her turn, Josefa Johnson was attracted to Mary

André: a curious *ménage à trois* formed. By the late summer of 1951 Kinser started pestering LBJ for money. LBJ – and lawyer Clark – suspected that it was the start of a long and dangerous shakedown. Giving Kinser money and favours would lead to blackmail. Between them Clark and LBJ came up with a final solution.

Mac Wallace, who worked in Washington, was advised that Kinser was bedding his wife. Two weeks later the supposedly angry and vengeful Wallace drove to Austin and shot Doug Kinser dead. The supposedly enraged husband then calmly drove off and was arrested by the County Police, not 10 miles away.

What followed next was bizarre in a legal sense. Two businessmen friends of LBJ stood bail. The District Attorney announced he could see no motive for the murder and therefore need not pursue that aspect in court. This meant that Josefa and the Kinsers' dirty laundry would not be aired in court, let alone tested in public as evidence. The jury got the message. After a brief spell as a hung jury, they convicted Mac

Wallace of 'murder with malice aforethought'. Eleven voted for the death penalty; one did not. The judge (who was firmly in Ed Clark's pocket) then had to intervene. He confirmed the verdict but sentenced Mac Wallace to five years in prison, suspended for five years.

There was a postscript to the story. In 1961 Josefa Johnson, still far too wild a card as far as the Vice President was concerned, attended a Christmas Eve party at her brother's spread at the LBJ Ranch. There was a row and Josefa left early. That very night LBJ's wayward sister died of a sudden and unexplained cerebral haemorrhage in her sleep. There was no autopsy.

***

Mac Wallace was to feature in a number of LBJ-linked murders before he himself was killed in 1971. The most notorious was the killing of Henry Marshall, a federal investigator for the US Department of Agriculture, who had got on to LBJ's money trail.

The scandal blew up over the clumsy fraud. Billy Sol Estes had made a lot of money by claiming Federal Cotton Support grants on behalf of non-existent farmers on land that was actually already owned by the US Department of Agriculture. The scam eventually became apparent and Henry Marshall was tasked with investigating the fraud. The danger was that LBJ had helped the scheme along and had received a cut of Sol Estes $1.7 million of Federal money for his trouble.

LBJ – now Vice President – and Mr Ed decided to ask Mac Wallace to have a word with Marshall. An offer of a Washington post as an Assistant Secretary of Agriculture was dangled as a bribe. Marshall refused all inducements. On 3 June 1961, Wallace met Marshall and clubbed him unconscious with his pistol. He then rigged a hose to the exhaust and started the car's engine before shooting Marshall five times. The local County Coroner ruled that Henry Marshall's death was 'suicide'.

If Texas shrugged its shoulders (Marshall 'was suicided' was the usual wisecrack), Washington did not. The US Department of Agriculture restarted their investigations and this time got the backing of the Justice Department and Robert Kennedy, the Attorney General. Murdering a federal official was not something that the Justice Department was prepared to see brushed under the carpet. Bobby Kennedy already detested LBJ, whom he thought was a crook, and behind his back referred to the tall Texan as 'old Uncle Cornpone'.

Now the Attorney General saw a chance to nail the Vice President once and for all. The FBI was asked to help. That was a serious mistake, because LBJ and Hoover were old buddies from way back and knew each other's secrets. Behind the scenes, J. Edgar Hoover alerted his long-term friend and ally that he, the Vice President, was now being investigated by J. Edgar's own boss, the Attorney General of the United States.

In October 1963 LBJ's past finally caught up with him. His personal aide Bobby Baker, Secretary to the Senate Majority, was indicted on a raft of allegations of corruption and pocketing campaign donations. The scandal erupted out of nowhere and brought the fire very close to LBJ, who was on record as saying (when he was Senate Majority Leader), 'Bobby Baker is my strong right arm.' Now his closest Senate staff aide was being indicted for Federal tax evasion, illegal payments and fraud. By early November, *Life* magazine ran a full page picture that showed LBJ and Bobby Baker close together under the headline, 'Bobby Baker Bombshell', for bombshell it was. Bobby Baker was the man on whom LBJ had relied, for years and very publicly, to make the wheels of the Senate go round.

Baker had started as a Senate page boy back in 1943 but, unlike the other interns, he stayed on and made a career out it. He was smart, hard-working and totally devoted to Lyndon Johnson. He eventually became LBJ's right-hand man on the Hill and rose to become his executive assistant. As Baker rose, so he prospered. He helped LBJ on 'sensitive' matters like helping Sam Giancana set up casinos, delivering briefcases of money between the Senate and the Mafia business bosses, and finally he established the

'Serve-U' corporation to place vending machines around the country. But Serve-U was a front for the Chicago mob. They manufactured the vending machines and Baker, through his network of contacts, placed the Mafia's machines in government buildings across the country. LBJ took a cut.

As if this profitable little sideline were not enough, across the street from the Senate Baker also ran the Quorum Club, which among other services provided a discreet chance for Senators and lobbyists to meet and mingle with pretty girls. This little racket not only provided a rich source of potential blackmail but also helped Baker to latch on to would-be investors for his own entrepreneurial activities. This was to prove his undoing. The expage boy turned Senate fixer became a little too over-confident. That made him careless and a Senate Committee eventually began an investigation into Baker and his dealings.

Baker got greedy. He shook down some of the investors in the Serve–U Corporation, demanding a cut of their profits. One Ralph Hill, owner of Capitol

Vending, suddenly found out even this wasn't enough. In 1962, Baker demanded the option to buy up the outstanding stock in Hill's company. Hill refused. Baker then terminated Capitol's contracts without explanation. Hill promptly sued Baker, naming several of Baker's other little rackets on the legal indictment. The press got wind of the story and suddenly all Baker's dirty laundry was going to be aired in court: that spelled big trouble for LBJ.

The problem for LBJ was that he had very publicly put his name to many of Baker's enterprises. He was a regular at the Quorum Club, he and Lady Bird had been guests at Baker's grand hotel openings, and many of Baker's money-grabbing initiatives were linked directly to him. Worse still, Baker's financial scams linked LBJ directly with Mafia crooks, lawless Texas oil men and corruption in high places. Bobby Kennedy briefed investigative journalists that it was 'open season on LBJ' and the Justice Department began a new investigation into the re-deploying of the $6.5 billion TFX fighter contract to various Texas companies linked to LBJ following the 1960 election. LBJ's highly public role as the Texans' front man and fixer in Washington provided the common link to the Bobby Baker scandal and all the other legal snowballs now rolling down the hill towards the Vice President.

Only one person could save him; but LBJ knew only too well that Jack Kennedy was being advised by his brother, the Attorney General, to use the chance to get rid of his now deeply compromised Vice President. The law was closing in for the kill and this time there would be no political top cover.

The final straw came in early November 1963. Newspapers and the Republican opposition had already begun to hint that LBJ's days as Vice President were numbered. Just five days before Kennedy's murder the President mused to his secretary, Mrs Lincoln, that he was thinking of dropping LBJ from the 1964 vice presidential ticket. At last the net was drawing tight around the big Texan. On the very day of Jack Kennedy's assassination a blue chip Capitol Hill Committee began investigating specific criminal allegations

against LBJ behind locked doors, and three major newspapers were openly discussing his links with Bobby Baker and with organised crime. The lanky, corrupt Texan was even greeted in Dallas on 22 November with the headline in the Dallas Morning News:
NIXON PREDICTS JFK MAY DROP JOHNSON

Only one thing looked possible to save LBJ's hide from disgrace and jail in the not-too-distant future. He was exposed, he was desperate and he had proved himself ruthless in the past. LBJ had ordered murders, he knew the Mafia's top men and he knew the President wanted to visit Texas on 22 November 1963. So did Kennedy's many other enemies.

And LBJ and Clark had one other consolation: as LBJ admitted to Claire Ince on the evening of Kennedy's inauguration, as Vice President he was now 'only a heartbeat away from the Presidency.'

12

ISRAEL AND HER FRIENDS

TRULY GOD IS LOVING UNTO ISRAEL...
PSALM 73

To add to the growing list of American organisations that had a major grievance against JFK, by mid-1963 Jack Kennedy had managed to anger another country as well. The country was Israel, whose Jewish supporters and agents owned or controlled larger chunks of the American media, big banks and corporations. Thanks to the Jews of America, Israel had a powerful voice in many matters American and had shown itself ruthless in attacking its critics, let alone its opponents.

Through agencies such as the Anti-Defamation League (ADL), the various Jewish defence committees and the American Israel Public Affairs Committee, the Jewish lobby in America hunted down any who dared to criticise

Israel or Zionism. They deliberately confused 'anti-Israeli' with 'anti-Jewish', knowing that the merest taint of anti-Semitism spelled the political death knell to any individual or cause, and would deter any other would-be critics.

The 'friends of Israel' monitored virtually all aspects of US life at both national and regional level. For instance, in 1993 the Anti-Defamation League in California was uncovered operating what many believed was a widespread spying network collecting domestic intelligence on America and Americans. The San Francisco police and the FBI, following up a separate espionage case, uncovered a secret cache of ADL files.

The seized documents revealed that the ADL was systematically snooping on the Civil Rights movement, the San Francisco police, anyone who dared to write to the newspapers criticising the Israeli government's behaviour and, more seriously, collecting America's defence secrets. The ADL forcefully denied any liability, claiming that they were merely acting like any journalist in keeping files on topics of interest to them, and insisting that the two individuals indicted by the police were acting as independent individuals. However the ADL agreed to an out of court settlement to the tune of $75,000, while still continuing to deny any liability.

With powerful and well-entrenched interests like this to watch out for, JFK originally trod very carefully with the Jewish lobby. He knew the power of Jewish influence in America only too well and he was burdened by his father's reputation as a notorious anti-Semite. Old Joe's anti-Semitism was undoubtedly going to be a major stumbling block in any bid by one of the family to run for president.

At the core of old Joe Kennedy's political problem and the Jewish penetration of American life stood the ambiguous figure of the 'King of the Jewish Gangsters', Meyer Lansky. Lansky, as both a Jew and an ardent Zionist, bore Joseph Kennedy little love from their Prohibition days and was only too aware that if Jack Kennedy got into the White House he might well spawn a Kennedy dynasty that could last from 1960 to 1984. The idea of the anti-Semitic Kennedys wielding such power in the White House for so long horrified much of Washington and the Kennedy clan's enemies. The Jewish lobby could be relied upon to oppose any 'Kennedy for President' ticket.

Joseph Kennedy solved the problem in 1956 by secretly asking a prominent media and entertainment business mogul called Joe Hooker to orchestrate a right-wing press campaign *against* his son, by accusing the then Senator Jack Kennedy of being a 'Jewish puppet', secretly in hock to Jewish interests and influences. Hooker and his neo-Fascist contacts duly smeared JFK in the Press. 'Kikes for Kennedy' ran one headline. The American Nazi party denounced him as a 'Jew lover'. The Jewish lobby was impressed and so, when the request for campaign funds duly appeared, Jewish political financiers decided to back Kennedy. In 1960 he was approached by Abraham Feinberg, representing a powerful group of New York Jews, who offered $500,000 in return for support for Israel. Feinberg later boasted of 'having bought political power' for Israel.

Kennedy took the money ... but he didn't sell his soul. Next morning he told Charles Bartlett, a newspaper man and close friend, that he was 'outraged' at such a crude attempt to buy his allegiance. Feinberg had actually demanded control of Kennedy's Middle East policy if JFK became President as a *quid pro quo* for handing over the money. Bartlett noted at the time that Kennedy had said that if he ever did become president he would do something about these special interest groups, and in particular the ones lobbying for foreign governments. The truth was that JFK was no particular friend of Israel. He just needed money to get elected.

Kennedy's true feelings about US links with Israel were made plain in a revealing letter to a critic of Israel, Alfred Lilienthal, a Jew himself. Kennedy wrote, 'I wholly agree with you that American partiality in the Arab/Israeli conflict is dangerous to the US and the Free World.' Kennedy was quite clear that American and Israeli interests were often clean different things.

But to John Kennedy's backers, the two were intimately linked, and still are to this day. This lockstep connection between Israeli and American interests is precisely what the ever-zealous Jewish lobby in America exists to promote. 'Israel's security is America's security' has been the mantra of one of the most powerful political pressure groups in the country, determined to bind America ever more closely to Israel at any political cost.

The respected Senator William F. Fulbright summed it all up for CBS News as far back as 1973: 'Israel controls the US Senate. The Senate is subservient, much too much; we should be more concerned about US interests rather than doing the bidding of Israel. The great majority of the Senate – somewhere around 80 per cent – is completely in support of Israel; anything Israel wants, Israel gets.' What Fulbright was also hinting at was that Senators could be bought. This was the growing power and influence that Jack Kennedy was taking on face-to-face in the early 1960s.

It was not always so. Although President Harry Truman had been the first to recognise the fledgling state of Israel in 1948, he did it primarily to head off a mass influx of immigrants into the United States. From that date on America had generally kept its distance from Israel and in the 1950s Israel's principal international backer was France. Rich Jewish industrialists like Marcel Dassault of France were Israel's key foreign friends and arms suppliers in the 1950s. But the Cold War changed all that.

Because later, with the Cold War in full swing and Gamal Abdel Nasser of Egypt cosying up to Moscow, the US needed a secure ally in the region. Israel as a functioning democracy threatened with annihilation by its Arab enemies was America's natural partner, and was only too willing to seal an ever closer alliance with the all-powerful United States. The emergence of a formal US/Israeli alliance in the late 1950s had a profound impact on American domestic politics.

From the 1960s onwards the 'Jewish lobby' morphed into the 'Support Israel at any cost lobby'. This was the foreign policy horizon John Kennedy looked out on as he moved into the Oval Office.

But first, the Jewish pro-Israeli lobby had to be paid off. Kennedy's reward to Feinberg and his Jewish backers appears to have been the appointment of the notoriously pro-Israeli Mike Feldman as his special adviser for Israeli affairs. State Department experts were appalled. Feldman's advice was frequently the same, word for word, as the official brief given by the Israeli Ambassador to Washington. But Kennedy had paid off his political debt.

Kennedy then turned his attention to the Middle East. He swiftly made it plain that he was not in the pocket of the pro-Israel lobby by sending personal letters to Arab leaders and by warmly welcoming newly independent Algeria. For Kennedy, America's relationship with Israel was always a two-way street. He reinforced this approach by establishing close links with Golda Meir (then Israeli Foreign Minister) to guarantee Israel's security, while at the same time putting out peace feelers to Israel's Arab enemies.

Israel and her friends in America watched these developments uneasily. They wanted exclusive rights – and control if possible – of American policy in the Middle East, not some even-handed 'America First' approach. For them it was always Israel first. Now Kennedy was putting America first. And he began to interfere with Israel's biggest secret of all: Kennedy had every reason to believe that Israel was secretly building a nuclear bomb. Even for the President who had said that America would 'support any friend' and 'pay any price', the idea of a nuclear armed nation in the powder keg of the Middle East was one step too far in the 1960s. From the White House the view was simple: the existence of more nuclear weapons was a bad thing, period. Nuclear weapons in a volatile area like the Middle East could only make the world a much more dangerous place.

Israel's Prime Minister did not agree. The ageing David Ben-Gurion had spent his life working to create a Jewish homeland in Palestine. In many ways he had been responsible for building the

State of Israel in the first place. To David Ben-Gurion, possession of nuclear weapons of mass destruction was essential for Israel's survival.

In 1957 he ordered a disguised nuclear facility to be built with French assistance at Dimona in the Negev Desert. Ben-Gurion also went secretly to the Chinese for the necessary expert backup and testing facilities. The combination of Chinese resources and Israeli scientists was formidable. Dimona was soon in operation, producing weapons-grade nuclear material.

Although Israel had tried to keep the Dimona nuclear plant a secret, the CIA was well aware of the clandestine nuclear programme and Israel's 'secret' nuclear plans were an open book to Jack Kennedy from the day he took over as president. It signalled the start of what was to become one of the most poisonous relationships between two supposedly friendly heads of state ever recorded. The truth was that, by 1963, JFK and the founding father of the State of Israel heartily detested each other. The starting point was that Israel wanted a bomb and Kennedy wanted to stop them from getting one. Ben-Gurion lied to both his own countrymen and to JFK. The ageing Zionist claimed to the Israeli parliament that the Dimona plant was a scientific research facility 'investigating the problems of fauna in arid regions'.

When Ben-Gurion met Kennedy in the Waldorf Astoria hotel in New York in 1961 Kennedy was forced to listen to blatant lies.

Behind the bland chat, neither man was impressed by the other. To Ben-Gurion, Kennedy appeared 'like a 25 year old boy'. He could not believe that such a youth could be a real politician, let alone the President of the United States. In his turn President Kennedy didn't like being lied to and patronised by the opinionated, patriarchal old man talking down to him. That faceto-face meeting in New York sowed the seeds of mutual dislike.

In an increasingly bitter exchange of letters, Kennedy and Ben-Gurion began what was virtually an exchange of hostilities. Over the next two years, the letters became blunter and less diplomatic. Even to this day, much of that correspondence remains locked away and marked 'classified'. What is available from the published record is the unswerving hostility of the Kennedy administration's foreign policy towards a nuclear-armed Israel.

As his anger grew with Ben-Gurion's lies and prevarications over the existence and purpose of Israel's Dimona facility, so Kennedy flexed his muscles. The collaboration between Israel and China – of which the CIA was well aware – also infuriated Jack Kennedy, as he was forced to listen to the cunning old man's bland but barefaced lies.

He also had a shrewd suspicion that an American company called NUMEC was secretly creaming off enriched uranium for the Israelis as well. The Nuclear Materials and Equipment Corporation of Pittsburg was owned by an American Jew called Zalman Shapiro, who quite clearly admitted to divided loyalties. After Kennedy's death the Atomic Energy commission found that NUMEC had managed to lose between 56 and 220 pounds of enriched uranium and couldn't remember where it had gone.

Significantly, these highly charged accusations against Shapiro, NUMEC and Israel went unchallenged by the normally vocal Jewish-Israeli lobby in the US. For once they kept strangely quiet. No one threatened to sue the newspapers who published the story.

Faced with supporting evidence of Israeli duplicity from the CIA, Kennedy decided to twist the knife. His demands to inspect the nuclear site and verify the true purpose of Dimona grew terser and more threatening. Ben-Gurion tried evasions, open lies and mobilising his vociferous pro-Israel lobby in the States to thwart the President, to no avail. Kennedy was adamant. He wanted his nuclear inspectors to check out Dimona – properly. Why exactly was an 'agricultural research establishment' being run by the Ministry of Defence? Why was it so tightly guarded?

Ben-Gurion finally caved in. However, he had one trick up his sleeve to deceive the ever-persistent American. He ordered a dummy plant built nearby. When the American inspectors finally arrived at Dimona they were greeted by polite and scientific hosts who showed them what was undoubtedly a secret nuclear plant – but one devoted to the production of cheap nuclear power, not atom bombs. But neither the CIA nor Kennedy were fooled and in early summer 1963 the President finally lost patience. On 18 May 1963 he blasted off what was described as a 'tough and extremely threatening' letter to the Prime Minister of Israel pointing out bluntly that if Ben-Gurion did not do what Kennedy required, then 'the US commitment to Israel would be seriously jeopardised'.

For Ben-Gurion this was the last straw. Domestic scandals had ripped his government apart and wrecked his reputation. He saw his legacy as the great Jewish patriarch and the 'Father of Israel' slipping away. Beset by enemies on every side, with the disaster of the 'Lavon scandal' (about the grubby details behind illegal secret orders from Ben-Gurion for a failed Mossad 'false flag' operation targeting British and US citizens in Egypt in the 1950s) breaking over his head and political rivals at home baying for his blood, Ben-Gurion succumbed to his own worst fears. David Ben-Gurion, founder of the State of Israel, resigned all his posts the day he received news of what he saw as an ultimatum from the President of the USA.

At 77 years of age he suddenly saw his life's work – building the Jewish State of Israel in his own image – threatened by some callow American *nebbish* who knew nothing about Israel and the harsh realities of survival in the Middle East. Like his father, young Kennedy was obviously just another anti-Semite. It was the only explanation.

Kennedy was undeterred and relentless. Once the inevitable Israeli political arguing and horse trading in the Knesset had settled down, a month later on 5 July he wrote to Ben-Gurion's successor, Levi Eshkol, with a letter that was regarded by all parties as effectively an ultimatum. After highlighting his abortive discussions with Ben-Gurion, Kennedy made an explicit threat:

> You are aware, I am sure, of the exchange which I had with

Prime Minister Ben-Gurion concerning American visits to Israel's nuclear facility at Dimona ... I am sure you will agree that these visits should be as nearly as possible in accord with international standards, thereby resolving all doubts as to the peaceful intent of the Dimona project. As I wrote Mr Ben-Gurion, *this Government's commitment to and support of Israel could be seriously jeopardized* if it should be thought that we were unable to obtain reliable information on a subject as vital to the peace as the question of Israel's effort in the nuclear field. [Emphasis added.]

The bottom line was clear: if Israel did not allow American nuclear inspectors into the secret site at Dimona, the President of the United States threatened to cut off US aid. It had the force of a diplomatic bombshell in Tel Aviv, where it was quite correctly seen as an order to 'cease and desist' – *or else*. 'This government's commitment to, and support of Israel would be seriously jeopardized' was nothing less than an ultimatum, and both sides knew it. Without US aid, and surrounded by Arabs sworn to its destruction, Israel might not be able to survive.

Kennedy's blunt letter seems to have finally tipped Ben-Gurion over the edge into paranoia. In continuing correspondence the Israeli spelled it out: 'Mr President, my people have the right to exist ... and this existence is now in danger'. To that most dangerous of political animals, a tired old man in a hurry, it seemed quite clear: by stopping Israel from developing a nuclear bomb, Jack Kennedy had now become a sworn enemy of Israel and, by extension, of the Jewish people.

But Israel had power too. Not only did the Jews of America support Israel and could be relied on to rally against any threat to their spiritual homeland, there were other powerful forces that could be mobilised to oppose any threat to Israel. Israel's secret service, Mossad, had links with a company called Permindex. Permindex's darker side was revealed in 1962 after it was uncovered shovelling money to the OAS and paying for assassination attempts on de Gaulle in an attempt to prevent Algerian independence. The plots failed and de Gaulle ran Permindex and its Mossad bankers out of France. In Canada the company now provided Mossad with a safe haven from which it could influence events and orchestrate any counter attack on anti-Israeli interests in the USA.

Sometime in the hot summer of 1963, Mossad's link with North America became aware that Mafia sources warned of a death threat already made against JFK. To Israel and its friends this could only be good news. It would remove the problem of JFK and – should anything untoward happen to Jack Kennedy – the successor would be Lyndon Johnson. Fortunately, LBJ was well known to be a strong supporter of Jewish interests – and therefore to Israel. The lanky Texan was even referred to as 'Israel's Texan friend'. If LBJ were to inherit Kennedy's throne, then Israel would have a real ally in the White House.

What was clear was that Ben-Gurion and the Israeli government, along with Jack Kennedy's many domestic enemies, desperately wanted him out of the way. By the summer of 1963 he was regarded as an enemy of the Israeli State and therefore by extension of the Jewish people.

Israel and its friends had effectively declared the President of the United States as the equivalent of a *din rodef,* or 'betrayer of Jewry'. One way or another, Jack Kennedy was now in mortal danger.

***

By the autumn of 1963 President John Kennedy had built up an impressive stable of enemies both at home and abroad. To lead is to choose, and Kennedy's choices and decisions as President had managed to alienate an extraordinarily wide constituency of individuals and organisations. His key mistake seems to have been that he not only overestimated his own power but to have seriously underestimated the influence of the non-governmental power centres of American society, life and politics.

Jack Kennedy had another problem too. From all the evidence it seems that he was becoming a genuine seeker after peace. For any Cold War American politician in the post-McCarthy era that was a brave, if not positively dangerous, position. In the aftermath of the Cuban missile crisis it seems that Kennedy was genuinely intent on ending the Cold War and trying to establish a more peaceful relationship with the Soviet Union.

According to Arthur Schlesinger, 'President Kennedy began to feel in the spring of 1963 that there was a possibility for some kind of new movement in our relations with the Soviet Union, and he began to look for an opportunity to make a "peace speech".' The outcome was a little-publicised speech at American University on 10 June 1963, where JFK spoke about his desire for world peace and talked of forging a new relationship with Khrushchev. He mused about the importance of a nuclear test ban treaty and the need for disarmament. He recognized that the Russian people wanted peace as much as the American people, saying 'we are all mortal.'

The discovery that the President was now signing documents to begin withdrawal from Vietnam, exchanging private letters with Khrushchev, and discreetly putting out peace feelers to Castro to explore some *rapprochement* with Cuba, posed a clear threat to the mindset and the agendas of the hard men and power brokers of Washington DC and New York. The fact that both Khrushchev and Castro were responding favourably alarmed them even more. Castro was actually due to meet a private JFK representative on the day that the President was murdered. Nowhere was there greater concern about these diplomatic manoeuvres than among the hardnosed men of his own US military-intelligence establishment in the Pentagon, who now regarded their President as 'a virtual traitor who had to be eliminated.'

For Kennedy the problem now was twofold. The various people who felt that they would be better off with Jack Kennedy removed from the scene were not only very powerful; the real threat was that they were all closely linked to one another too. Therein lay the real danger. Jack Kennedy had, without realising it, encouraged a broad coalition of his most bitter enemies both at home and abroad.

That coalition was united by a consensus of opinion and one common goal: Jack Kennedy was dangerous to their interests and had to go.

PART 3

THE PLOT IS HATCHED

13

THE ANTI-KENNEDY COALITION

'A CONSPIRACY!' CRIED THE DELIGHTED LADY, CLAPPING HER HANDS, 'OF ALL THINGS, I DO SO LIKE A CONSPIRACY! IT'S SO INTERESTING!'
LEWIS CARROLL

Part of the problem over the mystery surrounding John Kennedy's murder is the sheer number of individuals and organisations who would have been happy to see him out of the way. The list is a long one.

To get Cuban Exiles, the CIA, the Pentagon, J. Edgar Hoover and the FBI, the Mafia, the Texas oil barons, the Wall Street bankers, the South Vietnamese, the Israeli government and their influential American friends – plus his own Vice President – all to agree that 'Kennedy must go', was an impressive achievement.

It was never a formal alliance – nor could it ever be. It was more a shared sense of mission. In the end it didn't really matter who pulled the trigger to get rid of JFK or even how they did it. The important fact was that as long as someone in the anti-Kennedy coalition got rid of him, the other politically powerful groups were only too happy to give tacit support by looking the other way.

What Kennedy failed to understand was the real nature of power in the United States. In politics, as in the boudoir, once again Jack Kennedy took huge risks and gambled – but this time he was to lose. The man who timidly ordered President Diem of South Vietnam to be overthrown, then changed his mind, then agreed, and finally claimed that he never meant it really was, ironically, himself 'terminated with extreme prejudice' just three short weeks later.

***

The plot to kill Kennedy started, as these things often do, with an idle threat. The Cuban Exiles and their American friends felt abandoned by the new President's dithering over the Bay of Pigs. 'Someone should shoot that bastard Kennedy,' growled the hotheaded and vengeful survivors. Their view was echoed by the Cubans' many supporters in the Deep South.

The most murderous group in the coalition against JFK was the Mafia. Ever mindful of Stalin's dictum, 'If you have a man and he is a problem – kill the man! There, no problem,' the Mob applied this golden rule to their own lethal business dealings. In the constant struggle for power, influence and control of their illicit markets, the Mafia used murder as a straightforward business tool.

Some of the anti-Kennedy coalition was already firmly in place. The links between the Mafia and the Cuban Exiles in the Deep South were extensive and went back for at least four years. To the Exiles in Florida, Cuba was the lost golden homeland of their parents and their youth. To the Mafia, Cuba was their lost golden cash cow. It was therefore perfectly natural for the CIA to approach the Mafia for help when the agency was looking for a way of eliminating the new Cuban leader in 1959–60. The Mafia understood Cuba. Thus was born the unholy trinity at the heart of the coalition against Kennedy: the Cuban Exiles, the Mafia, and the CIA. At the time this tri-partite group was dedicated to furthering US foreign policy by killing Castro.

This link between American Intelligence and the Mafia was not new, either. Meyer Lansky, the brain behind much of the Mafia families' activities, admitted after the Second World War that he was the man who had helped to broker a deal between Lucky Luciano and the office of Naval Intelligence. Castro's overturning of the Mob's Havana casinos upset a delicate and tenuous link between the Mafia and the CIA. Because the truth was that after the war the CIA had never quite weaned itself off its clandestine addiction to the Mafia. Now with orders from the White House to go after Castro, the CIA turned once again to their old friends. The Mafia were experts on Cuba and Cubans; they had friends there and they were a good source of intelligence on that troubled island. If only one single factor united the anti-Kennedy plotters, it was Cuba.

By 1961 the key players in the anti-Kennedy coalition were already working together on the US government's secret anti-Castro projects: Mafia bosses Giancana and Rosselli; CIA officers David Morales, Frank Sturgis and Dave Atlee Phillips; ex-FBI agent Robert Maheu, acting as official government liaison officer between the CIA and the Mafia; and last but not least, the evervengeful Cuban Exiles. All were partners in the official US government policy of getting rid of Fidel Castro.

Or were they? The truth is that the US government had got itself – not for the first time – into an unholy political muddle. The Kennedy White House was asking the Mafia for secret help to kill

Fidel Castro at the very moment that Jack Kennedy was secretly offering to negotiate with the Cuban leader; while at the same time the Kennedy Administration was openly attacking the Mafia in the courts. The problem is best summed up by Jack Kennedy himself. During the period when his girlfriend Judith Exner was being cross-examined by the FBI, she complained to her presidential lover about her treatment at the hands of the Justice Department's investigators. 'Don't worry,' she claims Kennedy told her, 'They won't do anything to you. And don't worry about Sam [Giancana]. You know he works for us.' At a time when Robert Kennedy was trying to jail Giancana this was hardly a good advertisement for joined-up government, let alone brotherly communication inside the White House.

Any assessment of a threat rests on two key factors: capability and intention. Bar room threats to shoot Kennedy by disgruntled Cuban Exiles were one thing. But by the middle of 1962 a new and more sinister intention to actually *do* something and carry out the threat against the Kennedys began to surface. An official of Jimmy Hoffa's Teamster's Union told the FBI that Hoffa had openly discussed murdering his arch persecutor, Robert Kennedy.

The Teamsters enjoyed a curious status in American society and still do. The image of the tough, hard-driving trucker and his massive Mack rig thundering along the Interstate or Route 66 to keep American business on the move day and night is an enduring icon of America's mythology. Unfortunately, the Teamsters – which operated nationwide and moved most of America's goods from the 1940s to the 1980s – had by the late 1950s under Jimmy Hoffa become part of just another Mafia protection racket. Drivers' 'union dues' were really a lucrative source of revenue for the Union's senior officials, many of whom were plugged directly into the Mafia. Attempts to complain, break away or set up internal Union enquiries were met with beatings, 'accidents', or worse.

The Union gradually evolved into Hoffa's own private fiefdom, where he could milk his drivers and put large sums of Union money to illegal purposes, all benefiting Hoffa and his friends in organised crime.

The Teamsters was a magnet for the Mafia's interest for two clear reasons: first, it took in money every week from over a million individuals nationwide; second, the network of trucks pounding along the United States highways night and day was a natural way to transport illicit goods. And for the Mafia, that meant moving drugs. The Teamsters and the Mafia were made for each other.

By 1960 Hoffa was the link between the Mob's national drug distribution network and his drivers, taking money from both ends. The scale of the operation was vast. At one point 90 kilos of dope a month were being run for Mafia boss Carlos Marcello's local criminal empire in Louisiana and Texas. Hoffa associated and worked quite openly with organised crime syndicates, exchanging favours, laundering money, protecting key shipments, and providing illegal loans from Union funds. In 1957/58 he had organised gun-running to Cuba, using $300,000 of Union money to set up a deal for 'surplus' military guns and ammunition to be shipped to the Cuban rebels. The operation was backed by Santo Trafficante in Miami. One of the leg men for the deal was a smalltime Mafia gopher called Jack Ruby.

With a record like this, it was inevitable that the new Attorney General would come gunning for Hoffa. Robert Kennedy's crusading zeal to go after the Mob was redoubled once his brother put him in the Attorney General's chair. The leader of the Teamsters was one of his principal targets. One of his first acts as Attorney General was to set up a special 'get Hoffa' squad. However, the problem was that by then Hoffa was actively working for a different section of the federal government as part of the CIA's efforts to kill Castro.

Although the CIA's files remain firmly closed, there is now enough evidence from other sources to show that Jimmy Hoffa was one of the CIA's contacts and the man who recruited the Mafia to support the CIA in their anti-Castro campaign. Hoffa brokered a deal on behalf of the government that brought together five key Mafia leaders: Carlos Marcello; Sam Giancana; Santo Trafficante; Johnny Rosselli; and a little-known Mafia boss from the north east, Russell Bufalino. Jimmy Hoffa was in fact effectively acting as the 'liaison officer' between the CIA and organised crime. Yet this was the man Robert Kennedy was trying to put behind bars.

According to Ed Partin's statement, Jimmy Hoffa had said, 'Somebody needs to bump that son of a bitch off. You know I've got a run down on him ... his house is not guarded. He drives about in a convertible and swims by himself. I've got a .270 rifle with a high-power scope ... It would be easy to get him.'

By the middle of 1962 Hoffa was joined by a growing chorus of like-minded mobsters. José Alemán, a well-connected Cuban exile whose father had been one of the Mafia's top Cuban lawyers, later testified that Trafficante openly threatened the Kennedys in 1962 in Miami. According to him, Trafficante said, 'Have you seen how his brother is hitting Hoffa? Mark my word, this man Kennedy is in trouble and he will get what is coming to him.' Alémán claimed that he had told Trafficante that he thought Kennedy would probably be re-elected in 1964, to which the Mafia man replied, 'You don't understand me. Kennedy's not going to make it to the election. He's going to be hit.' Alémán was sufficiently disturbed at the time to warn the FBI, whose agents rated him as a reliable source and passed it on to Washington. J. Edgar Hoover ignored the intelligence.

At almost the same time a similar threat was being uttered in Louisiana. Carlos Marcello, the boss of the New Orleans Mafia and ruler of a crime empire that stretched from Texas to Florida told a visiting oil man called Ed Becker that he was going to 'get Kennedy'. Becker was, at first, not surprised. Marcello had a particular score to settle with Robert Kennedy. Shortly after taking office in 1961, the Attorney General had had Marcello deported as an illegal immigrant. In fact, Marcello had been virtually kidnapped during one of his routine visits to the Immigration and Nationalisation office in New Orleans.

Marcello and his companions were flown to the Mobster's supposed home country and dumped on the tarmac in Guatemala to find his own way back through the jungle.

Carlos Marcello survived his ordeal and was secretly flown back into the United States by his private pilot, the right-wing pederast David Ferrie. But from that day on, Carlos Marcello swore vengeance on Bobby Kennedy and his brother to anyone prepared to listen. This spelled serious danger to the Kennedys: not for nothing did The House Select Committee on Crime declare in 1972, 'We believe Carlos Marcello has become a formidable menace to the institution of government and the people of the United States.'

Ed Becker was therefore not surprised by Marcello's openly advertised intentions to kill the President. Marcello made a number of explicit threats while he ranted on over a few drinks. On one occasion Marcello called the Kennedy brothers 'dogs', explicitly threatening Bobby as the Attorney General harassing the Mafia. Then he quoted the old Sicilian proverb: 'If you really want to stop the dog wagging its tail, then cut the head off the dog.' Ed Becker was quite clear that the Mafia leader was 'clearly stating that he was going to arrange to have President Kennedy murdered.' Becker was so disturbed that he took his story to the FBI. Once again, just as with Alémán, they ignored the threats. J. Edgar Hoover not only failed to warn the President of the threats to his life, as the FBI chief was mandated by law to do, but after the assassination carefully filleted the FBI records and removed the copies of the Alémán and Becker warnings.

The threats from Marcello were backed up now by quite open discussions of the consequences of removing the Kennedys. In spring 1963 Hoffa asked his lawyers, 'What if something happened to the President. Instead of Booby [Hoffa's scornful nickname for Robert Kennedy]?' One of the lawyers said that Johnson would take over as Vice President and would get rid of Bobby Kennedy because he hated his guts. 'Damn right,' responded Hoffa. 'He hates him as much as I do. And don't forget. I've given a hell of a lot of money to Lyndon Johnson in the past.' Marcello, Hoffa and Trafficante's threats were soon joined by that of fellow Mobster Johnny Rosselli. By mid-1962 he too was being hounded by Bobby Kennedy's Federal Agents. With the IRS on his back he said to a colleague, 'I'm being run into the ground ... it's terrible ... Here I am helping the government, helping the country and that little son of a bitch is breaking my balls.' Rosselli's threats were important. Not only was he linked with the other top Mafia leaders; he too was also working closely with the CIA on their plan to assassinate Castro.

The problem was that all the Mafia men threatening Kennedy were in fact linked not just to each other, but they were also linked with the Florida CIA station dedicated to killing Castro. It was a tangled web, because if the Mafia was now threatening to get rid of Kennedy as well as Castro, then that suited some folk very well indeed, including Carlos Marcello's good friend Lyndon Johnson. LBJ's campaigns had benefited hugely from Marcello's and his good friend Jimmy Hoffa's 'political contributions' over the years. And Lyndon Johnson was a close friend and ally of the Jewish lobby in the US. The Mafia/CIA links, and the threats to JFK, all began to come together as 1962 turned into 1963. At the heart of it all was Johnny Rosselli.

Johnny Rosselli was a gangster's gangster. He started as one of Capone's gang and was sent to Los Angeles to begin a profitable career shaking down the big studios. Things went wrong in 1943. 'Handsome Johnny' was convicted of racketeering and got 10 years. He only served three and by 1947 was back on the film sets.

Rosselli rose through the ranks of the Mob in the 1950s by becoming the link between the Chicago syndicate and the new Tropicana Hotel Casino in Las Vegas. Having set up the Tropicana and made sure that Vegas worked for 'the boys', Rosselli moved back to Hollywood to continue his 'career in films'.

Rosselli prospered and by 1960 was based more and more in the South working for Santo Trafficante, the Mob's Cuban expert. This was about the time that he was formally recruited by the

CIA to help out over Cuba. Rosselli's handler and case officer was David Morales, the Miami office's Chief of Operations. He, in turn, worked closely with Dave Atlee Phillips, the CIA JM/WAVE officer with responsibility for specific anti-Cuban operations. Thus was forged another link in the chain of those who were later suspected of killing the President in Dallas. Morales and Phillips helped to run the Cuban Exiles and both were unhappy about the state of training of their teams. The men were fit and enthusiastic, but they weren't real soldiers. They asked Mafia link man Rosselli if he could help.

Captain Bradley Ayers was a US Army Ranger seconded in 1963 to beef up the CIA's secret training programme to overthrow Castro by teaching commando skills to selected Cuban exiles. There he met a 'Colonel Rosselli'. The gangster's smooth talk and easy manner impressed Ayers (who didn't realise that Rosselli was, in reality, a Mafia man) and Rosselli slotted easily into the hard male camaraderie of the training camps, striding around in his 'Bird Colonel' combat uniform. Ayers later remembered that Rosselli's primary interest was recruiting marksmen.

The result was that, by mid-1963, the anti-Kennedy coalition now not only had the stated intention to assassinate the President, but his sworn enemies, organised crime and the Cuban Exiles, were working together hand in hand.

All the would-be assassins had to do was to find the time and the place and then cover their tracks.

14

THE WIDENING CIRCLE

NO ENTERPRISE IS MORE LIKELY TO SUCCEED THAN THAT WHICH IS KEPT FROM THE FOE UNTIL THE MOMENT OF ITS EXECUTION.
NICCOLÒ MACHIAVELLI

The knowledge that the Mafia had taken out a contract to murder the President would have been of considerable interest to a number of people. It would soon be no secret to two key individuals in particular, Lyndon Baines Johnson and J. Edgar Hoover.

Lyndon Johnson would have known about the threats through the 8F Group in Texas; Hoover through his ubiquitous wire taps. Both men had much to gain from the President's demise. LBJ would get the presidency and would then have the power to sit on or quash any potential criminal charges against him. Hoover would get his old friend LBJ into the White House with a guarantee that he'd keep his job as head of the FBI. Hoover and LBJ were close friends and had been for many years. Both of them were completely united in one thought: 'If only Jack Kennedy goes, we'll be OK'. Sometime during the hot summer of 1963, the final plot was hatched.

One of the key figures in the plan turned out to be Ed Clark, LBJ's lawyer. For years Barr McClellan was a partner in Clark's Austin, Texas legal firm and learned some of its dirtiest secrets. In 2003 he published a set of explosive memoirs, revealing the truth behind the plot to kill the President. For over 20 years Clark and LBJ had been partners in a long-running Texan fraud on the Feds.

Johnson, the good ol' Southern boy-turned-politician, would represent Texan business interests in both the State and national capital. He sold his political services – or allowed himself to be bought – by powerful interest groups, business, banks, Big Oil and the Mafia. In return for his influence in securing profitable Federal contracts, blocking legislation that threatened his 'clients', and using his insider's knowledge to divert Federal tax dollars to benefit his friends, LBJ needed money to support both himself and his re-election campaigns – a great deal of money.

Big money duly flowed in to the 'Brazos-Tenth Street Company' of Austin, Texas. Its role was to hold LBJ's campaign funds in trust, with Don Thomas as the trustee (providing yet another layer of cut out), and then to make the cash sing. The campaign funds were then loaned, earned interest, or used to buy profitable chunks of land that LBJ knew from his backroom political contacts were earmarked for purchase by state or federal government. The profits from this insider trading were then re-invested in LBJ and Ed Clark's own bank accounts. Such a cosy (and highly illegal) reapplication of campaign funds made both men very rich. LBJ's personal fortune on becoming Vice President was estimated at not less than $20 million, a huge sum in 1960.

The danger to this highly agreeable illegal arrangement came from the

Internal Revenue Service and the courts. Clark had solved the problem neatly for himself and LBJ very early in their relationship. In 1946 he had bribed and supported Jack Roberts into becoming first District Attorney, then District Judge in Travis County. To 'own' the Travis County judge meant that Clark had power both inside and over the State of Texas legal system and any court actions.

The IRS – in some ways a potentially more dangerous opponent of crooked politicians, lawyers and gangsters alike – was bought off by Johnson's power of political patronage in his home state. He appointed a trusted friend as the chief accountant for the local IRS.

As further insurance, LBJ had for years made a point of being a good friend of the FBI Director, J. Edgar Hoover. In fact, it would be entirely accurate to describe the pair as being as 'thick as thieves', and J. Edgar Hoover had the inside dope and dirt on virtually every politician in the country. This unholy alliance therefore gave LBJ a powerful blackmail weapon as well, because many members of the State Legislature were as corrupt as LBJ himself.

But the unholy alliance between Ed Clark and LBJ went deeper. Ed Clark was also Lyndon's cut out and 'fall guy' for more serious crimes, including murder where necessary. Both men understood their role perfectly. LBJ discussed his objectives with his lawyer; Ed gave the orders behind the scenes. Clark organised murder for LBJ, using Mac Wallace, as a 1984 indictment was to prove.

The Texas Suite 8F Group membership represented 70 per cent of the anti-Kennedy coalition. The men around the table, although mainly Democrats, were deeply conservative men at heart. They believed in 'the great State of Texas', making money, and keeping 'nigras', liberals and 'karm-yew-nists' at bay. Above all, they believed that the right to make money their own way and without interference from central government and the dogooders in Washington was a God-given freedom, confirmed by the Constitution.

So the news that the Mafia had taken out a contract on the Kennedys would have been greeted with thoughtful nods by the Texan power elite. A problem was 'being taken care of'. If anyone needed funds for a project that might benefit them all, then the backing would be indirect and discreet. The big oil men, Giants like H.L. Hunt, Sid Richardson, 'Dry Hole' Byrd and Clint Murchison had plenty of what they called 'burn money'. Doubtless the idea that the Mafia were planning to get rid of a president who was threatening to take away their much-loved Oil Depletion Allowance would have seemed an attractive proposition to them and one worthy of their backing. In the 8F crowd there was little overt conspiracy, but much discreet *complicity.*

When the meeting was over, the members would retire to the 'Top of the Hill', a gambling casino operated by a Mafia leader – and associate of Sam Giancana and Meyer Lansky – called Lewis McWillie, sometimes helped by his good friend Jack Ruby (who called McWillie his 'idol'). All of them had close working relations with the Louisiana Don, Carlos Marcello, and the other Mafia networks around Dallas and New Orleans. Thus, in the 8F Group, the Mob met up with politics and big business; J. Edgar Hoover was friend to many of them, especially LBJ and the Texas Oil Millionaires like Billy Byars, with whom he shared his annual summer vacation.

The 8F Group's awareness of a threat to the President would have travelled rapidly to the company called Permindex, now based in Montreal, Canada. Permindex was originally funded by a banker who just happened to be Mossad's Director of Finance, Tibor Rosenbaum. Permindex in Texas was run by a man called Clay Shaw, manager of the New Orleans International Trade Mart and one of the associates of the 8F Group.

Clay Shaw had an unusual background. He had worked for the CIA and its forerunner, the OSS, during the war. He knew many of the senior CIA officials personally. He was a director of the Swiss registered Permindex and also a director of its banking partner CMC, the Centro Mondiale Commerciale.

Deeper examination of Permindex uncovers some other interesting details, too. Permindex's North American HQ in Montreal was run by Louis Bloomfield, a former British intelligence officer with close ties to Mossad.

Bloomfield had spied and soldiered for the Zionist cause from the beginning. Once America joined the Second World War Bloomfield was sent to work with the newly formed OSS as a major. After the war he returned to Canada and a legal career, working for ex-Mafia bootlegger and fellow Zionist, Sam Bronfmann, the billionaire boss of the Seagrams drinks empire and one of Mossad's strongest links in North America.

When the OSS became the CIA in 1947, Bloomfield continued doing work for them, plus the occasional State Department contract, as well as being a North American director of Permindex. This was a man who knew J. Edgar Hoover personally, had carried out sensitive FBI contracts and could pick up the telephone to the Prime Minister of Israel.

Permindex's board of directors all had links with the Bronfman family of Canada. The Jewish billionaire Sam Bronfman had made his money from bootleg liquor in the 1920s and the family were closely associated with Meyer Lansky, the Jewish gangster and the brains behind many of the Mob's more 'business-like' activities.

The links between the coalition of Kennedy's enemies were thus complete and traceable. The hot-blooded Cuban Exiles had sworn revenge on the Kennedys. The Cubans were working with the Mafia, who had taken out a contract to kill the Kennedys. The Mafia was hand-in-glove with Big Oil and LBJ. Big Oil and Wall Street connected with Permindex. Permindex was linked with the CIA, the Mafia, and Israel and its many supporters – which included the Big Banking Houses. The anti-Kennedy Coalition was complete and working together on many levels.

The link was Israel and Mossad. Not only was the Bronfman family one of the richest in North America, they were also dedicated Zionists and unquestioning supporters of Israel.

Edgar Bronfman had even been President of the World Jewish Congress. Like Louis Bloomfield, he knew Meyer Lansky and David Ben-Gurion very well. The collaboration between Israel and Permindex, Montreal (which meant Louis Bloomfield and Bronfman) was rock solid and the networks were personal.

Permindex's association with Israel was not even well hidden. Tibor Rosenbaum, Permindex fundraiser and one-time Financial Director of Mossad, also just happened to be a good friend of one Meyer Lansky. Rosenbaum and Lansky had used the BCI bank to hide and launder the Jewish Mobster's money, just as he and his Mossad friends used BCI to finance Mossad's overseas intelligence operations. The circle was complete and visible: Mafia-Permindex-Israeli intelligence.

Permindex was nothing less than the common link between organised crime, Israel and the CIA. After Kennedy's death, the Italian press began to probe the company's origins. Permindex did undoubtedly have links to the intelligence world and so did its 'banking arm', the CMC and the BCI. The former had been founded in Rome as the 'CMC' standing for *Centro Mondiale Commerciale* or (ominously) the 'World Trade Centre'. Italian journalists were unable to unravel CMC's complex layers of shareholders, directors and shell companies distributed around the world. They eventually gave up, describing CMC as a 'labyrinth'. In the world of intelligence, 'labyrinthine' is a compliment.

The Jewish connections with Clay Shaw and International Trade Mart in New Orleans were equally murky. Clay Shaw's boss was one Rudolph Hecht, a leading light in the small Jewish community of New Orleans and another ardent Zionist. Another board member of Permindex's New Orleans operation was Edgar Stern, Jr, whose activities on behalf of Israel and the Jewish lobby in the US were both very public and highly effective. The result was that through this network of well-placed Jews and Israeli sympathisers, Mossad could pick up intelligence and influence events far from Tel Aviv, even in the Deep South of the USA. And at its heart in the Southern States of America was

Permindex-Mossad's own employee, Clay Shaw of New Orleans, boss of the Texas Trade Mart.

As an ex-OSS man, Shaw knew Bloomfield in Montreal through Permindex and also through his CIA connections. Significantly, when Clay Shaw flew up to Montreal to see Bloomfield, the pilot for that flight was none other than an individual who had sworn to kill Kennedy. This was David Ferrie, the pilot who had worked for the CIA, the Cuban Exiles, and Carlos Marcello. Ferrie also knew Jack Ruby well, as well as a man called Lee Harvey Oswald. 'Captain' David Ferrie was the man who had first recruited the adolescent Oswald into the Civil Air Patrol in 1955. These many links and associations, both personal and commercial between Permindex, Israel, the 8F Group and the Mafia defy the laws of probability and go well beyond mere coincidence.

Clay Shaw may have had another link too, and one that once again went to the heart of the Israeli connection. He and James Jesus Angleton of the CIA had worked together in Europe during the last years of WW2. The Angleton link is important because James Jesus Angleton was also an uncritical admirer and supporter of the State of Israel. In fact, he was acknowledged within the CIA as the best connection of all with Mossad. In his position as the official liaison officer with responsibility for all Allied-CIA links, Angleton was able to exert enormous influence at home and abroad.

From this position he became ever more closely associated with Israel's political elite and Mossad. He had direct access to David Ben-Gurion and was openly called 'Israel's man in Washington' by many CIA officers behind his back. For a passionate, crusading anti-communist like Angleton, John Kennedy must have seemed a threat to both Israel and to the CIA alike.

American or not, Angleton's own loyalty to Israel was unquestioning. He had helped to ship arms to Palestine in the 1947/8 period and to run shiploads of Jewish refugees to Palestine in the early 1950s. The North American end of this gun-running operation had been masterminded and funded by Meyer Lansky and Louis Bloomfield of Montreal. The whole operation had been bankrolled by one Tibor Rosenbaum, Mossad's Director of Finance, founder of CMC-Permindex and friend of Angleton and the CIA. Angleton's Israeli connections were strong and so was his network of like-minded supporters in Israel, Canada and the pro-Zionist Mafia. Once again the same network of pro-Israeli links connects all those involved.

These were the Israeli sympathisers to whom Angleton talked regularly in the early 1960s when he had risen to be the head of the CIA's Counter Espionage department. That his sympathies lay with Israel is not in doubt. If proof were needed, the Israelis themselves provided it in spectacular and public form. When Angleton died he was given a memorial in Israel by the Israeli government for his 'services to the Jewish State'.

Angleton's other over-riding loyalty was to the CIA. The eruption of an angry John Kennedy onto the scene after the Bay of Pigs fiasco had come as a huge shock. So the arrival of JFK's National Security Action Memorandum 55 on 28 June 1961, which stripped the CIA of its Covert Action task, was the final straw for Angleton.

The 35th President of the USA had stripped his beloved agency of its secret power and was now threatening his adopted country. We know that Angleton was furious. He said so. What could he do? At best the CIA man could turn a blind eye to rumours of Mafia contracts on the Kennedys. At worst he might be able to use the Agency to facilitate the plotters' efforts. But what is clear is that any conspiracy to go for the President would need someone to act as the operations officer and controller.

With Angleton on their side, any conspiracy could easily handle the four principal tasks: recruiting an undercover team; planning a sophisticated assassination; ensuring a getaway plan; and lastly coordinating a widespread media cover-up. Any coalition dedicated to stopping the Kennedys didn't really have to do anything once the CIA, the Cubans and the Mafia came together under strong central management.

All they needed to do was wait and let events run their course. For Kennedy's enemies in the Cuban Exiles, the CIA, the Mafia, Wall Street, Texas Oil and Israel, James Jesus Angleton would have been the perfect secret coordinator. All that was needed was a chance to get rid of John Kennedy once and for all.

And all that was needed was a successful ambush.

15

PLANNING THE AMBUSH

IF YOUR ADVANCE IS GOING REALLY WELL – THEN YOU'RE WALKING INTO AN AMBUSH.
MURPHY'S UNOFFICIAL LAWS OF COMBAT

The Mafia's experience of murdering high-ranking government officials had not been a happy one. In 1951 the Mob had 'whacked' the Attorney General of Alabama. The effect of the murder on their business operations had been catastrophic.

Phenix City in Alabama was on the state border between Georgia and Alabama. Across the state line was Columbus, Georgia, a well-ordered city with a large military community based on Fort Benning. Phenix City on the other side of the Chattahoochee River was virtually a 'wide open town' offering 'Every conceivable vice: gambling, prostitution, bootleg whiskey, drug ... backroom abortions, and baby selling' (*Look* magazine, 4 October 1954). Phenix City was Mafia heaven. But by 1954 Phenix City was out of control. The outraged citizens of Alabama demanded action.

A local lawyer called Albert Patterson ran for the post of Attorney General of Alabama on a 'Clean Up Phenix City' ticket. He won and announced that his first step would be to move in on the organised crime syndicates operating in the town. Santo Trafficante's response to this threat to his criminal empire was swift and brutal. On 18 June 1954, the new Alabama State Attorney General was gunned down in a very obvious Mafia 'hit'.

The Alabama National Guard moved in to Phenix City and declared Martial Law. The Military Police raided the vice dens and arrested the low life. The Mob could take on and bribe politicians and businessmen, but the US Army on the warpath was out of their league. The Mafia leaders and their corrupt friends fled to safer States of the Union.

But for the Mafia leaders two lessons were clear from their 1954 experience: first, any overt Mafia hits or murders of politicians could bring the wrath and full might of the Federal authorities down around their ears; second, it followed logically that if there were to be any such future murders then they would have to look deniable.

The finger of suspicion should be pointed at a patsy, never at the Mob. Marcello and Trafficante, the two Mafia leaders most affected by the debacle of Phenix City, absorbed the lesson and went looking for their tame murderers, a convincing plan of action to kill Jack Kennedy, and to find some sucker to take all the blame.

***

Planning and setting an ambush involves at least 10 key elements for success: timely, accurate intelligence on the target and its movements; detailed descriptions of any protective arrangements; clear fields of fire; ideally triangulation of the target; an open kill zone; close target reconnaissance; concealed firing positions; good communications; covered withdrawal and escape routes; and if it is to be a 'deniable' operation, a carefully thought out deception and cover plan. In an ideal world, the ambush should also be rehearsed.

An operation of this nature is in fact a highly complex affair, demanding good command and control arrangements. It is a job for professionals who can not only shoot straight, but can also follow a plan and coolly make their escape. Dealey Plaza demonstrated all these characteristics on the day. Professional sharpshooters were readily available. 'Operation 40' and 'Alpha 66' were staffed by just such men and they all believed that Kennedy was a traitor to their cause. The CIA's renegade anti-Castro Exiles were ideal for any deniable operation. The Mafia set up the contract; the vengeful Cubans would do the hit and take the risks. It was perfect.

The next step was the target himself. JFK was a popular and populist president. Young, charismatic, with film star looks and a beautiful wife, he liked to display himself openly to the people.

This vanity offered many opportunities to shoot him from a distance. His visits to big cities and the big crowds he attracted seemed ideal. On these semi-royal progresses JFK liked to sit in an open car: an open and highly visible target to a sniper in a tall building with a well-zeroed rifle.

More problematic was the target's protection. Wherever the President travelled, the FBI and the Secret Service provided a threat assessment and the Secret Service provided 'close protection' on the presidential car operating to strict security procedures. Fortunately for the plotters this was not a problem. With an eye to the future, a worried LBJ had already provided the ever-busy 'Mr Ed' with a copy of the Secret Service's standard operating procedures for protecting the President over a year earlier.

LBJ had handed his lawyer a large envelope containing the official – and highly secret – manual of 'Instructions on Presidential Security'. In September 1961 Clark gave the manual to one of his junior partners called Martin Harris and tasked him with preparing a memorandum on 'The Threat to Vice-Presidential Security'.

According to Harris, he realised that his 'feasibility study on the security threat to the Vice President' could just as easily be used as a blueprint for an attack on any senior public figure. He was also puzzled that his recommendations never saw the light of day. To check out his hunch he reportedly asked Clark, 'How do I charge my time?' to which Clark replied, 'Charge it to the Firm.' Not the supposed client, LBJ – but to the Firm. Harris's suspicions were aroused.

That there was a clear threat to kill the President is no longer in any doubt. In March 1963 a New Orleans FBI informer called Eugene Lappara reported that he overheard three unidentified men in a known Mafia haunt run by Carlos Marcello discussing the contract to whack JFK and looking at advertisements for foreign rifles. He reported hearing one of them, a friend of Marcello's, saying, 'there is a price for the President's head' and that 'somebody will get Kennedy when he comes south.'

In the end the conspirators chose three venues for their attempts on the President's life, based on his well-publicised schedule for November 1963: Chicago, Illinois; Tampa, Florida; and Dallas, Texas. There had been a hushed-up threat to President Kennedy earlier that year in Chicago. On 29 March 1963, he had been scheduled to drive from O'Hare Airport to the Chicago Hilton. Nothing happened, but unusually, all the reports on the incident were swiftly classified and sent by urgent courier straight back to Washington.

Kennedy's subsequent visit to Chicago on 2 November 1963 was also a puzzle for the security authorities. The Cuban Exiles claimed that a team of four gunmen 'out of Montreal' were going to shoot the President. Montreal was Bloomfield and Permindex's base and a known French assassin called Michel Victor Mertz was operating a revived drugs smuggling racket out of the Canadian city at the time. Other likely candidates for the Chicago kill-team were Chuck Nicoletti, Sam Giancana's top trigger man, plus two unidentified Hispanic men. Significantly, both Michel Mertz and Chuck Nicoletti would later be identified in Dallas on 22 November.

Then, on the last day of October, the Secret Service received a telephoned warning claiming that the President would be shot at a sharp 90 degree turn on Jackson Street. The Secret Service reacted strongly and stepped up security. They also got a tip-off from the FBI that Thomas Arthur Valee had an apartment overlooking the motorcade route and 'owned an assortment of weapons'. Valee was arrested, hotly protesting his innocence.

Valee's story would later take on a grotesque significance. He was an ex-Marine, and he claimed that he had been recruited by the US government to help train dissident groups of Cuban exiles for the assassination of Fidel Castro. Confronted with the accusation that he had intended to shoot the President, Valee denied it strongly. On the contrary, he claimed he had been set up by 'someone with special knowledge about him, such as the CIA, because he had a government assignment to train Exiles to assassinate

Castro.' Someone had tried set up the unfortunate ex-Marine to be a patsy for the attempted murder of JFK.

In the event, the Kennedy trip to Chicago was called off as being too risky. The Secret Service eventually assessed the Valee story as a completely different case from any suspected four-man gun team. A worried White House cancelled the presidential visit to Chicago, citing 'health scares'.

One of the puzzles was why the story didn't come out at the time. A likely explanation is that the story was squashed to cover the White House's deadly secret. Kennedy was personally setting up the assassination of Castro and a secret coup and invasion in Cuba. At the time this was political dynamite.

If the Russians got wind of that it could mean war. Washington dare not admit that – ever. But what if Castro got his retaliation in first *or at least appeared to?* Even then the authorities could never admit the truth. They would still have to keep their own plan secret even if it went wrong. The truth was that in their meddling with the CIA's anti-Cuban plans, the Kennedy brothers had unwittingly given JFK's murderers a helping hand. The administration dare not admit that it was planning to kill Castro. All of which helpfully provided the perfect cover-up for a hit on John Kennedy as well...

16

THE KENNEDYS' COUP IN CUBA

FROM ALL DECEITS OF THE WORLD ...
GOOD LORD DELIVER US.
THE LITANY

For a 'deniable' hit, a good cover story is essential.

Jack Kennedy and his brother never really got over the shock of the Bay of Pigs. They felt betrayed on at least three levels. First, the new President realised that the CIA's great plan to invade Cuba was really just a sucker punch to draw him into committing regular US troops in support of the CIA's hare-brained scheme. The CIA had badly misjudged their plan and their man. On a second level, both brothers felt that the CIA was assuming far too much power. The President and Capitol Hill decided US foreign policy; not the CIA. Last, but not least, the Kennedys realised that the Bay of Pigs had damaged the Kennedy presidency. Remedial action was required.

It was against this background that Jack and Bobby Kennedy considered their options over the problem of Cuba in general and Castro in particular. In October 1962 the world had held its breath when Kennedy and Khrushchev had prepared for nuclear war after the Soviets had installed nuclear missiles in Cuba. After 13 nerve-wracking days, the two leaders had compromised. Khrushchev had agreed to remove his missiles from the island; Kennedy would pull the US's Jupiter missiles out of Turkey. Very few really noticed the fine print. Khrushchev agreed that UN inspectors could check on the withdrawal of the Cuban missiles; and Kennedy had promised not to invade Cuba – or to overthrow Castro.

Neither condition was met. Castro flatly refused to allow UN – or any other – inspectors in to Cuba and Kennedy continued to look for ways of overthrowing Castro. Kennedy's problem was primarily political. A presidential election was due in 1964, and, many observers were beginning to suspect, rightly, that not all the Soviets had left Cuba and that Kennedy was lying to them. Kennedy even feared that he could be impeached for misleading Congress.

Cuba was increasingly being identified as potentially the biggest problem in the Kennedys' preparations for the 1964 presidential election. Solve the problem of Cuba, went the thinking from the Oval office, and re-election would be assured. Fail to deal with the situation and Goldwater and the Republicans would carry the day.

The Kennedys then had an extraordinary stroke of luck. Out of the blue came a remarkable offer. Castro's number two, the hero of the revolution, put out tentative feelers in the middle of 1963. Trusted intermediaries indicated that Che Guevara might be prepared to consider – very discreetly, naturally – any ideas that the White House might have in mind to replace Fidel Castro with perhaps a more sympathetic regime.

Guevara was, and still is, an iconic figure. Che's image as a romantic, poetry-loving revolutionary has become a clichéd fantasy to a million sighing co-ed students. The truth about the amoral, psychopathic, murderous fanatic has been lost in the revolutionary legend. Nonetheless, Che's vague and ambiguous offer changed everything. Now, with a man like Che as the figurehead and at the helm of a new Cuba working with the United States, the Kennedys' problem of Cuba would suddenly change into the Kennedys' triumph of Cuba.

So when in 1963 the Kennedy boys were presented with this opportunity of solving their Cuban problem once and for all, they jumped at the chance. Especially, as the offer came from inside Cuba itself: a Cuban solution to a Cuban problem – perfect.

The Pentagon and State Department already had their contingency plans for any Cuban coup or major disturbances in any of their Caribbean neighbours. These suddenly became a very real possibility when in May 1963 Castro's Army Commander Juan Almeida let the Americans know that if anything were to happen to Castro, Almeida would be happy to put a more moderate government in its place; a government that would seek an accommodation with the US. So opportunity really stared the Kennedys in the face a month later in Paris, where a disgruntled Che Guevara met his old friend Carlo Franqui, a distinguished Cuban journalist who now wanted to defect from Castro's Socialist Paradise.

It was a seminal meeting. Franqui was openly defecting and Che was admitting that he too had had enough of Castro and his dictatorial ways. He wanted out of Cuba by 1 December 1963. The Joint Chiefs of Staff contingency plans to deal with any coup could be swiftly upgraded to become a real plan *to start* a real coup in Cuba. A Cuban must eliminate Castro; Almeida's Cuban army would then take over; Che Guevara would head up a new Provisional Government and invite the Exiles back; and if there was any trouble, the Provisional Government would ask America to help. The key was it had to be seen by the world as an *internal* Cuban matter and it had to be led, and carried out, by Cubans.

In the late spring of 1963 President Kennedy had ordered his brother to personally oversee the top secret task of planning a coup in Cuba to be run from the White House itself. Now the plotters had a solid offer out of Cuba. The Kennedys set to finetuning the so-called 'Contingency Plan' into a real plot to start a Cuban coup.

It was an audacious scheme. Not just because it would cause at least a generation's worth of posters and T-shirts to be re-printed to read 'Che, Che, CIA?' but also because the Kennedy brothers were risking war with the Soviet Union. If the Soviets ever found out that the Americans were behind a covert attempt to overthrow Castro, then the Kremlin would undoubtedly have moved to retaliate. In Berlin they had a vulnerable Western hostage and could have overrun it in two or three days – and Khrushchev had made it plain that is precisely what he would do if Kennedy didn't keep his word about not invading or interfering in Cuba.

The problem of killing Castro was easily solved: the CIA just happened to have a tame anti-Castro gunman up their sleeve already. His name was Rolando Cubela and he was a member of Castro's government in Havana. Together with Che Guevara and Castro he had helped to drive Batista from power. The revolution was long since over and Cubela was increasingly marginalized and disgruntled. In 1961 he had flirted with the CIA. In mid-1963 he offered to shoot Castro.

Codenamed AMLASH, Cubela became a major part of the Kennedys' plan for the Cuban coup. The CIA even sent one of their senior officers, Desmond FitzGerald, posing as a US Senator to Paris in mid-1963 to meet Cubela and brief him. Cubela agreed to shoot Castro for the Americans and was put under the wing of David Morales, CIA Miami's chief of Operations and drinking buddy of Mafia man Johnny Rosselli.

Just to make sure, the CIA had activated no less than three separate, but linked, murder projects in the summer of 1963. In addition to Cubela, they had activated their European gunman recruiter, the mysterious QJ/WIN and had also tasked Rosselli to step up the Mob's efforts to eliminate Castro. The key point was that each of these activities could proceed in isolation. Only Bobby Kennedy and a dozen other US officials actually knew about the whole scheme and its real deadly secret to assassinate Castro as part of a 'Cuban coup'.

But the CIA-trained Cubans had been completely penetrated by Castro's intelligence service, the DGI, as well as by the Mafia. The knowledge that something big was being planned for 1 December leaked. By autumn 1963 the Mafia picked up the deadly secret.

The most likely source of the leak was a Cuban exile leader named Tony Varona. He had been a member of the Cuban government before fleeing to America. An imposing, respected figure, he was a natural choice as a member of any post-Castro Provisional government. The problem was that Varona was closely tied in with the Mafia and had a grievance against JFK, because the American President had cut funding to Varona's Cuban Revolutionary Council in April 1963.

Sometime in the summer of 1963 Tony Varona told his old friend Johnny Rosselli – 'Colonel Rosselli' to the Cuban exile fighters – what he knew about the Kennedys' secret plans. A CIA memo confirms that between 12 and 27 August, Varona took a $200,000 bribe from the Chicago Mafia. The Cuban coup's value as a cover plan for the Mafia's own contract on Kennedy was obvious immediately.

Gunmen could be hired and presidents killed. But it could be made to look like a Cuban hit: and no one in the US government dare challenge that, for fear of revealing to the Russians the dark truth that the US had been planning to kill Castro and interfere in Cuba all along.

The KGB's antennae had already picked up something. On 7 November Khrushchev was reported as warning that 'any US attack on Cuba will lead to war.' One wrong move could spark another confrontation between the two superpowers. As a cover story the Cuban connection was perfect, as the Mafia prepared for their next ambush, in Tampa, Florida.

Tampa was an important visit for the President. Whatever the importance of the southern states for his re-election campaign in 1964, he had another much more important task to perform than crude local electioneering. John F. Kennedy had to pass a vital message to the leader of any coup.

Not unreasonably, the plotters 90 miles across the water wanted some reassurances from their powerful neighbour. They were contemplating treason, and the would-be Cuban traitors looked to Kennedy for a clear promise of support. The CIA spelled it out with pin-sharp clarity, noting that '[dissidents] must have solemn assurances from high level US spokesmen, especially the President, that the United States will exert its decisive influence during and immediately after [a] coup...' But first Kennedy had to survive a second ambush attempt.

That the Mafia were interested in the Florida trip is not in doubt. Jack Ruby, Sam Giancana's local Mafia manager and gopher in the South, was suddenly ordered to fly to Las Vegas to meet Johnny Rosselli the weekend before Kennedy's visit to Tampa, for urgent consultations before returning to Dallas. In Tampa, the police suddenly started to get ominous warnings of threats to the President's life.

Tampa police and the FBI recorded a conversation between a right wing racist activist, Joseph Adams Milteer, and a Miami Police informant called Willie Somersett. On 9 November 1963, Milteer told Somersett that it was 'in the working' that JFK would be killed on his visit to Miami, by 'someone with a rifle in a tall building'. He also added that someone would be arrested immediately after the killing to take the blame.

It was a remarkably accurate description of 'the guy who would be arrested' to take the rap. His name was Gilberto Lopez, and the physical similarities between him and Lee Harvey Oswald are striking. Like Oswald, Lopez was heavily involved with the Tampa Fair Play for Cuba Committee; like Oswald he had been involved in a public brawl because of his alleged support for Castro; and had made a mysterious trip to Cuba via Mexico – also like Oswald. Someone tipped off to the Florida police, so that they would know exactly who to arrest first. Lopez had been carefully set up as a pro-Castro patsy.

Tampa Police Chief Mullins is the main source for the story of the unsuccessful attempt at Tampa on 18 November. Talk of cancelling the motorcade was brushed aside by Kennedy. To be in Florida was to demonstrate his power and America's strength to the nervous coup plotters in Cuba. To cower away from yet another death threat would merely advertise weakness and show him not to be master in his own backyard.

Chief Mullins employed extraordinary measures to combat the threat. No fewer than 600 security men crowded the route in Tampa. The uniformed police were reinforced by 400 other agents, recruited from a variety of agencies. Tall Secret Service agents crowded around the President. The ambush was aborted and the President flew on to Miami to make his speech. Although, unsurprisingly, someone had helpfully tipped off the FBI and Tampa

Police that Gilberto Lopez – 'a Cuban nut' – was a threat to the President, fortunately there was no reason to pick him up.

The next day Kennedy spoke at the American Press Association in Miami. He made a ringing declaration of support for the *'genuine Cuban Revolution'* and called on Cubans to 'remove this obstacle'. In no uncertain terms he pledged American support to the Cuban people and their leaders *'once Cuban sovereignty has been restored'.* Out across the water in Havana, his words were crystal clear to his unseen audience: mount a coup and get rid of Castro, and we will come and help you. The President of the United States had said so. The coup was on. D-Day would be 1 December 1963.

But first the President had to make his long-planned trip to Dallas.

PART 4

TO KILL A PRESIDENT

17

THE ROAD TO DALLAS

O DIVINE ART OF SUBTLETY AND SECRECY! THROUGH YOU WE LEARN TO BE INVISIBLE.
SUN TZU, *THE ART OF WAR*

There are numerous intelligence indicators in the weeks and days before the assassination that something big was being planned. The cast of characters for Dallas is big; and the stage is crowded. The pressure for the President to go to Texas was of long standing. The final decision to go ahead with the visit was taken on 5 June 1963 by JFK, LBJ and Texas Governor John Connally. The date was only finally confirmed as late as 8 November that the visit to Dallas would be on 22 November 1963.

It was a bold decision. Dallas was a fiercely conservative, rightwing city. Kennedy was heading into trouble. Only a month before, the veteran Washington politician, Adlai Stevenson, had been set upon by a hate-filled crowd during a visit to Dallas. He had been hit with a placard and spat at. Not for nothing was intolerant, racist and bigoted Dallas, 'the hate capital of the USA'.

The main characters were all in place by the autumn of 1963. A young ex-Marine called Lee Harvey Oswald, who had defected to the USSR and then returned, had taken up residence during May. Also in Dallas was a small-time gangster called Jack Ruby who had been sent by his boss, Sam Giancana of the Chicago Mafia Syndicate, to 'look after Dallas' and to work with the Louisiana Don, Carlos Marcello. Jack Ruby was well known to the Dallas Police. Every Friday he took discreet brown envelopes round their lockers in the Police station.

Jack Ruby ensured that many of 'Dallas's Finest' were bought by Carlos Marcello and the Mob.

On 25 September a Cuban exile called Antonio Veciana turned up in Dallas to meet his CIA handler, 'Maurice Bishop'. Veciana was the founder and leader of a team of anti-Castro commandos called 'Alpha 66' which had carried out a number of highly effective attacks on Soviet and Cuban targets in Cuba. Indeed, they had been so successful that Moscow was now complaining officially. President Kennedy ordered the aggressive CIA-run exile attacks on Cuba to stop immediately. The FBI even raided one of the CIA's secret Cuban training camps at Lake Pontchartrain and closed it down.

The CIA was outraged at the notion of one US Intelligence Agency being asked to raid and close down another Agency's activities – even though the CIA's operations on US soil were in many cases completely illegal. In their turn, the Cuban Exiles were furious at this curtailment of their commando raids and the loss of their money supply from the US government. The Exiles were suspicious and angry. Was Kennedy going to abandon them? Were they being betrayed – yet again – by the double dealing and gutless US President who had failed and abandoned them at the Bay of Pigs? Renegade elements talked of 'getting Kennedy'. Alpha 66's angry gang members sought a meeting with their CIA boss.

Veciana had met his handler over a hundred times and he later testified that it was the mysterious 'Mr Bishop' of the CIA who had always given him the targets to strike at Cuba. To this day, still no one knows – officially – the identity of 'Maurice Bishop'. His identity is important, however, for two reasons. One, Veciana says that 'Bishop' was, on 25 September, talking to man who he later identified as Lee Harvey Oswald. Second, Veciana was adamant that 'Mr Bishop' looked like the local CIA boss for Cuban Mafia operations, Dave Atlee Phillips. Dave Atlee Phillips denied being 'Maurice Bishop' until his dying day and even sued the *Observer* newspaper in London for printing that he was. He won his case. But Veciana was adamant that it was 'Mr Bishop' of the CIA who gave him his orders and described Dave Atlee Phillips very accurately. Thanks to the testimony of another CIA officer, Ron Crozier, we also know that that 'Maurice Bishop' was one of Dave Atlee Phillips' work names.

The very next day, confirmation of the President's forthcoming Dallas trip was blazoned all over the Texas newspapers. Unusually it went into some detail of the route and the timings. The Dallas Citizens' Council sponsored Jack Kennedy's trip to town. And the Dallas Citizens' Council just happened to be controlled by two very rich Jews, Julius Schepps and Sam Bloom. More interesting still, Schepps was Seagram's distribution agent in Dallas and was plugged directly into the Bronfman empire in Canada. He knew Louis Bloomfield and Sam Bronfman very well indeed. It would be naïve to the point of incredulity to think that a committed Zionist like Schepps was not aware of Israel's concerns over Jack Kennedy and the US President's ultimatum to Israel.

The mysterious Lee Harvey Oswald popped up again in late September. The trouble was he popped up in two places at the same time. On 26 September a Cuban exile named Sylvia Odio had a visit from three men in Dallas. One of the men was introduced as 'Leon Oswald' and was allegedly helping the Cuban cause. After the assassination, Mrs Odio realised that the TV pictures of the alleged assassin showed the man she had met that day. The Odio incident clearly indicates that either Oswald was involved with anti-Castro Cuban exiles who were talking about killing Kennedy, or that someone was impersonating Oswald while he was in Mexico City.

Because the problem with Odio's testimony was that on 26 September 'Lee Harvey Oswald' seems to have crossed the Mexican border. On 27 September someone calling himself 'Lee Harvey Oswald' applied for a visa for Cuba at the Cuban embassy in Mexico City. The 'Lee Harvey Oswald' in Mexico got into a shouting match with Cuban and Soviet officials and could hardly speak Russian. The conclusion is that it wasn't Lee Harvey Oswald – unless he was two people. None of the men filmed going into either embassy can be shown to bear any resemblance to Lee Harvey Oswald.

The road to Dallas was littered with key events as well as individuals. On 11 October 1963, Kennedy signed a crucial National Security Action Memorandum, number 263, signalling his intention to pull 1,000 US troops out of Vietnam by the end of the year and eventually run down the US's commitment to Vietnam. Pulling back from Vietnam meant a reduction in government orders for weapons. That meant a loss of profits for the arms manufacturers. That meant a drop in share prices for some of the big boys on Wall Street. Coupled with the reports of the closure of 52 military bases across the country, this spelled a major cutback in military expenditure. Vietnam was good business for a lot of people.

We now know that Kennedy was seriously considering getting *all* US troops out of Vietnam by the end of 1965, after the presidential election. There were only 16,000 American soldiers in Vietnam at that time, so that removing over 1,000 represented a significant withdrawal. It got a reaction, without doubt, but not the one Kennedy expected. To Kennedy's enemies, NSAM 263 was clear proof. Kennedy was going to abandon South Vietnam. The Pentagon's voice was now firmly added to the growing chorus of disapproval. Kennedy was a liability.

***

Another curious and unexplained piece of evidence was the cable from Dave Atlee Phillips to Washington reporting the 'Lee Harvey Oswald' visit to Mexico. Philips swears he signed off on the CIA cable at 7.43p.m. on 10 October, but he didn't. He was on leave in Miami at the time, not Mexico. Philips was either lying or the existing cable is a forgery placed in the CIA files later. The whole affair is wrong, because shortly afterwards an official CIA teletype hit the State Department, the FBI, the Navy Department and the US Immigration Service, informing them that 'an American who identified himself as Lee Harvey Oswald contacted the Soviet embassy in Mexico City ... it is believed that Oswald may be identical to Lee Harvey Oswald, born on 18 October 1939 in New Orleans.'

'It is believed' is the wording that is designed to get bureaucrats out of trouble at boards of enquiry because there is little solid evidence that the real Oswald visited Mexico City at the time. There is however hard evidence that an impostor was laying a false trail.

The real Lee Harvey Oswald was now back in Dallas and very visible. He had been befriended by Michael and Ruth Paine who were part of Dallas's Russian community. Ruth Paine had provided board to Oswald's Russian wife Marina, and had arranged for Lee to get a job at the Texas School Book Depository. The Paines seem to have been remarkably obliging and helpful both before and after Oswald's murder. The suspicion must be that they were part of some wider operation to control the hapless agent. It was Mrs Paine who took Oswald for a driving lesson and noted that he was both lacking in confidence and was 'unskilled' as a driver.

This is yet another puzzle, because on 9 November, a man calling himself

'Lee Oswald' visited Downtown Lincoln Car Sales in Dallas and took a car for a high-speed test drive. The real Lee Harvey Oswald was at work at the time, didn't have a driving licence and couldn't drive. Clearly, someone was impersonating Lee Harvey Oswald. Taken together with the visit of a noisy man calling himself 'Oswald' – and looking like him, too – to a Dallas rifle range, it all looks very odd. The man at the rifle range fired on a neighbour's target, got into an argument and left. At that time on that day, Lee Harvey Oswald was at work at the book depository.

To reinforce the legend of this second Oswald, a man cashed a large cheque in Irving, Texas and made sure that he was remembered. The only problem was that Lee never cashed a cheque there. On that same date, a man calling himself 'Oswald' took a Mannlicher-Carcano rifle into the Irving sports shop and asked for it to be drilled to accept a telescopic sight. The gun shop bored three small holes to accept a sniper scope. The evidence is clear: if someone was trying to implicate Oswald *before* the assassination, then someone knew there was going to be an attempt on the President's life.

The Cuban Exiles in Chicago definitely knew that something was in the wind. A Secret Service's undercover informant told Maurice Martineau, the local agent in charge, that some militant Cubans were trying to buy machine guns. According to the informant, the Cubans claimed to have plenty of money, and would pay for the guns as soon as they 'took care' of Kennedy. Martineau warned his headquarters and launched an investigation. After the assassination the Secret Service was ordered to hand over all its files to the FBI where they swiftly disappeared.

More confirmation of the threat to the President came from a CIA source. On 10 November 1963 David Ferrie's boyfriend, Eladio del Valle, told CIA agent Robert Monrow that the three Mannlicher-Carcano rifles he had got had been passed to David Ferrie and are to be used, 'for the big one ... in Dallas ... Kennedy's going to get it when he comes to Dallas'. Del Valle was leader of Florida's Free Cuba Committee and knew Santo Trafficante.

Ferrie is one of the key links in the whole Dallas puzzle. He knew Oswald, having recruited him into the Civil Air Patrol years before. He was homosexual, had alopecia and had to paint heavy eyebrows, and was a brilliant pilot and a pathological anticommunist. Ferrie also had links with the CIA, he was directly employed by Mafia boss Carlos Marcello and his private detective, ex-Chicago FBI man Guy Banister, and he knew Oswald.

Banister, like his boss William Harvey, was a hard drinking psychopath. Banister's job in 1962–63 was to carry out undercover investigative work for Carlos Marcello's businesses. But Banister was also a CIA asset. From his 544 Camp Street address in New Orleans, he ran a network of intelligence reporting operations in the South on behalf of the US government's intelligence agencies. One of them was the New Orleans chapter of the 'Fair Play for Cuba Committee' with its single member, Lee Harvey Oswald. But

Banister's sympathies were entirely *opposed* to Castro's Cuba.

Delphine Roberts was Banister's secretary in 1963. She confirms that Banister, Lee Harvey Oswald and Ferrie often held meetings behind closed doors and that Banister allowed Oswald to use his third floor office for the FPCC. Lee Harvey Oswald appears to have acted as an *'agent provocateur'* for the Federal government, being run through Banister's private security company. On 22 January 1964 Waggoner Carr of Texas called the Warren Commission to warn them that the FBI had confirmed that Lee was FBI Agent 'S-179' and on an FBI retainer of $200 a month. As one Warren Commission member said at the time, 'the implications are fantastic.'

More proof of Oswald's undercover role comes from Adrian Alba who in 1963 ran the Crescent City garage in New Orleans. Alba's garage had a classified government contract to service and maintain the local undercover pool of federal automobiles. In the early summer of 1963 Alba remembers an 'FBI agent from Washington' drawing a green Studebaker from the pool. Next day he witnessed the same agent hand a thick white envelope to Oswald, whom Alba knew well as he worked across the street.

After the assassination Alba confessed himself astonished that none of this appeared in the Warren Commission report. The irony is that Oswald, the 'lone nut' and the 'hapless patsy', turns out almost certainly to have been a rather good undercover agent until he was betrayed by his supposed colleagues and employers. What also emerges from the events on the way to Dallas is that the truth about the Mexico trip by 'Lee Harvey Oswald' is crucial. Oswald cannot have been in Texas and Mexico City at the same time. The balance of evidence is that someone was impersonating the real Oswald in Mexico.

Added to oddities like the $32 receipt from the Laredo clothes shop on the Mexican border found in Oswald's possessions by the FBI after his arrest, it raises the suspicion that the receipt might have been planted. But if the CIA and FBI were planting or fabricating evidence against Oswald *before* the assassination that points to a more explosive deduction.

For while it is quite clear that Carlos Marcello and his Mafia gunmen could take out a contract to kill the President of the USA, it is equally clear that the Mafia could not organise a sophisticated international impersonation to create a false legend and plant evidence in FBI and CIA files. The whole Mexico story smacks of an undercover intelligence operation to set up a cover and deception plan for some forthcoming event and one that had been going on – and had therefore been *planned* – for some time. The implications of piecing this jigsaw together lead only to one conclusion: there was a conspiracy to kill the President and it involved more than a few disgruntled leaders of organised crime or unhappy Cubans.

***

In the first week of November, three Corsican gunmen slipped across the Mexican border using Italian passports. According to one source they were ensconced in a CIA house by Roscoe

White, a Dallas policeman acting for the CIA. Jack Ruby's number of interstate calls did not just double in the first weeks of November. They increased to *25 times* their normal rate. Ruby's telephone calls are not the only sign of activity in the underworld. Jimmy Hoffa paid the anti-Castro exile and professional gunman, Rolando Masferrer, $500,000 for some undisclosed services. Masferrer was the killer who recruited assassination teams to eliminate Fidel Castro for Santo Trafficante on behalf of the CIA. Within 24 hours Hoffa and Ruby were on the telephone to each other and within another day Ruby flew to Miami where he was seen talking to Murray Miller, Hoffa's link with organised crime in the south east.

On the 12th, an irate Lee Harvey Oswald – the real one – stomped into the Dallas FBI office and left a note for agent Jim Hosty, who had been tasked with interviewing him. The note said that if Hosty wanted to know anything about him, then come and ask him directly. One explanation might be that Oswald couldn't understand why the 'overt' FBI was asking questions about him in public while he was secretly working for them behind the scenes. There is a school of thought that the note to Hosty also contained a warning about the plan to assassinate the President, which has since been suppressed.

Odd things were stirring on the other side of the Atlantic, too. A US Army cryptographic communications operator in France claimed that he had seen signals traffic that proved that 'the military' were going to kill the President. On 22 October Pfc. Eugene B. Dinkin had written to Robert Kennedy and then gone AWOL from his signals unit in Metz, Eastern France. Dinkin warned that there would be an attempt to assassinate the President on 28 November and that if it were to succeed 'the blame would be placed on a communist or a negro.' Dinkin eventually gave himself up in early November. He was put under close arrest and then examined by an Army psychiatrist, diagnosed as 'mentally ill' and placed under armed guard in Walter Reed Hospital in Washington. Dinkin was eventually released and has since refused to talk about his case.

A cynic might conclude that Private Dinkin had been muzzled while in the Psychiatric ward and realised that the only way to get out was to keep his mouth shut or change his story to suit the Feds. This assessment of the Dinkin case is given weight by the fact that all the papers on his case are still classified as top secret in the US National Archive: an unusual bureaucratic handling of a mere private soldier's absence and 'wild allegations'.

Back in Dallas the initial checks were being made on the route of the presidential motorcade. In a breach of procedures Secret Service agent Winston Lawson asked Dallas Chief of Police Jesse Curry to provide only four motorcycle outriders instead of the usual eight and requested that they drive 'on the rear fender' of the limousine, not alongside as was normal. The House Assassinations Committee later stigmatised Agent Lawson's security arrangements as 'uniquely insecure'.

On 14 November a Ku Klux Klan member told the FBI that 'a bunch of right-wingers' were going to try and kill the President. That was also the day that Jack Ruby hosted a friendly little business meeting in his Carousel Club. Present were Bernard Weissman, the sponsor of the black bordered anti-JFK poster that would appear in the *Dallas Morning News* the day the President came to town, plus a good friend of Jack Ruby's: Officer J.D. Tippit of the Dallas Police Force.

Ruby was in good spirits. He had bought a safe and began to talk about getting some real money soon. (In fact within the week he would receive $7,000: exactly the same amount that David Ferrie received from Carlos Marcello when the two met at Marcello's ranch 'Churchill Farms' the weekend before the murder.)

Meanwhile, in Dealey Plaza on 16 November, it looks as though someone might have been taking their rehearsal a little too seriously. As Mrs Joe Bailly Blackwell and her sister were approaching the triple underpass in Dealey Plaza, someone shot at them. The Police could find nothing except evidence that a bullet had definitely hit their car. The duty operator at FBI HQ received a specific warning about a threat to assassinate President Kennedy on 22–23 November in Dallas, by 'a militant revolutionary group'. In the early hours of 17 November, agent William S. Walter of the FBI passed the message on to all interested parties.

In Abilene on 18 November a man called Harry Reynolds picked up a note that had been slipped under his door. It was meant for one of his neighbours, Pedro Gonzalez. The note was a request to call two Dallas telephone numbers urgently and the signature was 'Lee Oswald'. Gonzalez was closely linked to Tony Varona, the now disaffected leader of the CIA-backed Cuban Revolutionary Council. Both the embittered Varona (who also had close links to Rosselli and the Mafia) and Gonzalez had uttered threats to 'get Kennedy' for cutting off CRC money.

One of the more curious stories of the impending assassination came from a CIA asset called Richard Nagell, who years later told the New Orleans DA Jim Garrison that he had been undercover, to investigate a major plot to kill the

President in 1963. He claims that he got close to Oswald (whom he says he only knew as 'Aleksei Hidell') and who reportedly told Nagell that 'they were going to get him within a month'. Nagell claims that he passed this information on to his CIA Controller, Robert Graham, who told Nagell to 'take care of Oswald' and 'stop the clock'.

On 20 September 1963 Nagell walked into an El Paso bank, fired two shots into the ceiling, then sat down and waited for the cops to arrive. He expected a 'criminal mischief' charge with a light sentence that would keep him away from Oswald and the CIA. Instead, Nagell was held in the local County jail for nine months without trial and the original judge was substituted for a newly appointed Judge Thornberry, who just happened to be a very close friend of the new president, Lyndon Johnson. To everyone's astonishment, Thornberry sent Nagell down for 10 years for a first offence to which he had pleaded 'guilty' and to which he had surrendered voluntarily. Nagell served three years and later told Garrison that in 1963 he had been working with Guy Banister, David Ferrie and Clay Shaw at the time – and that they all knew about the plot.

Years afterwards it emerged from Nagell's trial documents that the FBI had discovered a Minolta camera, 'Fair Play for Cuba' leaflets and an ID card for 'Lee Oswald' in Nagell's car. The paperwork has long since disappeared, doubtless into the secret archives or shredders of the FBI. Nagell also swore blind that he sent a registered letter off with all the details of the plot marked, 'Personal for the Director of the FBI' on 13 September 1963. The FBI and Hoover denied ever receiving such a communication.

The other curious fact is that the FBI found seven unexplained names in Nagell's address book. They all turned out to be active CIA contacts and when the FBI routinely checked the names with the CIA, the Agency angrily demanded how the FBI had come into their possession. Nagell died of a sudden heart attack in 1995; oddly enough on the very day he was summoned to testify at the Assassinations Records Review Board.

By the time he was found, someone had already searched his apartment and taken all his papers.

Back in Dallas the final plans for the motorcade were being laid. In yet another of the long list of curious coincidences surrounding Kennedy's murder, the Dallas hosting committee was organised and run by the pro-Israel Sam Bloom. It was he who suggested that Kennedy should speak at the Trade Mart instead of the planned Women's Building at lunch, and he is also implicated in the suggestion that the motorcade swing off the clear straight road onto Elm Street and make the tight turns in front of the book depository leading down to the grassy knoll. The result was that the route of the motorcade (which had already been released to the press) was changed at the last minute.

Forrest Sorrels or Chief Rowley of the Secret Service are usually blamed as the men who finally ordered the 90-degree dogleg to the right into Dealey Plaza, followed by a 120-degree hard left turn onto Elm Street underneath the book depository and in front of the grassy knoll. From the Commission testimony it appears that the person who was ultimately responsible for the final selection of the new route and the Trade Centre turns out to have been one of LBJ's aides, Bill Moyers.

The route confirmed by Moyers and the Secret Service was in direct contravention of the Secret Service protection detail's standing security instructions, as was the open memorandum from Secret Service agent Winston Lawson that agents 'will wear their red and white permanent lapel pin' in Dallas as identification. The note went out to the Dallas Police for information, in advance, thus making it possible for anyone to impersonate a Secret Service agent on the day and make any assassin's escape much easier. Suddenly the protection detail in Dallas looks remarkably unprofessional, careless or something worse.

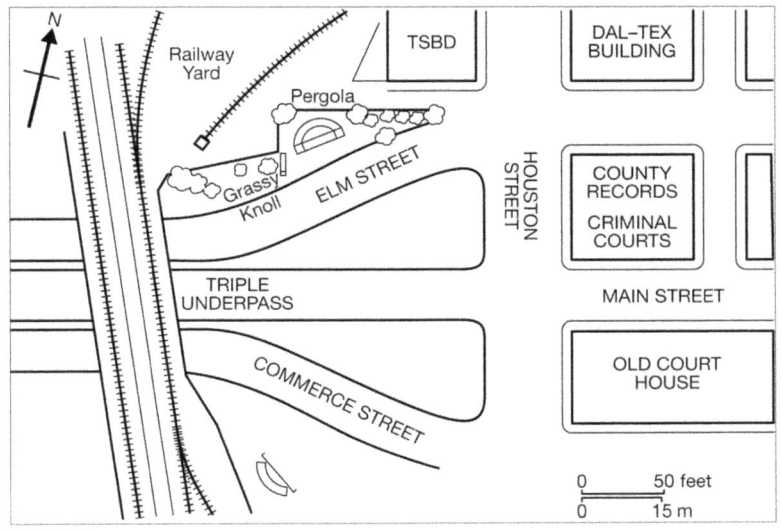

Dealey Plaza, Dallas: the 120-degree left turn from Houston on to Elm would slow the motorcade.

In 1991 JFK investigator Matthew Smith interviewed Wayne January at Redbird Airfield in Dallas on terms of strict confidentiality. Mr January has since died and his full story has been made public. On 18 November he claimed that a USAF colonel turned up in civilian clothes with a civilian pilot to inspect a Douglas DC-3 that Wayne's aviation company had sold. The pilot's job was to check out the aeroplane. The pilot was Cuban and admitted to having done work for the CIA. He and Wayne became friendly and on 21

November told Wayne that he had been involved in the Bay of Pigs. He added, 'your President is going to be killed.' Not unnaturally, Wayne said that he couldn't see it happening.

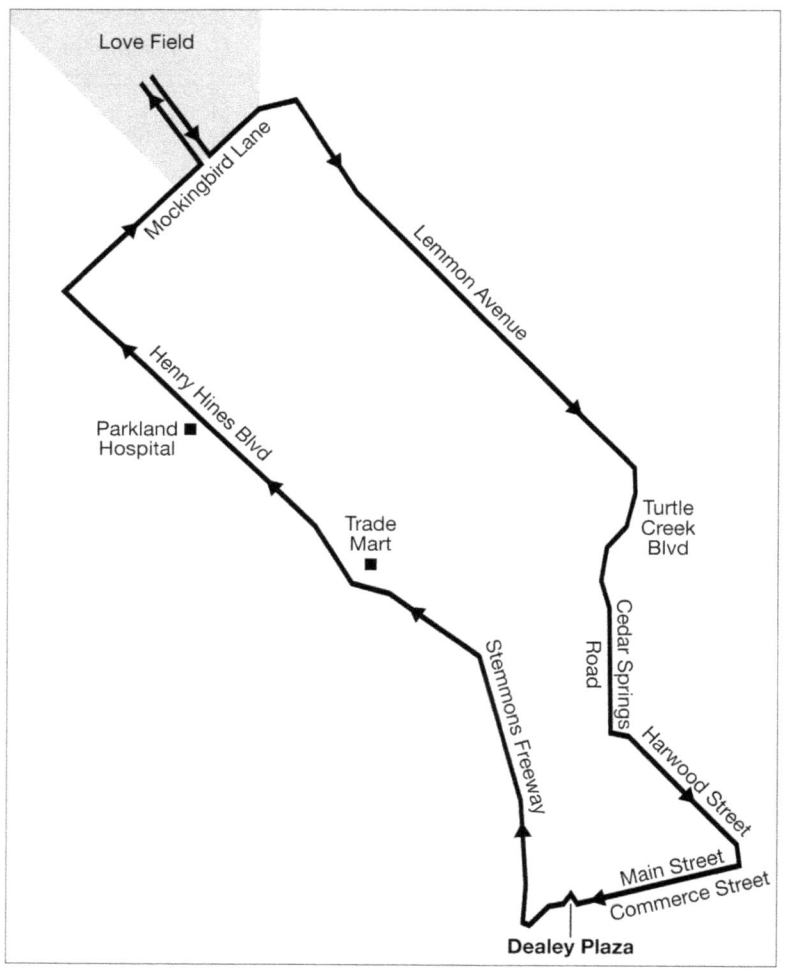

President John F. Kennedy's final, fatal, motorcade route through Dallas.

Next day, the 22nd, a friend told Wayne what had just happened in Dealey Plaza. Wayne was stunned, but the fact was the Cuban had warned him *before* the event. Matthew Smith later checked the plane's registration number, N-17888. Tracking N-17888 turned out to be difficult. The DC-3 had been purchased by the 'Houston Air Center'. That turned out to be one of the CIA's many front companies. But the pilot's warning had been spot on. The final pieces of the jigsaw now slotted into place. A Cuban CIA agent called Marita Lorenz arrived in Dallas from Miami. Lorenz had been Castro's mistress but had fled Cuba after being recruited by Frank Sturgis, contract agent of the CIA. She claimed that the two-car convoy was a CIA/Cuban hit team delivering weapons and gunmen to Dallas. The men she identified were members of 'Operation 40', the CIA secret group trained in assassination, sabotage and commando operations. According to Lorenz they were holed up in a motel when 'Jack Ruby' and CIA agent E. Howard Hunt came by with maps and money. The men began spreading their maps of Dallas on the table and discussing the ambush. Realising what they were planning, Lorenz claims she wanted out and went straight back to Miami on her own. Curiously, Ms Lorenz was adamant that 'Lee Oswald' had accompanied them in the cars from Miami, but that was impossible. Lee Harvey Oswald was going to work every day at the book depository.

Later Ms Lorenz added another piece to the puzzle. In 1977 she testified on oath during a defamation suit brought by E. Howard Hunt against *Spotlight* magazine, that after the assassination Sturgis said to her, 'You missed the really big one ... we killed the President that day ... you could have been part of it – you know, part of history. You should have stayed. It was safe. Everything was covered in advance ... No arrests, no real newspaper investigation. It was all covered, very professional.'

The CIA men Sturgis and Hunt denied her allegations that they had been involved; but the jury didn't believe either of them. The court ruled in favour of the *Spotlight* story; and that meant that, in law, Frank Sturgis had been party to a plot to kill President Kennedy.

Another unusual visitor to Dallas was Frenchman Michel Roux, better known by his work names 'Jean le Souetre' and 'Michel Mertz'. Roux is logged as having entered the USA through New York on 19 November and promptly headed south for Fort Worth, Texas. Michel Mertz-Roux was a notorious French gunman, and a close associate of both the Mafia and the CIA through his international narcotics dealing. At the time he was based in Quebec; a natural place for a French speaker in North America and, coincidentally, the home of Louis Bloomfield, Sam Bronfman, Permindex and the Canadian links to Mossad. The presumption that he came in courtesy of Permindex is strong.

All the actors were now waiting in the wings and the stage was set for what was to become known as 'the crime of the century'.

***

On the night of 20/21 November 1963. Louisiana State Police traffic patrol picked up a woman calling herself 'Rose Charamie', who worked for Jack Ruby as a hostess. The injured woman was taken to the East Louisiana State Hospital where Lt Francis Fruge and a secretary took her statement.

Rose Charamie admitted to being a low-level drug runner for the Mafia and Ruby and claimed that she had been abandoned on the road by two 'Italians'. In the hospital she warned that the President was going to be killed in Dallas in two days' time. The Chief Psychiatric Consultant heard her story too, but sadly Dr Victor Weiss assumed that the heroin addict was semi-delirious and rambling. He should have paid more attention.

Because Rose Charamie was telling him and anyone else who cared to listen on the morning of 21 November 1963 that 'the word was out in the New Orleans underworld that the contract on Kennedy had been let – and it's on for Dallas tomorrow.'

18

DALLAS ON THE DAY

AS MANY ARROWS, LOOSED SEVERAL WAYS FLY TO ONE MARK AS MANY WAYS MEET IN ONE TOWN...
SHAKESPEARE, *HENRY V*

One of the more curious aspects of the JFK assassination is the way that suggestion of conclusive or suspicious evidence of US establishment involvement is promptly challenged, criticised or rubbished. Nowhere is this more evident than in the Texas party supposedly held the night before the Dallas motorcade.

Madeleine Brown was LBJ's mistress for over 20 years and bore him a son, Steven. LBJ's attorney Ed Clark 'fixed the problem' by paying her off with $500 a month. For years Madeleine Brown claimed that she had attended a reception at oil millionaire Clint Murchison's house the night before the assassination.

According to Brown, at about midnight LBJ appeared:

Tension filled the room on his arrival. The group immediately went behind closed doors. A short time later Lyndon, anxious and red-faced, re-appeared ... squeezing my hand so hard it felt crushed from the pressure, he spoke in a whisper, a quiet growl, into my ear: 'After tomorrow those goddamn Kennedys will never embarrass me again.'

The problem with Ms Brown's oft-quoted account is that, based on the evidence, LBJ could not have been at the party. So it is not surprising that Brown's 1992 TV account of the party was promptly challenged. Researchers claimed that she was either lying, forgetful, or exaggerating. (She was 'puffing' a book about her affair with LBJ when she made her revelations.)

According to her critics there was no party at Clint Murchison Senior's house and that LBJ and Nixon were firmly identified in the Houston Coliseum at 10p.m. Richard Nixon too was seen in Houston at about 11p.m. on the 21st, squiring Joan Crawford. However,

Ms Brown's story does get confirmation from two other sources. There definitely was a major convention of soft drink bottling manufacturers in Dallas on 21/22 November, at which Nixon had been a speaker. According to Barr McClellan, one of LBJ's attorneys, there was a party that night, but at Clint Murchison *Junior's* house at Turtle Creek, less than an hour's drive from Fort Worth. McClellan is positive that there was a reception that night and, given the occasion of a local presidential visit with so many bigwigs in town and the bottlers' convention, such an event would be both normal and credible.

What is clear is that Clint Murchison Junior probably did host a reception of some kind at his house. Partial corroboration of the event does come from Robert G. Ross, who claimed that the guest list that night also included George Brown of Brown & Root; Earle Cabell, Mayor of Dallas; Mac Wallace and Ed Clark of LBJ's private firm; Carlos Marcello of New Orleans and his underling Joe Civello of the Dallas Mafia; John Connally, Governor of

Texas; plus a brief appearance by LBJ and Jack Ruby.

***

Not far from the smoke-filled reception salon of Texas's great and not-so-good, another party was in full swing. In downtown Dallas the presidential protection detail were quietly getting drunk. Standing Regulations for the US Secret Service are quite specific: 'the use of intoxicating liquor of any kind, including beer or wine, by members of the White House detail ... while they are in travel status (i.e. on a mission to protect the President) is prohibited.' The penalty for infringement was instant dismissal.

Despite this stern warning, the presidential detail decided to leave a couple of Fort Worth firemen to stand sentry over the President's bedroom and head off downtown. They went to a club called 'The Cellar' which was run by a good friend of Jack Ruby's called Pat Kirkwood. Kirkwood had a wide range of contacts, including Lee Harvey Oswald, who would sometimes come over and help wash the glasses. But

Kirkwood knew the Big Boys as well. He was on speaking terms with Meyer Lansky, Carlos Marcello and local Mafia boss Dino Cellini. He drank with the big oil men H.L. Hunt, Sid Richardson and Clint Murchison, and he was well plugged into serious politicians too, counting LBJ and Governor John Connally among his acquaintances.

Kirkwood got round the problem of having no liquor licence by simply giving it away. He broke no laws, but claims that The Cellar was a dry establishment are way wide of the mark. Kirkwood's motives for such largesse were clear. In a 1984 article he said, 'we had strange rules. We'd give drinks to doctors, lawyers, politicians, stag girls (sic), policemen, anybody we thought we might need.' Free drinks can buy a lot of favours.

This was the club that entertained the presidential Protection team the night before the murder. Kirkwood later told the Fort Worth Star Telegram, 'about 3.30 in the morning these Secret Service men were sitting around giggling about how the firemen were guarding the President ... we didn't say anything, but those guys were bombed. They were drinking pure Everclear.' (Distilled Vodka-like alcohol, designed to be added to and mixed with other drinks.)

This was the handpicked team of dedicated security professionals for the safety of the most powerful man on earth. Interestingly, not one member of Vice President Lyndon Baines Johnson's protection detail was at the boozy gathering.

***

Next day dawned bright and clear. The President went outside the Hotel Texas in Fort Worth and made a brief speech to a group of curious passers-by on their way to work. He noted that his brother Robert, the US Attorney General, had the day before ordered the American Zionist Council to register as an 'Israeli foreign agent', much to the fury of the Jewish lobby. After breakfast he spoke to the Chamber of Commerce in the grand ballroom. To genuine laughter and applause, the President moved on to Dallas.

Over in New Orleans, Carlos Marcello was finally facing Federal charges as an illegal immigrant and 22 November was the day that the jury would return their verdict. Marcello had few worries about the outcome. For powerful, rich New Orleans Dons, juries could always be encouraged to vote the right way.

Dallas shares the same airport as Fort Worth. For PR reasons the President decided to make a grand entrance to Dallas by flying in on Air Force One, and landed at Love Field. The presidential party then boarded their vehicles for the half hour ride through Dallas. The next stop was to be a speech at the Texas Trade Mart, just the far side of Dealey Plaza, a wide, grassy, open space where three roads came together.

***

News that the President was coming to town had been widely reported in the local Dallas newspapers, along with a map of his route. Despite the protests of the Secret Service, the ever-helpful Sam Bloom of the Dallas Citizen's Council had released a map showing the change of route to the press, including the lastminute alteration that would take the presidential motorcade off Main Street around the sharp turn to Elm Street to head for the Trade Mart.

Lee Harvey Oswald was at work early that day in the Texas School Book Depository, attending to his menial duties. He had been given a lift into work that morning by a work colleague, Buell Frazier. Frazier later told investigators that Lee was carrying a 'long, bulky package' into work. Oswald had told him that it contained curtain rods for his rooming house.

A number of people witnessed some unusual activity that only took on a sinister significance after the gunfire in Dealey later that morning. Two days before, on 20 November, two Dallas policemen had reported a group of men standing behind the wooden fence on top of the grassy knoll in Dealey Plaza 'practising aiming rifles' over the fence. It was not until a FOIA request in 1978, 15 years later, that the FBI suddenly 'discovered' the Dallas Police report.

Just before 11a.m. on the morning of the 22nd, a woman named Julia Ann Mercer was driving down from the direction of the depository towards the railway underpass when she was stopped by a green van with Texas plates pulled over on the righthand kerb. She stopped to pull out and saw a man taking a rifle case out of the back and starting up the grassy knoll. Twenty-four hours later she picked out a photograph of the man she had seen from the Dallas Police book of mug shots. It was their official ID picture of Jack Ruby.

She was not alone in observing unusual goings-on in Dealey Plaza. A man called Julius Hardee also saw 'three men with rifles and shotguns' on top of the triple underpass. Philip Hathaway and John Lawrence reported seeing a 'very big man ... 6'5" and built like a football player' carrying a rifle in a case into Dealey Plaza. They both thought that the man must have been a Secret Service agent taking up his position.

Lee Bowers was a signalman in the railroad control tower just behind the grassy knoll. About an hour before the shooting he spotted at least three separate cars drift into the parking area between the underpass and the book depository. This parking lot backed on to the grassy knoll and from Bower's signal box he could see it all from the rear. The first car was an Oldsmobile with a 'Goldwater for '64' bumper sticker. It circled the area, then left. Shortly afterwards a black Ford appeared. The driver was talking into a microphone and he too checked out the area, then left. Finally at about 12.20p.m., a Chevrolet Impala with a 1964 Goldwater sticker appeared and parked up behind the grassy knoll.

Other pre-shooting witnesses were not so credible. One man called Howard Leslie Brennan later swore that he had seen a 5'10" slim, white male answering Oswald's description in an upper floor window at the book depository. However as Brennan had bad eyesight, and the window in question was 40 yards away and six floors up, his claims must be treated with considerable caution. Despite this he would go on to become a star witness for the Warren Commission.

Steelworker Richard Carr claimed that he saw a man on the sixth floor of the depository long before the shooting. The man Mr Carr saw was nothing like Lee Harvey Oswald. This man was wearing a hat and horn-rimmed glasses. After Carr had noticed him, he later saw the man, who was wearing a distinctive 'tancoloured sports coat' hurrying away with two other men on the sidewalk. They got into a grey Rambler station wagon with Texas plates and were driven away. Carr's account was supported by at least three other witnesses, one of them being Roger Craig, a Dallas Deputy Sheriff.

A youth called Amos Euins reported seeing a 'black man with a rifle' in a window of the depository. Edward Fischer and Robert Edwards reported seeing a man with a rifle leaning out of an upper window in the depository.

As the final minutes ticked away, a vital record of the scene – as it was before the gunfire – was filmed by Charles L. Bronson. He recorded shadowy figures moving on the sixth floor of the depository. Bronson's film is supported by a couple of high school students (who later married), Arnold and Barbara Rowland. At about 12.15

they remembered seeing a man with a high-powered rifle in an upper window on the *left* -hand side of the depository, and a dark-skinned man, older ('about 55'), standing on the right of the building. At the time the Rowlands assumed that the gunmen they had seen were Secret Service guards.

A woman called Ruby Henderson saw them too. She pinned the time down exactly to 12.24. That was the time that prisoners in the Dallas County Jail overlooking Dealey Plaza noticed two men, 'one dark-skinned or Mexican looking' in a window on the sixth floor of the depository. One of the men was checking the telescopic sight on a rifle. It was precisely the moment that a curious diversion occurred in Dealey Plaza. The watchers saw Jerry Boyd Belknap being lifted into an ambulance in front of the depository. Belknap had had a very public epileptic seizure.

The curious thing was that on arrival at Parkland Hospital he calmly got off the stretcher and walked away from the baffled ambulance crew saying nothing to anyone.

***

The motorcade had gone well, apart from a couple of misunderstandings. On the previous evening in Fort Worth, LBJ and JFK had had a row. LBJ wanted Governor Connally, his friend and ally in his home state, to ride with him in the Vice President's car. Kennedy forbade it; the Governor's place was with the President. They argued loudly enough to be heard outside. Next morning LBJ tried to encourage his rival Senator Yarborough to travel in the presidential limousine until the White House protocol staff ushered Yarborough into Lady Bird Johnson's car and settled the Connallys in the front of the President's car.

The other puzzling mix-up involved the Secret Service. As Agent Rybka clambered onto the rear fender foot rail of the presidential Lincoln, the Agent in Charge, Emory P. Roberts, abruptly ordered him off. A mystified Secret Service agent Rybka can be seen on film spreading his hands in astonishment as the big Lincoln pulls away, unprotected.

There was another oddity about the Dallas motorcade. Normally the lower ranks such as the Mayor went first and the President's limo was towards the rear. For some inexplicable reason JFK rode up front – totally exposed.

The motorcade had been greeted by cheering, happy crowds. John Kennedy was visibly relaxed and Jackie, in her pink suit and pillbox hat, smiled and waved. Although a few hostile placards could be seen, Dallas had given the presidential couple a glorious welcome. The motorcade turned slowly to the right into Houston and then, under the tall red brick block of the depository, swung hard left to begin the run down to the railway triple underpass and on to the Trade Mart and the President's lunchtime speech. Mrs Connally, sitting in the front left seat of the stretched limo, looked back over her right shoulder and said, 'Mr President, you can't say that Dallas doesn't love you,' to which Jack Kennedy smiled and replied, 'No, you certainly can't...'

'Looks like we made it OK,' muttered one of the Secret Service detail.

But they hadn't. As the big limo came to a road sign for Stemmons Freeway, shots rang out. A bullet hit

Jack Kennedy in the throat. The stricken President clawed at his throat and choked, 'My God, I'm hit!'. The Secret Service men in the car shouted to the driver, 'Let's get out of here – we're hit,' and radioed to the Secret Service backup car, 'Lawson, this is Kellerman, we're hit. Get us to the hospital immediately.' Unfortunately the limo driver, Greer, did not accelerate. He slowed down for a second or two and looked back at the President. In those vital seconds a volley of shots ripped into the car.

The next shot hit Governor Connally in the back and blew a hole out of the front of his chest. Despite the shock he later remembered the crack and thump of incoming high-velocity bullets and believed, 'that there were either two or three people involved or more in this or else someone was shooting with an automatic rifle,' as he was hit again. He then heard a distinct boom and was sprayed with blood and brain tissue from the back seat. 'My God,' he shouted, 'They are trying to kill us all!' and then collapsed unconscious into his wife's lap, wounded in the chest, wrist and thigh.

The 'boom' Connally remembered was the mortal shot. A highvelocity soft point bullet hit the President on the right temple above the eye. As the bullet travelling at well over 2,000 feet per second transferred its kinetic energy to the static flesh and bone of the target and disintegrated, it blew a massive exit wound out of the back of the John Kennedy's head and sprayed blood, brain and fragments of bone into the air. Officer Hargis of the Dallas Police, riding left rear on his motorcycle, was hit by bits of skull and blood hit his face and helmet. Film of the day shows an explosion of red around the President's head as it blows apart.

Secret Service agent Clint Hill reacted quickly, racing forward from the car behind and leaping onto the rear fender of the presidential limo, shouting, 'Go! Go!' to the driver, Agent Greer. Abe Zapruder's film shows a distraught Jackie Kennedy clambering over the back of the car and grabbing a chunk of her mortally wounded husband's skull. The limo finally sped away under the railway underpass, leaving a stunned crowd and a thin haze of gun smoke drifting over the grassy knoll.

It had been a highly successful ambush. The President of the United States had been gunned down and assassinated in public, in broad daylight.

19

AFTERSHOCKS

AFTERSHOCK – A FURTHER REACTION FOLLOWING AN EARTHQUAKE OR THE SHOCK OF A DEEPLY DISTURBING OCCURRENCE...
THE AMERICAN DICTIONARY

Paul Landis was a Secret Service agent in the backup car immediately behind the limousine.

'I heard what sounded like a high-powered rifle shot from behind me ... then I heard a second report and saw the President's head split open and pieces of flesh and blood flying through the air. My reaction ... was that the shot came from somewhere to the front ... and looked toward the right-hand side of the road.'

Also to the front of the President's car was a young soldier, Gordon Arnold, home on leave after finishing basic infantry training. He claimed that he was trying to get up on to the grassy knoll to reach the underpass bridge when a man walked up, showed him a Secret Service badge and told him to move back, further down the slope.

When the motorcade arrived Arnold said he felt rather than heard the crack and whiz of a bullet passing over his shoulder. The infantryman's instinctive training took over and he hit the dirt. What is curious about Arnold's story is what he claimed happened after the shooting. Two 'policemen' supposedly booted him to his feet and confiscated his film. The Dallas police had not run onto the grassy knoll at that time and both they and the FBI deny any knowledge of any film.

Others identified the shots as coming from behind the motorcade. Canadian journalist Norman Similas heard the gunfire and instinctively swivelled towards the noise and clicked his camera. According to Similas the photograph clearly showed two men and a rifle barrel sticking out of a sixth floor window of the depository. When Similas got home to Toronto he submitted the pictures – as negatives – to *Liberty* magazine. In his own words:

I phoned and asked for them to be returned. Later I received a fat cheque in the mail, but the one negative which clearly showed what I believe to be two figures in the window was missing. When I pressed for it, I was told that this negative had somehow become lost. It has never been returned to me.

Similas's account has been challenged by those seeking to downplay any evidence that conflicts with the official version of events and he has been denounced as a fraud and publicity seeker by some.

Unfortunately this seems to be a not uncommon experience of those who claim to have uncovered embarrassing facts about the events in Dealey Plaza. Philip Willis, a WW2 combat veteran, had a similar experience to Similas. He was adamant that he heard shooting from the area of the depository. Willis swore that there were shots from both ahead of and behind the President's car. He saw Kennedy fall back after the fatal shot. Willis's photographs form an important record of events. One of the clearest descriptions of the fatal event comes from A.J. Millican, who was standing halfway between Houston and Elm, and who said: 'Just as the President's car had passed, I heard three shots from up towards Elm right by the Book Store Depository building. Then I immediately heard two or more shots from the arcade [in] the same direction only further back. It sounded like a .45 automatic or a high-powered rifle.'

This number of shots, far in excess of the three claimed by the Warren Commission, is backed by a great deal of evidence. Sandy Speaker was quite clear:

> I was less than half a block away and heard the shots. I heard at least five shots and they came from different locations. I was a Combat Marine with 1st Marine Division in WW2, hand-to-hand combat ... and I know what I'm talking about ... I've said for years that there were more than three shots fired.

Years later, Sandy Speaker said that Howard Brennan, the man who claimed he had seen someone like Oswald in the depository sixth floor window, had been 'got at' by the Feds.

They took (Brennan) off for about three weeks. I don't know if they were Secret Service or FBI, but they were federal people. He came back a nervous wreck and within a year his hair had turned snow white. He wouldn't talk about it after that. He was scared to death. They made him say what they wanted him to say.

Whatever coaching he did receive from the FBI, the Secret Service or the CIA, Howard Brennan's testimony was to figure large in the report of the Warren Commission. However, all the evidence points to a well-set, professional ambush with two or three different teams of gunmen and firing *at least* five or six shots. This kind of ambush requires more than one gunman with a finger on the trigger. It also needs lookouts, guards, a controller and good communications.

On the sidewalk below the grassy knoll, two men attracted attention by their odd behaviour. One, known as the 'Umbrella Man', opens an umbrella when the presidential car draws level with him. His dark-skinned companion holds his hand up as a signal, and then drops it. While everyone else in Dealey Plaza is either frozen in shock, hurling themselves to the ground or running as the gunshots ring out, the two men calmly sit down on the ground and the dark-skinned one appears to talk into a walkie-talkie. Once the motorcade had started moving again, the pair split up and calmly walk away. Even LBJ's actions at the time are curious. As they turned into Elm Street, LBJ suddenly 'leaned down listening into a walkie-talkie radio with the mike turned down low.'

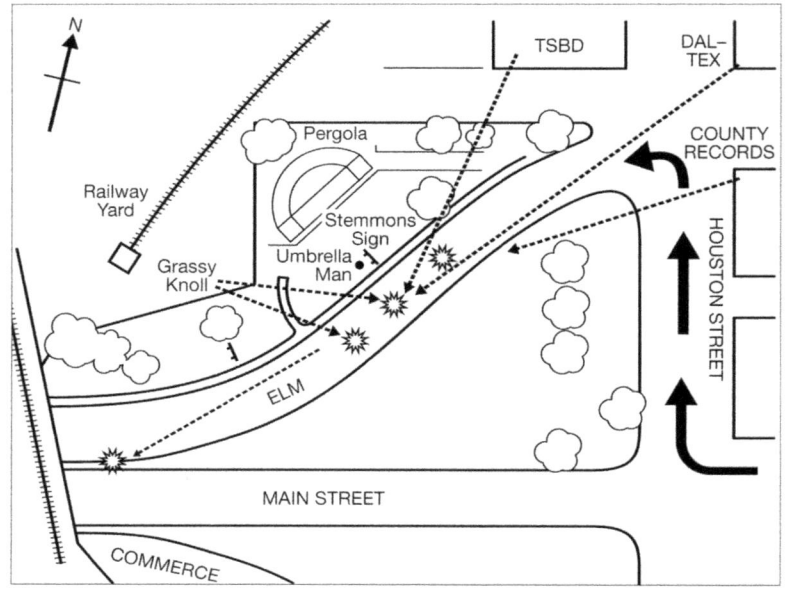

The successful ambush, with at least three firing positions.

A deaf-mute man named Ed Hoffman was standing up on the grassy bank near the railway underpass. He could see Elm, the grassy knoll and the railway yard behind it. Immediately after the shots were fired, he saw a man wearing a suit and tie with a rifle in his hand run along the back of the grassy knoll fence towards the underpass and toss the rifle to a waiting accomplice dressed as a railway worker. Hoffman saw the second man crouch down, disassemble the rifle and put it into a bag before walking calmly across the rail yard. Hoffman tried to explain to police but in the heat and confusion of the moment few could understand him because of his difficulties communicating. JFK researcher Jim Marrs eventually published Hoffman's account in 1985 and in 1991 Hoffman admitted that the FBI had tried to bribe him into *not* going public with his story.

Hoffman's story confirms Lee Bowers' account. At about 12.28 from his control tower behind the grassy knoll the railway signal worker saw two men at the picket fence in the bushes. As the motorcade appeared Bowers saw a flash and puff of smoke where the two men were standing, followed by a flurry of activity. He saw a man run along the fence past the cars. The whole story is further backed by the evidence of Sam Holland, the railway signal supervisor standing on top of the triple underpass bridge, with a good view of Elm, the grassy knoll, the car park behind and the railway yard. It also matches the testimony of James L. Simmons, standing watching on the triple underpass, who distinctly remembered 'a puff of smoke that came from underneath the trees on the embankment directly in front of the wooden fence.'

As the President's car and its bloody cargo sped away from the scene, one last curious event occurred as the wave of policemen and passers-by surged to the grassy knoll. Police Officer Joe Smith smelt cordite in the air and was confronted by a man in a sports jacket. Smith had drawn his revolver but the stranger reassured him, flashing his Secret Service badge. The only problem is that there were no Secret Service men assigned to the grassy knoll that day. Smith appears to have encountered one of the gunmen's backup men with impeccable forged credentials. There were a lot of men reported throwing rifles to each other or pretending to be Secret Service agents around the grassy knoll or the depository at 12.32 on 22 November 1963. They cannot all have been Lee Harvey Oswald.

***

At Parkland Hospital four miles away the bleeding President, unconscious but still breathing, was wheeled into Trauma Room 1 and Governor Connally into Trauma Room 2. Parkland's medical team was skilled and experienced in treating fresh bullet wounds. The President presented a mortally wounded casualty. A small entrance wound at the base of the throat was swiftly sliced open to allow for a tracheostomy to aid his breathing. Unfortunately as the doctors enlarged the small puncture wound they destroyed the evidence.

It was the gaping wound at the back of the skull that horrified the doctors and nurses. No one at Parkland even noticed the entrance puncture at the bottom of Kennedy's right shoulder blade, as the body was flat on its back on the table. Doctors Paul Peters and Robert McClelland took up a position at the head of the table and 'were shocked at what they saw'. A palm-sized chunk at the back of the President's skull had been blown out and brain tissue was bulging from the wound as blood leaked onto the operating table. The doctors reckoned up to 25 per cent of the brain had been blasted out.

John Kennedy's wounds proved to be too much for medical science, then and now. There is little doubt that he was dead by 12.50p.m., although the time was put back so that could be given the last rites by the local Catholic Priest. John Fitzgerald Kennedy, 35th President of the United States, officially expired of his dreadful head wound at 1p.m. Dallas time.

While the doctors struggled with their hopeless task, back at Dealey Plaza the shocked spectators were beginning to return to normal. As Marvin Robinson and his friend Roy Cooper were slowly driving past the depository, a light coloured Nash Rambler station wagon suddenly stopped in front of them, forcing Robinson to slam the brakes on, and a 'white male, somewhere between 20 and 30 years of age' ran down the slope from the book store building to the kerb at Elm Street and jumped into the Nash, which accelerated quickly away. A Mrs Helen Frost, who was looking back from the crowd gathered at the base of the grassy knoll, also witnessed the event, saying later, 'If it wasn't Oswald, then it was his identical twin.'

As the police follow-up operation in the area of the grassy knoll and the railway yards widened they made an extraordinary find; inside a boxcar were three scruffily dressed men. The police dragged them out, promptly dubbed them 'the three tramps' and then marched them off to the Sheriff's office. We have a photograph of the three being escorted by shotgun-toting cops.

The tramps look remarkably relaxed and at least one of them has been identified as a known gunman. The tall tramp is unmistakably Charles Harrelson, a contract killer. Lois Gibson worked for the Houston Police as an internationally renowned facial reconstruction artist and identification specialist. In 2003 Ms Gibson ran the 'three tramps' through her computers and graphics and came up with a 90–95 per cent match for Chauncey Holt, Charles Rogers and Harrelson. The significance is that Holt and Rogers both had links to the CIA. Holt in particular was of note; he had been one of Meyer Lansky's trusted 'accountants' before working for the CIA in Cuba. What was he doing running away and hiding in a railway box car, not two hundred yards from the site of the assassination of the President of the United States?

Later in the day the three tramps were quietly released without charge and with very little record of their detention. The whole incident has provoked a storm of claim and counterclaim in the incestuous world of Kennedy assassination research. But the tramps' suspiciously smart and shiny shoes, allied to Ms Gibson's international reputation and professional record, prove that there was something decidedly odd about them.

While the 'tramps' were being marched away, outside the Parkland the announcement went out that the President was dead. The shockwaves went round the world. Secret Service agent Hill was telephoned by the President's brother, to find out if the newsflash reports were true. Hill told a shocked Attorney General that, 'it looks about as bad as it can be.' Few people later failed to recall where they were in 1963 when they learned that the

President of the United States had been assassinated. Curiously, two men were extremely vague as to their whereabouts that day: Richard Milhous Nixon and George Herbert Walker Bush.

What followed next was one of the most extraordinary events on an extraordinary day. The Secret Service kidnapped the President's body. At the time, murdering the President of the United States was not a federal crime. However, homicide in Texas most definitely was. Legally, the body, the autopsy, the evidential chain and the whole investigation of the crime all now fell under the jurisdiction of the State of Texas. Despite this, Secret Service agent Roy Kellerman confronted the Dallas Police and demanded the body for an autopsy in Washington. The Dallas County Medical Examiner Earl Rose explained the law and sent for a Justice of the Peace. An extraordinary and ugly confrontation ensued between the Secret Service and the Texans. A Dallas policeman began to un-holster his pistol. Secret Service men brandished their submachine guns. A hearse suddenly appeared at the door and the Secret Service barged past with the corpse of the leader they had so signally failed to protect in life in a heavy bronze casket and bulldozed their way out of the building.

At Parkland the Assistant Press Secretary to the White House called a hasty press conference in the hospital. In sombre terms Malcolm Kilduff described the dramatic events and with the doctors' help explained the wounds. In the photographs Kilduff can be seen pointing to his head, quite clearly indicating that the fatal bullet had hit the President in the right temple.

But the events of that extraordinary day had claimed another victim. At about 12.45, Dallas Police officer J.D. Tippit took his patrol car away from his assigned beat and headed, for some unknown reason, towards the Oak Cliff area of Dallas. Oak Cliff was the district where Lee Harvey Oswald rented a room, where the CIA and the Cuban Exiles kept safe houses, and where Jack Ruby lived.

A few minutes later Mrs Earlene Roberts, Oswald's landlady, said she saw a DPD car drive slowly away.

Shortly afterwards Oswald ran out of his room and dashed to the bus stop. He was next spotted entering the Texas movie theatre about a mile away at about 13.15. The timing is important because at about 13.11 someone shot and killed officer Tippit at the 400 block of East Tenth Street, between Denver and Patton (see map in chapter 19). Meanwhile Lee Harvey Oswald sat in the Texas Movie Theatre watching *War is Hell* and waiting for – what? But the net was closing in. By 13.16 the call had gone out that a police officer was down and by 13.22, officers at the scene were already broadcasting APBs for 'a white male about 30 years old, black wavy hair, 5'9" to 5'10", wearing a white jacket, white shirt and dark slacks.' How did they know this accurate description of Oswald so quickly?

The Warren Commission Report claimed that Oswald was cornered due to the vigilance of a shoe store owner, who called the police. At 13.45 the DPD broadcast a message to surround the Texas theatre and at about 13.50 he was seized and arrested after a scuffle. By 14.00 Lee Harvey Oswald was at

Dallas Police Station. He was carrying very little, except a .38 revolver that didn't work and, allegedly, David Ferrie's library card and significantly a federal cheque for $200. A later search of his room unearthed a sea bag containing a Minox spy camera, three other cameras, binoculars, a high-power telescope, a compass, a pedometer and several rolls of exposed film. Even to the untrained eye it looks suspiciously like a spy's kit.

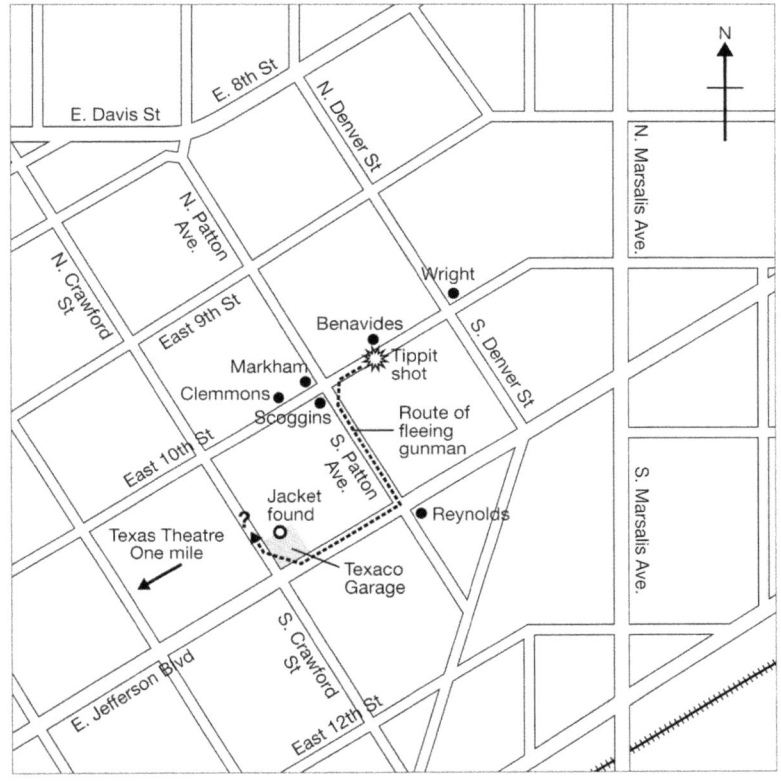

Oak Hill, Dallas: the murder of Officer J.D. Tippit.

While Oswald sat stunned in the Police headquarters, at 14.00 a CIA undercover DC-3 was taking off from Redbird Airfield piloted by a CIA and ex-intelligence contract pilot called 'Tosh' Plumlee. He had flown in to Dallas that morning with a mixed Cuban/CIA team from the JM/WAVE base in Florida. Plumlee claims his group's mission was to try to stop any attempt on the

President's life. As one of the passengers he picked up that day and flew into Dallas was 'Colonel' Johnny Rosselli – whom he knew – many think that the group of silent men that Tosh flew into Dallas that morning was in fact one of the teams of gunmen.

Plumlee does however offer some interesting corroboration in two areas: firstly, he says that he heard 'at least four or five shots' fired; secondly, he recognised Lee Harvey Oswald on the television later. Oswald had been on the same intelligence training course at Nag's Head, Carolina some years before. Testifying to the various committees later, Plumlee told them that he had also met the real Oswald 'at a CIA safe house on North Beckley Street in Oak Cliff, Dallas which was run by the Cuban Exiles' Alpha 66 Group'. As the aircraft flew out of Dallas, Plumlee noticed something else: the group he flew back no longer had Johnny Rosselli on board, and the passengers 'seemed very quiet and shocked'.

Plumlee's plane was not the only strange flight out of Dallas that afternoon. A USAF Crypto operator named Robert Vinson had hitched a lift that morning from Washington DC trying to get a quick flight back to his post at NORAD headquarters. Vinson was puzzled at the strange markings on the C-54 and understood the aircraft to be a CIA admin flight. The crew didn't speak to him and he was the only passenger. Suddenly over the mid-west the plane diverted in mid-afternoon and flew south to land at Dallas. They waited on the tarmac at Dallas and a jeep drew up. Two men wearing coveralls got out and hurried aboard. They didn't speak to Vinson and the plane landed at Roswell, New Mexico, where the two anonymous passengers got off and Vinson had to stay the night. Only later, when he saw the TV pictures, did he realise that one of the men was the 'spitting image of Lee Harvey Oswald'.

***

The shock news of the President's assassination rippled outwards. A French journalist was having lunch with Fidel Castro in Havana when an aide burst in with the news of the killing. Castro, clearly troubled said, 'This is very bad news'. For a brief period all US forces went into 'DefCon 3' – the third highest alert condition. Jimmy Hoffa gloated and ordered Teamsters' flags to fly at the masthead. 'You realise that cocksucker [Bobby Kennedy] is just another goddamn lawyer now?' he said to an aide.

In New Orleans, Carlos Marcello walked out of the court a free man. A colleague told him the news from Dallas. Marcello smiled and ordered a celebration dinner. At a nearby US Army base the Israeli Army's Chief of Staff Yitzhak Rabin – who coincidentally just happened to be in Dallas on the day – diplomatically expressed his surprise and shock at the news.

Back in Dallas, after being informed at Parkland Hospital that Kennedy was dead, Johnson climbed aboard Air Force One, to the surprise of some of the Kennedy aides who thought that he would go back on Air Force Two and let Jackie Kennedy take her dead husband back and grieve in private. LBJ was having none of it. LBJ was insistent that he be sworn in immediately as the new president.

He called the Attorney General to inform him that his brother was dead. LBJ then called an old friend and Texas Justice of the Peace, Judge Sarah Hughes, and demanded that she come to Love Field to take the Oath of Office and swear him in as president aboard the aeroplane, claiming that, 'The Attorney General of the United States had insisted I do this as soon as possible.' This was a downright lie. Robert Kennedy was later insistent that he had done nothing of the kind.

On board Air Force One, presidential aide McHugh went looking for Johnson. But Johnson was nowhere to be seen. Eventually McHugh checked the presidential lavatory. 'I walked in the toilet ... and there he was hiding, with the curtain closed ... He was hysterical, sitting down on the john there alone.'

Eventually LBJ emerged to take the oath of office. The famous photograph records a hangdog and lugubrious LBJ standing alongside a dazed and grief-stricken Jackie Kennedy, with her dead husband's blood still spattered on her pink woollen suit.

When the oath-swearing ceremony was over, Johnson then did an extraordinary thing and was again caught on camera. He turned to his right and to the bow-tied figure of one of his old Texas cronies, Congressman Albert Thomas. Then, astonishingly, he clearly winked at him, as if to say, 'We made it,' and Thomas winked back. That LBJ-Thomas wink speaks volumes for what was really going through the minds of those Texan politicians in the know. Now officially President of the USA, Johnson ordered Air Force one to take off for Washington DC bearing its tragic load and its new leader – safe at last.

Someone else sighed with relief that afternoon. J. Edgar Hoover realised that his job was now safe with his old friend, fellow Freemason and companion safely in the White House. The FBI Chief only made three main telephone calls that afternoon: one to Bobby Kennedy, barely commiserating. He made another to his old crony, Texas oil baron Billy Byars, and a third to LBJ telling the new President that the FBI had caught the President's killer ... Lee Harvey Oswald. He also issued a memorandum at 17.15 EST saying that the Dallas police 'very probably' had JFK's killer in custody.

At about this time in Dallas Lee Harvey Oswald was being fingerprinted and having a paraffin test to check if he had fired a gun recently. The paraffin test proved conclusively that Oswald had not fired anything that day. His .38 revolver had a defective firing pin and had not been fired either. It mattered not: J. Edgar Hoover had already announced to the new President, the dead President's brother, and helpfully to the media, that Oswald was the prime suspect.

Hoover's action in going public so quickly completely changed the focus of the investigation. Now that the 'FeeBees' had got their man, or rather the Dallas Police had, there was no more need for any big manhunt. To make absolutely sure that he had total control over the Texas legal case against the murderer of the President, by midnight on 22/23 November, J. Edgar Hoover's FBI had effectively taken over the investigation and was having the evidence flown direct to Washington. J. Edgar Hoover was, within two hours of the assassination, giving Robert Kennedy and the Dallas Police a background brief on the ex-Marine, 'lone nut' who was solely responsible for the murder of the Attorney General's brother.

However, back in Dallas, sitting in a lavatory cubicle, a teenage boy may have heard something significant. Mike Robinson was 14 at the time. He and his friends had heard that the President had been shot and rushed to police headquarters where a friend's father worked. After a while Mike had to go to the lavatory. His friend's father showed him down to the policemen's locker room in the basement.

Mike Robinson claims that while he was in the lavatory he heard two policemen talking in low voices. One said, 'you were supposed to kill Lee ... you stupid son of a bitch, then you go and kill a cop.' The men started talking again and 'the one with the nasty voice' said, 'well, Lee will have to be killed before he goes to Washington.' The men then left and after a decent interval Mike said he crept out to be glowered at by a cop in the changing room. The boy stayed quiet about what he had heard and seen. It only came to light in 1993 while under a hypnosis session for something else. When he was shown pictures of the Dallas policemen back in 1963, Mike Robinson picked out Officer Roscoe White as the scowling man he had seen in the locker room on the afternoon of 22 November 1963.

Someone else was in Dallas that day too: a French hitman called Jean Souetre. He and another gunman called Mertz were bitter rivals. Souetre himself hotly denied being anywhere near Dallas on the day and had an alibi. He swore that it was Mertz using Souetre's name. Within 48 hours of the assassination FBI documents confirm that a known OAS French gunman was picked up in Texas by US federal authorities and expelled immediately from the United States. If it was Mertz, as seems likely, it seems that his CIA friends had effectively given him a 'get out of jail free' card and allowed him to flee to Canada.

While tracing 'Souetre' the FBI discovered that Dr Lawrence Alderson had met Souetre while stationed in France with the US Army. Years later, Dr Alderson claimed that the FBI agents who interviewed him informed him that the FBI felt that Souetre, or the man who used his name, 'had either killed JFK – or knew who had done it.'

***

By midnight Lee Harvey Oswald was charged with the murders of Officer J.D. Tippit and President John F. Kennedy. In far-off Washington the autopsy on the body of their slain leader was being completed by the Navy's resident doctors. From what they could see, the President had been shot from behind. Killer and victim: it all fitted very neatly.

None of it was true.

20

SILENT WITNESSES – THE WOUNDS

IF YOU WALK ON SNOW, YOU CANNOT HIDE THE FOOTPRINTS.
GEORGE HERBERT

The most compelling evidence of a murder is often the size and nature of the wounds.

At Parkland, the President had a small entrance wound in the throat, which had been cut and enlarged to make way for a tracheotomy, and an entrance wound in the right temple with a massive exit wound at the rear of the skull.

Although the President's body had been filmed being loaded onto Air Force One at Dallas in a formal bronze casket, the body that was wheeled into the Bethesda Naval Hospital was in a standard transportation coffin. Sixteen years afterwards Lt Richard Lipsey, US Navy, confirmed that the real body had been brought into Bethesda by the *back* door while a shaken Jacqueline Kennedy was still waiting for the arrival of the bronze casket at the front. The testimony of the medical orderlies at Parkland and the sworn evidence of Paul O'Connor at Bethesda confirms that the body he handled arrived in a 'plain shipping casket' and was zipped into a 'military type body bag'.

The body left Dallas wrapped in a sheet and in a bronze casket. The body that was received by the medical assistants in Washington DC was in a body bag inside a routine transporting coffin.

We know from the Bethesda Hospital log that X-rays of the President's body were already being processed at the time the bronze casket was filmed arriving at the hospital. The bronze casket appears by then to have been nothing more than an empty decoy by the time it arrived at Bethesda in Washington.

The wounds that Surgeon Commander James Humes of the US Navy and Doctor Thornton Boswell found on the mortuary slab at Bethesda in

Washington were not the same as those recorded at Dallas. Neither man had ever conducted an autopsy before, and neither was an expert on gunshot wounds. To make matters worse, the autopsy room was crowded with spectators: medical assistants, photographers, FBI agents, plus senior officers barking orders. The atmosphere at times was noisy, 'like a crap game'.

FBI special agents Silbert and O'Neill were on duty as observers and noted in their official report that there appeared to have been 'surgery of the head area'. No head surgery had been performed in Dallas. They – and several others – commented on the unusual fresh blood flow from the dead man's head and a straight V-shaped incision laying open the scalp between the right ear and the temple on the front right of the skull. They also took official possession of a 'missile or bullet' that Commander Humes had removed. He handed it to an FBI officer and even got a receipt for it. That 'missile' has never been seen again.

At Dallas all six doctors swore that the right rear of the President's skull had been blown out. The two X-ray technicians at Washington confirmed this. They were among the first to handle the body on arrival in Washington, and both recall the gaping hole at the back of the head. One said, 'It was enormous. I could put both my hands into the wound.'

Paul Kennedy O'Connor was the laboratory technician at the Bethesda responsible for taking the President's body out of its shipping coffin, and preparing it for autopsy. O'Connor recorded his action at 8p.m. in the 'Autopsy Log' and then turned to the grisly task of removing the brain and weighing it before passing it on to the pathologists for examination. O'Connor then produced his bombshell during his interview with researcher David Lifton. He said that there was a massive hole eight by four inches in Jack Kennedy's skull and his brain had pretty well gone completely. O'Connor assumed that the force of the gunshot 'had just sucked the whole brain out.' He was also adamant that the huge wound he saw was in the back of the head and that the only damage at the front right was a flap of skin which someone had cut and pulled down.

As a relatively junior enlisted man O'Connor was in the background throughout but could see clearly what went on and watch the reactions of the admirals and doctors crowding into the autopsy room. He felt that Dr Humes was 'scared to death' and that there was something odd about the whole autopsy. He also said he had been ordered not to talk.

This was later confirmed in writing individually to each enlisted man (a most unusual procedure) in a letter signed by Captain John Stover, Commanding Officer of the Naval Hospital, on 26 November. The letter had to be signed by the recipient and returned. O'Connor's colleague Jim Jenkins confirmed this and added that there had been 'a row' at the end of the autopsy between the three doctors and some unnamed civilians who had insisted that they change their report. Jenkins admitted to being scared by what he witnessed overall: clear evidence of a shot from the front being splashed all over the papers next day as a shot from the rear. That, coupled with the heated argument at the end of the autopsy, plus the extraordinary gagging order from his CO, frightened him.

By the time the Bethesda autopsy was finished, someone had pulled the loose flap of skin at the back of the President's head forward to give, with the crude incision of the front of the scalp, the impression of a much smaller wound at the rear. Some of the official photographs from the autopsy support this. In the words of US journalist Stanhope Gould,

> [The] evidence is that the President's body left Dallas in one coffin and arrived at Bethesda in another ... with the discrepancy between the autopsy photographs and the recollection of several witnesses as to the location of the head wounds ... it seems clear that there was a conspiracy to cover up the essential facts.

JFK's body had two other wounds: a shot in the throat and a bullet wound *below* the right shoulder blade. This back wound was probed by Humes and turned out to be very shallow, 'not the length of his little finger'. According to Medical Corpsman Jenkins, who had assisted Doctor Humes in probing the back wound with a gloved finger, it had not even penetrated the pleura (chest lining). If the bullet or missile that hit John Kennedy in the back hadn't even punctured the lining of the chest cavity, then it could not possibly have gone through his lungs and burst out of his throat then go on to inflict five wounds on Governor Connally. There was no exit wound at all from Kennedy's chest.

The President's third wound could not be examined properly at Bethesda because the Parkland Doctors in Dallas had enlarged the small bullet hole in the throat into a tracheostomy.

The evidence of the wounds, therefore, is quite conclusive. John Kennedy was hit by three bullets: one in the throat from the front; one below the right shoulder blade from behind; and one in the temple from the front. There was proof positive that from the very beginning there were at least two or more gunmen, one front and one back.

***

Governor Connally's three wounds are equally revealing. The first was an entrance wound in his back near his right armpit and an exit wound where the bullet had exited below the right nipple. His right wrist had been shattered by a descending bullet and there was a minor wound in the left thigh caused by fragments that slid under the skin. The position and nature of Connally's wounds are important because later the Warren Commission would claim that they were all caused by a single bullet *after* it had already passed through John Kennedy's body.

This so-called 'magic bullet' stretches credibility to its limits. It was completely unmarked and yet had supposedly gone through the solid flesh and bones of two grown men. LBJ himself doubted it. In a September 1964 telephone call to Richard Russell, a member of the Warren Commission, both men aired their doubts. It is a startling exchange. Could a single bullet have caused all those wounds? 'Well, I don't believe it,' said Senator Russell. Johnson replied, 'Well, I don't either.'

Yet the single bullet theory had allegedly caused no less than seven separate wounds, including contact, at least three times, with bone mass, and changed direction five times and still remained completely undamaged. Bullet CE 399's history is revealing.

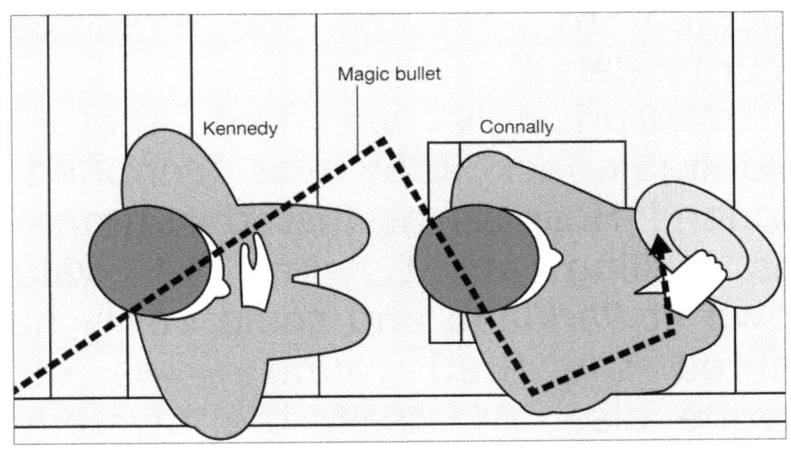

The mysterious path of Exhibit CE 399, Warren's 'magic bullet'.

'Exhibit CE 399' was in fact found on a stretcher at the Dallas Parkland Hospital by an engineer, Dwight C. Tomlinson. He saw a used stretcher against the wall. US government investigators claimed later that this 'must have been Governor Connally's stretcher.'

However, Connally's stretcher had been placed empty in Trauma Room 2, according to Diana Bowron, the nurse who tended to the President. The stretcher in the hallway had been used by a small boy who had been treated next to TR1. As Tomlinson pushed the stretcher to one side a bullet rolled on to the floor. He picked it up and it was collected by one of the President's security detail.

Unsurprisingly we find that the ubiquitous Jack Ruby was identified at Parkland Hospital at just this time. He was milling about with the waiting crowd at Parkland and could easily have planted the fired round – as could anyone else. By itself, the mysterious loose bullet on the stretcher at Parkland Hospital proves nothing.

But that 6.5mm bullet, and the circumstances of its discovery, were to become central to the government's case. According to them, the bullet found on the stretcher must have fallen out of Governor Connally's thigh wound. If it did, it must truly have been a magic bullet, because when the weight of the minor fragments of copper and lead left in Connally's thigh and wrist are added to the 100% correct weight of CE 399, then it would prove that the bullet had somehow managed to put on weight after being fired...

Any claim that CE 399 was the bullet that caused all the wounds can be shown to be completely false. First of all, any bullet found outside a body is circumstantial evidence, by definition. Secondly, the trajectories of the bullets and the wounds don't match up. The sixth floor of the depository is 60ft high. When the rounds struck the presidential car 150ft away, they came from different heights. (See diagram p.185.) By tracking the wounds back, we can get a clear indication of where the gunmen really were. Projecting a laser back from the key points of impact and at the angle of the wounds provides some interesting results. The first shot into Kennedy's throat came from the front, from a point slightly above the limousine in the grassy knoll area. The second shot, which hit Kennedy in the back, appears to have come from a second floor window in the Dal-Tex building, not the depository. The third and fatal shot came from slightly above and to the right, from the area of the picket fence on the grassy knoll. That is the bullet that blew his head apart.

Governor Connally's wounds are less conclusive. But what is clear is that the bullet that hit him in the right back and blew out part of his chest was fired from behind. However the flat path of the bullet rules out a hit from the top windows of the depository. From the sixth floor to the car, the angle varies from 17 to 25 degrees downwards. Connally's chest wound is nearly flat and straight through, indicating a shot from the Dal-Tex building.

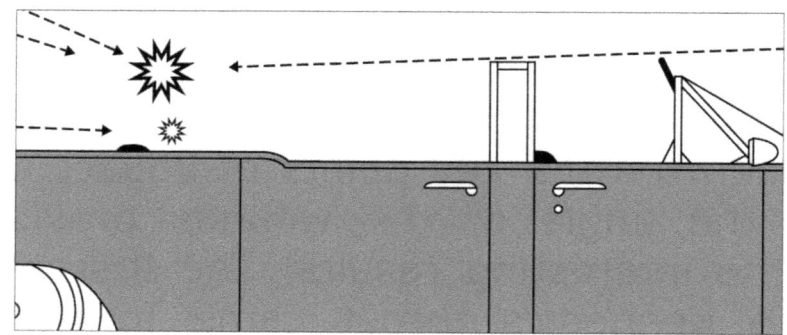

The bullets struck at several different angles.

There was another wound in Dealey Plaza that day. James Tague was standing on the far side of Elm Street and watching the approaching motorcade (see diagram p.198). A bullet hit the concrete kerbstone to his right front, striking sparks and sending a fragment flying into Tague's cheek. A police officer called Buddy Walthers saw Tague mopping blood from his face and searched for the bullet strike. He found evidence of a bullet mark on the edge of the road 'at the top edge of the kerb on Main Street near the underpass.'

Back-tracking the angle of this shot puts the firer near the second floor of the Dal-Tex building. Officer Walthers promptly went to the area of the strike, accompanied by two men in suits, assumed to be federal agents. A sequence of photographs shows him pick an object out of the grass and put it into his pocket. Walthers reported that 'they had found a bullet' but later claimed that it was all a mistake and that they had really found a piece of Kennedy's skull. Whatever Walthers and the two men pocketed that day has never been seen since.

Tague's sliced cheek, Governor Connally's punctured chest and President Kennedy's shattered skull all point to gunfire coming from more than one location. Their wounds cannot all have been inflicted by a single gunman. Dallas Chief of Police Curry and DA Henry Wade believed that the Warren Report was a government whitewash. According to FBI records, Police Chief Curry told Lt Revill (of the Dallas Police) that 'two men were involved in the shooting.'

Paul O'Connor and Jim Jenkins, the two Bethesda medical corpsmen, corroborate this view in their account of what they saw and what happened in the autopsy. The facts seem incontrovertible: the body arrived in a different coffin from the one in which it left Dallas; the head wound pointed clearly to a shot from the front; someone had tampered with the body; someone ordered the doctors to write a false report; and then the Navy slapped a gagging order on junior ranks present. The result was that the tampered wounds remained as mute testimony to what really happened that day. But they are not alone.

For if the wounds are silent witnesses, then the guns of Dealey Plaza spoke volumes.

21

THE VOICE OF THE GUNS

THE PROBLEM WITH GUNS THAT ARE HIDDEN IS THAT YOU CAN'T SEE THEIR SMOKE.
ARI FLEISCHER

From the moment that the echoes of the gunfire died away in Dealey Plaza, there has been controversy about the number of shots fired. The official US government report on the assassination claimed that there were only three shots and they all came from the same rifle: an old-fashioned single shot, bolt action Mannlicher-Carcano of Italian manufacture, fired from the depository.

The Mannlicher-Carcano model 91/38 is an unlikely weapon of choice for any would-be assassin. The version supposedly owned by Lee Harvey Oswald was 40 inches long, weighed 8 pounds and was purchased by mail order from Klein's Sporting Goods in Chicago. The Mannlicher-Carcano advertised in the magazine, however, was a different model completely; a 36 inch, 5.5 pound carbine model. At the same time Oswald, using the alias 'A.J. Hidell', bought a .38 Smith & Wesson revolver for $29.95. All were sent to his post office box number in Dallas.

Why anyone would want to send off for a second rate, oldfashioned rifle from out of state remains a mystery, when it was possible at the time just to walk into any gun store in Texas and buy any gun in the catalogue. That is, however, precisely what Lee Harvey Oswald, posing as 'A.J. Hidell', is alleged to have done. That Mannlicher-Carcano is, supposedly, the only weapon to have been fired in Dealey Plaza on the day.

The problem is that there are more bullets counted in Dealey Plaza than either the official version admits or Oswald's obsolete rifle was capable of firing in the time. When we count the actual bullet strikes, a very different picture emerges of what really took place that day.

The **first bullet** struck sparks behind Kennedy's car and was observed by Royce Skelton and Austin Miller. The **second shot** hit the kerb on the north side of Elm and sent a fragment of something sharp flying into James Tague's face, cutting his cheek. The **third shot** splashed against a manhole cover in the street and embedded itself in the grass; policemen were later photographed removing a bullet. The story ran in the Dallas newspapers the next day but was never confirmed officially.

The **fourth shot** came from the front and hit the President in the throat. This was the wound that would later be widened into a tracheotomy at the Parkland Hospital; but before they did so, the experienced doctors observed that it was an unusually small entrance wound. This raised important questions about the calibre of the guns on the grassy knoll area.

The **fifth shot** is probably the one that hit Kennedy in the back. It came from behind on a relatively flat trajectory. It is possible that this bullet had lost speed, possibly as a result of hitting something, or passing through something first.

The **sixth shot** is probably the one that caused an often-overlooked bullet strike on the President's car. A bullet punched a neat hole through the limousine's windscreen 'just left of centre', according to the two policemen Sgt Ellis and Patrolman Freeman, who noticed the hole while the limo was parked at Parkland.

There are at least **four other recorded strikes.** One was a bullet hole through the metal road sign for Stemmons Freeway at the base of the grassy knoll. The bullet had punched through from the direction of the grassy knoll and blown the rim backwards.

Governor Connally received at least two bullets and possibly three. The shot from the back that smashed through his chest brings the number of bullet strikes up to at least eight and the shot that shattered his wrist adds up to nine.

The final shot is the fatal gunshot, as what looks like a highvelocity bullet blows the President's head open. This comes from the front, from the evidence of the gaping exit hole in the back of his head. The bullet broke up on impact as fragments were found in JFK's cranium at the autopsy.

This last shot has caused more controversy than all the others put together because the Warren Commission fought tooth and nail to establish that the bullet came from behind, even to the extent of getting a scientific Nobel Laureate talking about 'propulsive jet effect' and by J. Edgar Hoover deliberately transposing the two key frames on the film of the incident to make it look as if Kennedy was knocked forward. (He was later caught out by researchers and in 1965 had to admit, shamefacedly, that 'there had been an accidental mix-up in the FBI laboratory.')

This final shot appears to be different from the other gunshots in two significant areas. First, the report of the gun sounded louder; second, the bullet's horrific consequences on flesh and bone. Governor Connally thought that the final shot was a 'boom' and the observers in the railroad signals control tower heard a bang and saw 'a flash of light' on the grassy knoll and a distinct puff of smoke.

Despite the use of so-called 'smokeless powder' as a propellant, the cordite charge used to propel bullets can produce visible smoke. The most common causes are oil in the rifle barrel and unburned propellant. A professional sniper ensures that his rifle barrel is spotlessly clean. Therefore that leaves unburned propellant as the most likely cause of the flash, smoke puff and louder report heard on the fatal final shot.

By the time the bullet emerges from a short barrel, not all the cordite propellant has been burned off; in long-barrelled weapons it usually has. This raises the question: was a short-barrelled rifle present on the grassy knoll? Intriguingly, there may have been. A convicted murderer in Stateville Prison in Illinois called James Files claimed that he fired the fatal shot with a very special gun: a Remington XP-100 'Fireball'.

The Remington Fireball is an unusual gun. The first models were bored to accept a powerful new cartridge, the

.222 round. The designer noted that this cartridge's propellant was not all burned off in the XP-100's short (14") barrel and so in 1964 marketed the Fireball with a slightly weaker cartridge. The Fireball's muzzle velocity of 2,650 feet per second still made it a perfect close quarter sniper's gun accurate to 150 yards.

The right bullets 'blossom' or break up in impact, delivering their energy instantly to the luckless target. The original prototypes of the XP-100 were chambered for .222 long case bullets, didn't burn all their powder and reportedly had a distinct flash, bang and puff of smoke. That original ammunition was far too powerful for the gun, hence the name 'Fireball'. To add to the pile of circumstantial evidence, only 1,000 XP-100s were built in 1962/63 as experimental models, and these were all chambered for .222 rounds. Some of these unique weapons were acquired by the CIA in 1963 for evaluation purposes. James Files is adamant that he fired a .222 XP Fireball from the grassy knoll with an exploding-type bullet. The question remains: is Jim Files telling the truth?

Files never volunteered his story. He was implicated by an FBI informant who warned the FBI that Files knew something about the assassination of JFK. The FBI approached him indirectly using an agent called Zack Skelton. He in turn briefed a private investigator called Joe West to interview Files. West informed FBI man Skelton that he felt that Files did know something about the assassination.

Something odd then happened to Joe West after that. The investigator went to hospital for routine heart surgery, recovered, and then suffered an unexplained relapse followed by a coma and death. Just before he died, he scribbled a desperate note to his family, 'Get me out of here, they are trying to kill me'. So the only witness to the Files confession was dead. However, the story about the XP-100 at the grassy knoll does appear to fit the known facts. But the XP-100 and the Mannlicher-Carcano were not the only guns in Dealey Plaza, not by a long way.

***

When police burst onto the sixth floor of the depository, to discover the 'sniper's nest', Deputy Sheriff Roger Craig spotted three used 6.5mm Mannlicher-Carcano shell cases on the floor and, together with Deputy Sheriff E. Lee Boone, began a search. Near the stairwell Boone called out 'Here it is. Here's the rifle.' Captain Fritz and Lt Day were called, the site was photographed and Fritz then carefully handed the rifle out by its sling. Constable Seymour Weitzmann was called over. He was an expert on weapons. Later, Fritz held the gun in the air and Weitzmann said, according to Craig, 'There. On the barrel. "7.65 Mauser".'

The first official police reports of the rifle found in the depository sixth floor sniper's nest were of a 7.65 German Mauser rifle, with a 4:18 telescopic sight and a thick leather sling. There was no mention whatsoever of a Mannlicher-Carcano, except for the three 6.5mm empty cases found by Craig. Years afterwards a researcher called

Anne-Marie Kuhns Walko discovered an old envelope from the Dallas FBI office labelled '7.65mm shell found in Dealey Plaza 12/02/63 [2 December 1963] ... determined as of no value and destroyed'. No one has ever explained how a vital bit of evidence, found only 10 days after the murder, came to be ignored.

The gun later photographed and held up by the Dallas Police as the murder weapon was a Mannlicher-Carcano 6.5mm. The gun photographed being taken out of the depository by Lt Day is indeed a Mannlicher-Carcano, but it cannot be Oswald's. The rifle in Day's hands suddenly has a full ammunition clip and sling swivels on the left-hand side of the weapon. The picture of Oswald with 'his' rifle taken in his back garden and later used as part of the Warren Commission's evidence is a different model Mannlicher-Carcano with sling swivels on the bottom of the gun.

There are other discrepancies as well. Checks on 'Oswald's rifle' revealed that its firing pin was defective: the telescopic sight had not been zeroed and it was missing its ammunition clip magazine, so every bullet would need to have been fed in by hand. It would have been a very poor choice as an assassin's weapon, even in the hands of an experienced, skilled marksman, which Oswald certainly was not. On test the Mannlicher-Carcano defeated the best efforts of America's finest professional snipers; not only to hit the target, but to get the necessary shots off in the time the Zapruder film indicated that they had.

Craig Roberts was a United States Marine Corps sniper in Vietnam. He is adamant that Oswald did not and *could not* replicate the official version of the three aimed shots from the Mannlicher-Carcano rifle in question at a moving target going down-range in the seven seconds available. Given the Mannlicher-Carcano's clumsy top sliding bolt, the need to take the eye out of the aim to manoeuvre the bolt action and then resight, firing three well-aimed shots is just plain impossible in the time. Moreover the FBI lab had to put in three shims just to realign the telescope – and only then it was discovered that the sights on the rifle had been adjusted for a *left-handed* firer – Oswald was right-handed.

Gunnery Sergeant Hathcock, an ex-senior instructor at the USMC Sniper School at Quantico – with 93 kills in Vietnam – confirms this judgement: 'We have reconstructed the whole thing: angle, range, moving target, time limit, obstacles, everything ... but we couldn't duplicate what the Warren Commission said Oswald did.'

According to all the ballistic and expert evidence, Oswald's Mannlicher-Carcano was the wrong gun for the job and was incapable of doing what it was claimed to have done. Most damning of all, the rifle had none of Oswald's fingerprints on it. Oswald had not fired a shot from a rifle – and could prove it. After his arrest, the Dallas Police performed routine paraffin tests (the so-called 'GSR' Gunshot Residue Test) on his hands and cheeks.

When a rifle is fired, minute particles of nitrates from the bullet's explosion and ejection are embedded in the hands or cheek of the firer. Oswald's cheek was 100% clean. The paraffin tests proved conclusively that he hadn't fired a rifle that day. The evidence of the guns and the blasts of gunfire in Dealey Plaza conflicts sharply with the FBI's testimony and the US government's official report.

And much of the incident had been caught on film.

21

THE CAMERA CANNOT LIE – CAN IT?

A PHOTOGRAPH IS A SECRET ABOUT A SECRET. THE MORE IT TELLS YOU THE LESS YOU KNOW.
DIANE ARBUS

Many photographs were taken of President Kennedy as his car drove through Dealey Plaza. As a result we have an extensive photographic record of events from a number of sources, both moving and still. The important sources are: (see diagram for individual locations, p.203):

1. The Zapruder film. An 8mm colour sequence of 486 frames recording most of the incident. Often referred to as the 'Rosetta Stone' for decoding the assassination.
2. Major Philip Willis's 12 slides.

3. James 'Ike' Altgens was an Associated Press photographer and recorded the scene as it happened.
4. Mary Ann Moorman was snapping away with her Polaroid camera across Elm Street from the President looking towards the grassy knoll.
5. Orville Nix was facing the grassy knoll and took a motion picture of Kennedy being shot.
6. Robert Hughes' movie showed the depository moments before the shooting.
7. Tom Alyea was a WFAA-TV cameraman who filmed immediately after the assassination, particularly in the depository.
8. Bill Allen of the *Dallas Times Herald* photographed the aftermath of the assassination in Dealey Plaza.
9. Wilma Bond took a series of 35mm slides with Mary Muchmore from the corner of Elm and Houston.

10. Mary Muchmore filmed the fatal sequence, including the motorcade's reactions.
11. Norman Similas, the Toronto journalist, took a sequence of photographs throughout the shooting.
12. Beverley Oliver filmed the whole series of events from a position facing Zapruder and the grassy knoll.

Their combined story is one that casts further doubt on the official US government version of events.

By far the most important is the Zapruder film. It would be even more telling if it could be viewed in conjunction with Beverly Oliver's film, taken on a Ashica Super 8 facing towards the Pergola and grassy knoll. Unfortunately it cannot. She can be clearly seen on the Zapruder and Muchmore film and claimed to be the 'Babushka Lady'. The film she says she took on the day (the Yashica Super 8 was a far superior camera to Zapruder's Bell and Howell) would have been vital, but on 25 November, she alleged that two federal agents door-stepped her and demanded her film 'as evidence'.

When later she tried to draw the authorities' attention to this, she was told that no one knew anything about the incident, or her film. Eventually she identified FBI Agent Regis Kennedy as the man who had taken her cine-camera. This was the New Orleans FBI agent who steadfastly testified that Mafia Boss Carlos Marcello was 'only a tomato salesman' to J. Edgar Hoover and who was later given permission by LBJ not to testify before a New Orleans Grand Jury investigating the assassination, citing 'executive privilege'. Beverly Oliver's film was has never been heard of again. Zapruder's film therefore stands alone as the best record.

Abe Zapruder was a clothing manufacturer who worked out of Sam Bloom's Dal-Tex building. His model 414 Bell & Howell camera was a fairly simple machine that took good pictures for its day and had a 9-27mm f/1.8 zoom lens. It photographed on a double strip of 16mm celluloid film, exposing 25 feet to give two strips of 8mm home movie which, after being professionally developed and sliced down the middle, made one single reel of film. Zapruder filmed from the Pergola with his receptionist Marilyn Sitzman.

They were about 60 feet from the road, with the depository to their left and the grassy knoll to their right (see plan p.203). Zapruder set the zoom lens to x4 magnification and started filming as the presidential motorcade began to turn from Houston into Elm. He kept his viewfinder on the President throughout and recorded Jack Kennedy's murder.

That record is important because Zapruder's B & H camera filmed at exactly 18.3 frames per second. That gives a very precise and irrefutable timeline. When combined with the other photographs taken in Dealey Plaza, the evidence points to a very different story from the official version. The Zapruder film showed, frame by numbered frame, what happened, from Kennedy clutching at his throat, Governor Connally collapsing and then, at frame Z313, the President's head exploding. Zapruder filmed it all then walked around in a daze mumbling, 'They shot the President

... they shot him...' before returning to his office. It was there that the *Dallas Times Herald* interviewed him as an eyewitness.

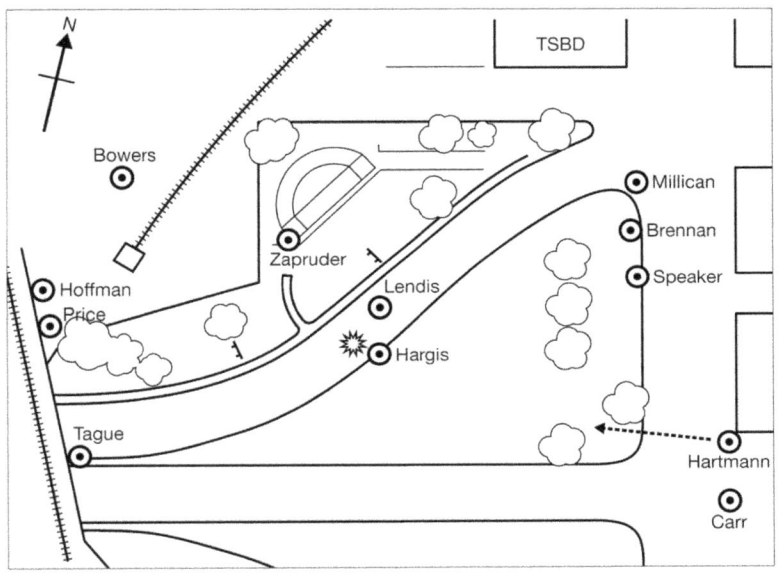

There were numerous witnesses; Warren ignored most of them, and the rest are long forgotten.

As a shocked Zapruder sat in his office, the Secret Service and a couple of Dallas policemen arrived and demanded the film. Zapruder refused to hand it over and the group set off in a police car to get the film developed at the local Kodak plant. Somewhere along the line Abe Zapruder realised that he was sitting on a goldmine. By early evening he briefed his lawyer – who told the Dallas Police that if they wanted the film they would have to take out a court order – and acquired three authentic copies to add to the original 8mm film, split and spliced, as one long piece of footage. Abe Zapruder had in his hands the single most important piece of news footage ever filmed in the USA.

By 11 the following morning Zapruder had sold the film to *Life* magazine for $150,000 – a huge sum in 1963. A private company with close links to the CIA and the American political establishment now legally owned America's most historic piece of film. They printed their own copies, destroyed five frames (allegedly by 'a technician breaking the film'), and printed off 'scores' of black and white stills, from which they selected 31 pictures to go in the special edition of *Life* due out on 29 November.

Amazingly, Time-Life then sat on the film and locked it away. No one saw it again for 12 years except for an abbreviated version, which was shown to the Warren Commissioners. To say that their behaviour doesn't make a shred of corporate or business sense is an understatement. Considering the size of their investment, it seems perverse – unless Time-Life had acquired the film solely to suppress it?

That however throws up some serious questions. Who would want – or who would need – to suppress it? And why? Closer examination reveals that there was more to the purchase of the film than met the eye. For a start, a copy of Zapruder's film had been flown by a fast military jet to the top secret National Photographic Interpretation Centre (NPIC) in Washington within hours. By dawn on 23 November, 'Official Washington' knew exactly what had been recorded on the film. Time-Life's generous offer to Zapruder turns out to be both timely and convenient if someone wanted the Zapruder film held back or suppressed.

Life was strongly anti-Kennedy. What was not so well known was that *Life* was also one of the CIA's major media assets, with several CIA men on the staff. C.D. Jackson, the man who authorised the purchase for Time-Life, turns out to have been an undercover American intelligence agent with both the forerunner of the CIA, but also while working in publishing after the war. *Life* magazine fought for over 10 years to keep the film it had bought so expensively from being seen either by the public or by photographic experts seeking to analyse the film. *Life* even went as far as the US Supreme Court when New Orleans DA Jim Garrison sought to have it subpoenaed as evidence for his indictment of Clay Shaw. Why all the fuss?

Perhaps a clue can be found in frames Z314 and Z315, which show President Kennedy's head jerking sharply *backwards* as the fatal bullet impacts. For some strange reason these were transposed at the first Warren Commission showings, giving the impression that he had been shot from *behind*. J. Edgar Hoover later claimed that it was just a 'printing error'. The reporter Dan Rather described how he had been privileged to be given a private viewing of the Zapruder film on the 23rd – the day after the assassination – and how he had seen the President's head 'go forward ... at considerable speed.' This is curious because Rather could not have seen the original and the copies were with Time-Life and the Secret Service. Nevertheless Rather's misleading assertion that the President's head fell forward gave immediate emphasis to that fact that the shots came from behind the car, and became the accepted truth from the start. Rather's broadcasting career prospered mightily thereafter.

The Zapruder film provides another useful piece of evidence to identify the number of shots fired in Dealey Plaza. When a gun is fired people react physically to the 'bang' and the camera 'jiggles.' The 'jiggle' analysis of Abe Zapruder's camera film shows that Zapruder reacted no less than seven times. Because his camera was running at a constant 18.3 frames per second it is possible to tie in the number of the film frame to a specific time. These jiggles also reveal the crucial point that the first shot was fired, well before Warren's alleged 'first shot' at frame Z 210. The first recorded jiggle at frames

Z 165-168 indicates that the first shot was fired around frame Z 160 and the second at Z 190. This is crucial, because the time interval between those frames is only 1.6 seconds: the fastest marksman in the world could not fire a clapped out Mannlicher-Carcano rifle in less than 2.3 seconds. That 1.6 seconds between the first two shots proves there had to be at least two gunmen firing in Dealey Plaza.

    Perhaps the most blatant example of tampering with the film evidence is the fact that the driver of the limousine, Bill Greer, is looking straight ahead in frame Z302. According to the commercially available version of the film, in the next frame, Z303, he is looking over his shoulder: an absolute physical impossibility in one sixteenth of a second. It therefore follows that some versions of the Zapruder film have been tampered with.

    As well as the five destroyed frames, two early frames, Z155 and Z156, mysteriously went missing as well. These probably recorded the time of the real first shot. When Time-Life was eventually forced to produce the film (it was *prima facie* evidence in a first degree murder trial) these two frames had allegedly been damaged, supposedly 'cut and spliced by an apprentice'. The House Assassinations Committee looked at the case again in 1977 and confirmed that the first shot had been fired much earlier than the Warren Commission admitted. It must have been fired at about Z155 and Z156. But to admit that meant that there must have been more than three shots: and that meant more than one gunman in the time allotted. To make matters worse for the official version of events, these two frames of the Zapruder film supposedly destroyed by Time-Life later turned up in FBI files, an embarrassing fact which has never been fully explained.

More support for the earlier shot however comes from the stills photographic record. Major Willis's fifth picture coincides with Zapruder's frames Z210-Z213. (The two men were facing each other on opposite sides of Elm.) Someone has already fired a shot. Given the speed of Zapruder's film, it must have been fired before frame Z190. (The time elapsed between frames Z190 and Z203 is less than one second.) Willis's picture number 5 is taken at the same moment as the first shot.

Willis's eighth photograph also records Jack Ruby – or someone remarkably like him – standing at the door of the depository at 12.30. Ruby's alibi (that he was around the corner in the newsroom of the *Dallas Morning News* at the time) is highly suspect. Ruby could easily have been on the depository corner and back in the offices in less than five minutes: and no one noticed him in the office at exactly 12.30. The FBI dealt with Willis's photograph of 'Ruby' by cropping it out in their official report.

The other photographs are equally important as evidence. Mary Moorman was snapping away with her Polaroid at the roadside and recorded someone or something in the bushes on the grassy knoll. Willis's pictures support the existence of this figure. Robert Hughes's cine film also caught a flicker of action on the sixth floor of the depository seconds before the shooting. The Warren Commission, despite Hughes's protests, said he must have been mistaken in his timings. However, a man called Jack Weaver took a still photograph at the same time that shows what seems to be a gunman at the sixth-floor window.

Ike Altgens was a professional AP photographer on the corner of Elm and Houston. He caught the motorcade head-on at the moment the first shot hit the President in the back. The Secret Servicemen's heads are quite clearly turned to look back towards the sound of a shot in the direction of the Dal-Tex and depository buildings. The picture was taken long before Zapruder's frame Z210.

Orville Nix's cine film was shot looking across Dealey Plaza towards the Pergola and the grassy knoll. He clearly picks up a figure running up the last steps and disappearing behind the grassy knoll after the last shot was fired, backing Willis's and Moorman's photographic claims of something in the grassy knoll bushes. His claim that he filmed a gunman hiding in the grassy knoll was checked by a company called ITEK who said that the film showed only 'shadows from a tree', despite Nix pointing out that the 'shadow from a tree' appeared to have walked off and disappeared 10 frames later; unusual behaviour for a tree. Only afterwards did Nix discover that ITEK did contract work for the CIA.

Mary Moorman's camera caught the final headshot on Kennedy, the braking to a stop of the presidential limo and the chaos as it then sped away. Another set of still photographs was taken by Wilma Bond, standing behind Moorman. They show men running up the Grassy Knoll, families lying down, but curiously, no Gordon Arnold, the soldier who reported 'a shot past his left ear' and claimed that two policemen had impounded his film. In the close-knit world of Kennedy Assassination researchers this had led to allegations against Arnold of lying in the surprisingly bitter personal attacks on witnesses that seems to dog the research community.

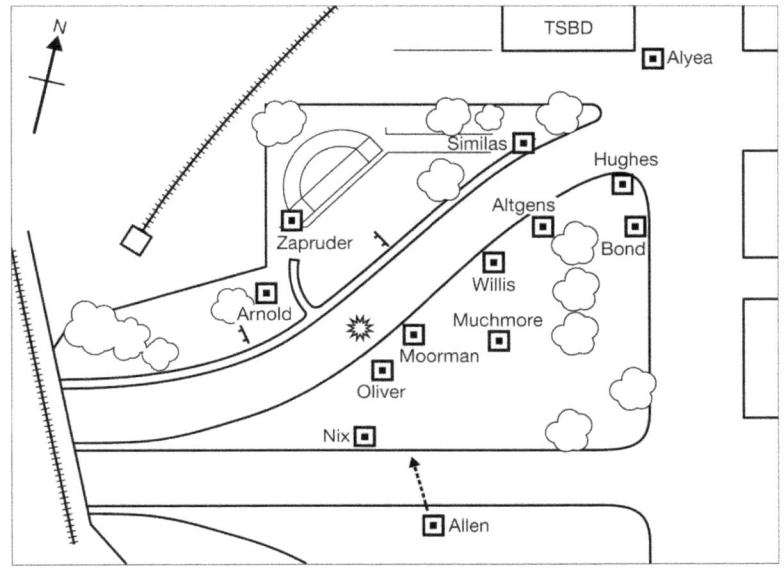

The assassination was photographed from all angles.

However, the photographs of the shooting in Dallas on 22 November are not the only interesting photographic record of that dreadful day. The official photographs and X-rays taken at the autopsy in Washington later have been doctored, too. In 1978 Robert Groden, official photographic expert of the House Select Committee on Assassinations, testified:

> When I saw the autopsy photographs, I was shocked. After years in photo-optic work I know what I saw, and what I saw was a

soft edged matte insertion forgery of very high quality which made it appear as if there were a small wound of entry in the rear of the President's head.

Groden claims that he informed the HSCA Chairman that in his expert opinion the 'official' photographs of the Kennedy autopsy had been faked.

The final piece of photographic evidence is the curious experience of Norman Similas. Taken by itself it might be accepted as coincidence or just bad luck. But if a key intelligence indicator is the absence of the normal or the presence of the abnormal, there is much that seems abnormal if not plain suspicious about the way Kennedy murder was investigated or covered up.

The photographic evidence of the assassination is no exception. The conclusion is chilling but thoroughly documented: the films were ignored or fixed. The Zapruder film in particular has been doctored, pointing to a meticulously planned, high-tech falsification of evidence.

But by whom? And why?

23

ANOTHER 'SHOT HEARD ROUND THE WORLD'

WHEN A DISTINGUISHED BUT ELDERLY SCIENTIST STATES THAT SOMETHING IS POSSIBLE HE IS ALMOST CERTAINLY RIGHT. WHEN HE STATES THAT SOMETHING IS IMPOSSIBLE, HE IS VERY PROBABLY WRONG.
ARTHUR C. CLARKE'S FIRST LAW

The Warren Commission claimed in its official report that there were only three shots fired in Dealey Plaza. For years the US government clung tenaciously to this position despite the photographic evidence. That they did not believe it themselves was made clear in 1978 when Robert Blakey, the Chief Counsel and Director of the House Select Committee on Assassinations, admitted that he believed 'there were six or seven shots on the day, but begged him not to make this public.' This astonishing admission was prompted by the inclusion of new acoustic evidence.

A 'Dictabelt' (a primitive recording device) ran all day in the Dallas Police radio room and was changed daily. The blue Dictabelts were numbered and stored. The Warren Commission listened to the tape for 22 November 1963 and heard the usual muddled mixture of voices, traffic sounds and routine police radio transmissions. Unfortunately at the vital moment, a policeman's microphone had jammed open in the transmit position for eight minutes. Officer H.B. McLain admitted that it was his motorcycle as he rode front left of Kennedy. A researcher called Gary Mack got hold of a copy of the Dictabelt and was convinced that he could pick out no less than seven gunshots, even from his poor copy. The Dallas Police Intelligence Division turned the original copy over to an firm called BBN Acoustic Sciences, which specialised in identifying sensitive acoustic signals for US Navy submarines.

BBN's top scientists turned the old Dallas police recording into a digital signal, removed all the extraneous 'noise' and electronically highlighted the frequencies of gunshots. At least seven spikes of 'powerful acoustic signals' can be seen on the recording. (See diagram below.)

Some of the scientists claimed they could see *nine* gunshots on the tape. A series of test recordings, with Dallas policemen firing at sandbags one quiet Sunday morning, proved with 95% confidence that some shots had indeed been fired from the area of the grassy knoll and that there were at the very least four shots. That meant more than one gunman. With great reluctance the House Select Committee accepted the firm's findings.

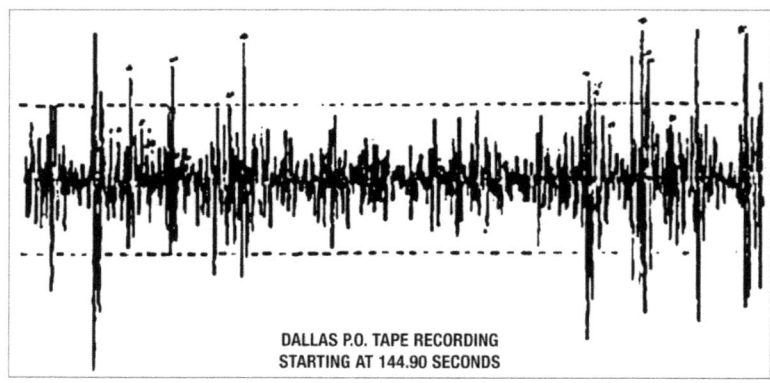

Only three shots? The damning evidence of the Dallas Police Dictabelt recording.

The familiar campaign to rubbish any finding that challenged the official version of Kennedy's assassination swung into action. The FBI leaked news stories to its mouthpieces in the US press that BBN's work had been 'invalid' and the Committee's conclusions were 'misplaced'.

Official Washington now entered the ring. Out of the blue a blue chip panel under Harvard Professor of Physics Norman Ramsey suddenly received a $25,000 award from the National Science Foundation to 're-examine the acoustic evidence'. The US Justice Department (the FBI's bosses) sponsored the study. Unsurprisingly, the Ramsey Panel found the Police Dictabelt tape 'unreliable'. The government's Professor Ramsey concluded loftily that, 'the acoustic analyses (therefore) do not demonstrate that there was a grassy knoll shot ... and do not support a conclusion that there was a second gunman.'

BBN Acoustic Sciences were furious at this criticism of their professional competence. It mattered not. Once again, someone had denounced the new findings, setting up expert against expert and planting doubts against any criticism of the official government line that there were no shots from the grassy knoll and Lee Harvey Oswald, acting alone, killed the President with an old-fashioned, unsighted and decrepit rifle.

That war of words goes on to this day, but the damage has been done. Forty years after the assassination, the press carried reports of a new evaluation by Don Thomas, a statistician, who reexamined the crucial 18 seconds that ended with the Dallas Police Chief saying, 'Go to the hospital' into his microphone. Dr Thomas specifically focussed on the fact that the two channels on the Dictabelt were clearly out of synchronisation. He picked on a key transmission when Sergeant Bellah of the Dallas Police asks: 'You want me to hold this traffic on Stemmons until we find out something or let it go?' On Channel 1, that question was nearly 3 minutes (171 seconds) out of synch with the rest of the tape.

Dr Thomas re-synchronised the speech on the two channels and came to the conclusion that the gunshots on the tape were real. The Thomas findings tallied with Zapruder's film running at 18.3 frames a second, giving a gap of 4.8 seconds between the bullet that seriously wounded Senator Connally, and the fatal Kennedy headshot. Dr Thomas's new analysis of the Dictabelt sounds matched the Zapruder film timings exactly.

Sure enough, in 2003 other scientists and researchers weighed in, challenging Thomas's work. The wrangle over the acoustic evidence continues to this day. Behind the internet spats and the learned scientific papers, important issues lurk and what might normally be treated as a bitchy fight between academics assumes, in the case of Kennedy's assassination, a more sombre tone. For someone, somewhere, it seems to be vital to challenge, contest and rubbish any suggestion that Lee Harvey Oswald did not do it all on his own. That immediately begs the question: *why?* If it were confined solely to the acoustic evidence, that would be just another squabble between the notoriously vain egos of rival PhDs seeking public prominence.

But, combined with the conflicting medical evidence, the photographic evidence and the testimony of the eyewitnesses, it all looks most odd.

What secret is so important that it must be covered by a bodyguard of lies?

24

OFFICER TIPPIT

A POLICEMAN'S LOT IS NOT A HAPPY ONE.
W.S. GILBERT

John Kennedy wasn't the only person shot in Dallas that day. Someone else had his head blown open by a gunshot, too: Dallas Police Officer J.D. Tippit.

The US government's line has always been to link the Tippit murder to the Kennedy assassination, and it was the Assistant Counsel to the Warren Commission who forged that link. David Belin said in 1964 that 'the Rosetta Stone to the solution of President Kennedy's murder is the murder of Officer J.D. Tippit ... once [this] is admitted there can be no doubt that the overall evidence shows that Lee Harvey Oswald was the assassin of John F. Kennedy.'

This deliberate attempt to link the two is illogical. Whoever pulled the trigger, Officer Tippit's is a separate murder, both in time and in location, and, on the evidence, it is hard to see just how Lee Harvey Oswald could have done it.

***

At 12.45 Tippit's Dallas Police patrol car was reportedly in the Oak Cliff area about four miles from the Kennedy murder. At about 13.10 his car was observed by a witness called Jack Tatum who was in his car and stopped at the intersection of 10th and Denver. (See map of the area, in chapter 19.) He saw 'a squad car pulling over to the kerb and a man walking east down the sidewalk...' He said that the uniformed policeman leaned over and spoke to the pedestrian through the passenger window.

The policeman then got out of his car and was shot three times in the chest. As he lay on the ground, his attacker walked round the car and administered a *coup de grâce* by shooting Tippit in the right side of the skull. The killer then fled west towards the junction of 10th and Patton, leaving appalled eyewitnesses to call the police.

The Warren Commission relied on highly selective evidence to implicate Oswald. Firstly, they drew heavily from eyewitness testimony; secondly, they accepted four spent cartridge cases found near the scene as definitely coming from the revolver Oswald had in his possession when he was arrested. Lastly, the Warren Commission said that a zip-up jacket, found nearby, also belonged to Oswald.

None of these claims would survive scrutiny in a courtroom. The government's chief witness was a Mrs Helen Markham. She claimed that she saw everything and gave a lurid description of Tippit talking to a pedestrian who then shot him and 'trotted off', after 'fooling with his gun.' She claimed to have rushed over to the mortally wounded policeman and 'comforted him as he lay dying'. However she had been observed by two other eyewitnesses to have slumped down and covered her face when the shooting started. Mrs Markham was still in hysterics when the police and ambulance arrived shortly afterwards. At the subsequent identification line-up at the police station she eventually picked out Oswald as the man she had seen, but only after coaching from a friendly police officer who had to prompt her to pick out 'number two' from the row of four men. For the Dallas Police Department and the government, however, that amounted to a positive identification.

Mrs Markham's testimony was contradicted by at least three other witnesses. Bill Scoggins was a Dallas taxi driver who had stopped on the corner where Patton joins 10th (see map in chapter 19) to grab a snack lunch. Some shrubbery obscured his view of the actual shooting but he heard the shots and saw the gunman run past him, heading south on 10th: 'I saw him kinda coming toward me ... I could see his face, his features and everything plain ... kind of loping, trotting ... He had a pistol in his left hand ... I heard him mutter something like "poor damn cop" or "poor dumb cop". He said that twice.'

Scoggins later identified the man he saw as Lee Harvey Oswald or his double.

Even more confusing is the testimony of Mrs Acquilla Clemons, who lived nearby and who heard gunshots. She ran out of her door and saw a 'kind of chunky ... kind of heavy' man with a handgun. That description certainly does not fit Oswald. But Mrs Clemons reported seeing another, 'taller, thinner' man across the street to whom the gunman called out, 'Go on. Go on!' waving his hand. The two men split up. The police and FBI ignored Mrs Clemons's story and later she was called by an unidentified man who claimed to be a member of Dallas Police Department, warning her to keep her mouth shut or she would get hurt.

Further down the street, Frank Wright and his wife heard gunshots. Mr Wright stared up East 10th Street, where about 100 yards away he saw Tippit's body roll over after the headshot. Then he saw a man 'in a long coat' run away down the passenger side of Tippit's car, jump into a 'gray coupe ... Maybe a Plymouth '50-'51' and drive away. His testimony was ignored.

Two women who lived on the corner of 10th and Patton also heard the shooting. They saw a man cutting across the grass and heading for Patton, scattering spent shell cases as he fled. Barbara and Virginia Davis later swore that the man they saw was Lee Harvey Oswald.

Another eyewitness was Warren Reynolds, who was a block away on Jefferson when he saw a man walking and reloading a pistol. He and another witness, B M Paterson, decided to follow, heading west at a discreet distance. That was a mistake, because he later told the authorities that the man he trailed looked nothing like Lee Harvey Oswald. Two months later Reynolds was shot in the head for his pains, but miraculously survived the wound. From then on Warren Reynolds had no problem remembering that the man he chased looked 'just like Lee Harvey Oswald'.

There was yet another witness to the killing. Domingo Benavides was a car mechanic. He had pulled his truck to a stop on the opposite side of the road from the shooting. He saw a gunman dropping empty cartridge cases as he fled. Benavides waited until the coast was clear, then rushed to Tippit's side. Grabbing the police radio in Tippit's car, Benavides tried to call in to Dallas Police HQ but he couldn't work the radio. A passing motorist ran over and finally got through. The DPD operations room timed it at 13.16. That means that the shooting must have taken place at around 13.12-13.14.

This critical timing was corroborated by the hysterical Mrs Markham. She worked as a waitress and normally caught the 13.12 bus to get to work. She had just been leaving the house to catch that bus when she saw the shooting. That, therefore, places the killing at nearer 13.10, not 13.15. This rules out Lee Harvey Oswald as the perpetrator if he was walking from his rooming house. Oswald had left, on foot, a mile away, at about 13.04-13.05. There was no way he could have covered that distance on foot in 6 or 7 minutes.

There are two clear possibilities: one, that Oswald had been given a lift; or, two, that it was not Oswald. According to his landlady, Earlene Roberts, Oswald had come rushing into the rooming house at exactly 13.00 – the TV news was just starting – and went straight to his room. After three or four minutes Oswald dashed out again, having changed his clothes and grabbed a .38 revolver. Mrs Roberts noticed something strange.

A Dallas Police patrol car drifted slowly to a halt outside her house and beeped the horn twice before driving away. As the only known police car in the area was that of Officer Tippit, it could, theoretically, have been his car. However, by the time Oswald left the house at 13.05 to stand by a bus stop, the police car had gone. Witnesses who saw Tippit's car on 10th Street said that he was cruising up slowly 'as if looking for somebody'.

J.D. Tippit had come on duty at 7.00. His beat patrol area was #78. By 12.17 he was reported attending a possible burglary at Bonny View and cleared this incident at 12.20 when the dispatcher logged him as, '78, clear'. What Tippit did next was very strange. At least five witnesses (who knew the officer well) placed him static at the GLOCO petrol station right at the north of the Oak Cliff area at 12.45 watching the bridge leading from downtown Dallas and the area of the depository. However, according to the DPD dispatch records, Tippit claimed to be in Oak Cliff at that time. Suddenly at about 12.55, he 'tore off' down Lancaster at high speed, reporting to the dispatcher that he was 'in the area of Keist and Bonny View' – which wasn't true.

His next reported sighting was when he rushed into the Top Ten Record Shop and asked to use the store phone. In the days before mobile phones this was a fairly regular practice by policemen in a hurry. The question is, why didn't Tippit use the car radio? It cannot, therefore, have been official business. According to the store clerk, Tippit dialled a number, 'waited for seven or eight rings,' then, receiving no reply, rushed out of the shop.

What is important about this incident is that it places Tippit firmly at the Top Ten Record Store at about 13.00. It is therefore virtually impossible for him to have been in the police car that drifted by Mrs Roberts's rooming house and beeped its horn twice. It is too far, if the reported timings are as accurate as they appear to be.

At about 13.02, insurance worker Jim Andrews was driving west along West 10th Street on his way back to work after lunch. Suddenly a police car overtook him and forced him to stop at the kerbside. The patrolman – wearing a badge with the name 'Tippit' on it – jumped out and without a word scanned the backseat of Andrews's car as though looking for something. He then jumped into his patrol car and accelerated away. A slightly stunned Andrews reported that Tippit seemed 'very upset [and] agitated' and was 'acting wild'.

All the evidence points to the conclusion that Officer Tippit's behaviour after lunch is consistent with a worried man looking for someone or something. He was away from his usual patrol area. He missed at least two radio calls that afternoon (a serious offence – he had only missed one call a year in his previous service). Jim Andrews reported that the policeman who hurriedly scanned the back of his car seemed anxious and in a rush, and when Tippet finally stopped his patrol car in West

10th Street, the policeman was so pre-occupied he never bothered to even remonstrate with, let alone book, a civilian who rear-ended him, however gently. All the signs are that J.D. Tippit had other things on his mind that day.

The other evidence that the Warren Commission brought out to 'prove' that Oswald shot Tippit is equally flimsy. Oswald had a .38 special Smith & Wesson revolver on him when he was arrested. This is important because the cartridge cases at the Tippit murder scene were originally reported as being from a .38 *automatic* pistol, not a revolver. Mrs Markham reported the gunman 'fiddling with his gun' as he fled. It is highly unlikely that someone using a revolver would stop after a killing in the street, snap open the revolving chamber of his gun and eject the spent brass cases on the ground (plus the two unfired bullets of a standard six round load) as a useful bit of evidence for the cops later, fingerprints and all. This looks much more like an attempt to plant evidence.

The four empty shell cases were collected at the scene. Police officer Poe scratched his initials onto the soft brass of two empty cases to preserve the evidential chain and bagged them. By the time the FBI 'analysed' them months later, Policeman Poe's marks had mysteriously vanished from the brass cases and the fired rounds had definitely become revolver bullets. Unfortunately the bullets removed from the luckless Tippit's body didn't match. They consisted of three Winchester-Western bullets and a single Remington-Peters .38 round. The problem is that the four empty shell cases handed over to the FBI don't match the bullets from the body. There are two Winchester-Western cases and two Remington-Peters cases. It does not make sense unless, of course, the evidence has been interfered with or planted.

The final piece of evidence, the zip-up jacket found at the Texaco garage on Jefferson, turns out to be the wrong colour – it is white, and Oswald's zip-up jackets were either blue or grey. It had a dry-cleaning tag from another state; the policeman who allegedly found it couldn't explain how it got there before he picked it up; and finally the owner of the Texaco garage pointed out that could have been anyone's jacket. There is no chain of evidence. No court of law would admit it as evidence.

The killing of Officer Tippit was a muddle at the time and remains a muddle now. When we factor in the murder of Domingo Benavides' brother 6 months later – apparently in a mistaken 'hit' intended for Domingo himself – the affair becomes even messier. It has all the hallmarks of a bungled gangland attempt at silencing a man who saw too much.

Tippit had a troubled record. He was running a mistress with an angry husband and he was mixed up with some dubious characters. He had another police uniform in his patrol car for no good reason and was certainly up to something that afternoon. He may even have known Oswald. Two days before the killing, Tippit had been eating breakfast at the Dodds House restaurant where he was a regular and well known to the staff. Also in the restaurant was a young man later identified by the waitress as being Lee Harvey Oswald. They remembered him because he made a scene that day, 'was nasty and used cuss words' and drew attention to himself by complaining loudly that his eggs were not cooked properly. Tippit 'stared hard at Oswald' according to the waitress.

If Tippit had been instructed to pick up Oswald and move him on 22 November 1963 – since Oswald couldn't drive – then an encounter such as the attention-grabbing fuss at the restaurant would have offered a perfect chance for him to identify his passenger in advance. It would also fit in with eyewitnesses reports that Tippit seemed to be looking for someone on the afternoon he was killed, and Oswald's pointless hanging around at the bus stop.

***

Whether or not Oswald was at the scene of Officer Tippit's murder, he was now about to encounter the full force of the law. Five blocks to the south west, twenty minutes later at about 13.35, a young store manager named

John Brewer on West Jefferson claimed he saw a man behaving suspiciously as he ducked back in the doorway and then slipped into the Texas Movie Theatre behind the back of the ticket collector, Julie Postal, who had come out into the street. Brewer asked her if she had sold the man a ticket. She hadn't, so Julie Postal decided to phone the police, saying, 'I know you are very busy but I have a man in the theatre who is running from you for some reason.'

She later claimed that she thought the 'suspicious-looking' man might be something to do with the killing of the President. 'The officer asked me if the man fit the description of the suspect.'

The people and the police force in Dallas were in an ugly mood that afternoon. The murder of the President was bad enough, but the knowledge that one of their own had been gunned down too raised police tempers to boiling point and within minutes, at about 14.45, the police investigating Tippit's death arrived mob-handed to arrest his killer at the Texas Movie Theatre. A crowd gathered in reaction to all the activity as the police surrounded the building and drew their guns to begin the search for what they believed to be an armed and dangerous gunman.

FBI agent Bob Barrett was with them at the cinema and recorded what happened as armed police flooded into the cinema, to the consternation of half a dozen schoolboys in the balcony playing truant. On the ground floor the police found their suspect, who stood up saying, 'I guess it's all over now', before punching police officer MacDonald in the face. After a brief struggle, the officers seized their man as he tried to pull a .38 pistol from his belt. He was swiftly overpowered by half a dozen cops, who took advantage of his resistance to work off some of their frustrations. In the struggle Oswald sustained cuts and bruises and a black eye.

The Theatre Manager told the police that the individual they had arrested had been in the cinema since about 13.05 – which, if true, means that Oswald could not have been involved in the Tippit murder and raises questions about the timing of the Julie Postal telephone call to the police. FBI Agent Barrett had been called to the scene of Tippit's murder (he specialised in Mafia related crime for the Dallas area.) There Captain Westbrook of the DPD then showed him a wallet the police claimed to have found near Officer Tippit's body. It belonged to a 'Lee Oswald' and also had identification for an 'A.J. Hidell'.

Shortly afterwards, Barrett was at the Texas Theatre and witnessed the arrest of Oswald without realising that it was the same man. The arresting officers claim to have searched Oswald and found his wallet. The arresting officer mistakenly logged it as having been 'taken from Oswald at the scene of his arrest'. Either that or it had been deliberately dropped by the killer at Tippit's murder to incriminate Oswald.

The prisoner was eventually restrained and led away loudly protesting that his civil rights were being violated and that 'I am not resisting arrest!' As Oswald emerged blinking into the sunlight, he was greeted with shouts of 'Kill him!

Murderer!' and 'Kill the son of a bitch ... we'll do it'. The police quickly hustled their handcuffed prisoner into a car and sped away from what looked like turning into an old-fashioned Texas lynch mob. As far as the Dallas Police were concerned, they had got their man.

Lee Harvey Oswald was under arrest for the murder of Officer Tippit.

25

DEAD MEN TELL NO TALES – LEE HARVEY OSWALD

TO THE DEAD WE OWE ONLY TRUTH.
VOLTAIRE

Despite Warren Commission Assistant Counsel David Belin's confident assertion that the Tippit murder was the 'Rosetta Stone' of the Kennedy assassination, the true key to the whole affair is really the enigmatic figure of Lee Harvey Oswald, and he is dead, the first of many witnesses of the Kennedy saga to meet an unexpected and violent death. Oswald carried his secrets to the grave, and dead men tell no tales.

***

Lee Harvey Oswald was born in New Orleans, Louisiana in 1939. He was a poor southerner by upbringing. The family moved to New York City, where

Lee was diagnosed with 'learning difficulties' (he had an IQ of 118, but suffered from dyslexia) and spent some time in a 'youth house' for truancy. Mrs Oswald returned to New Orleans in 1954 when Lee was 13. It was the height of the McCarthy anti-communist witch hunt, with scare stories of 'Reds under the bed'. Lee was apparently much taken with *I Led Three Lives,* a radio series featuring an undercover Mr Ordinary America who, while pretending to be a secret communist, was really a double agent for the FBI. Lee allegedly listened to all 117 episodes and saw the film of the series several times. From an early age, he wanted to be a secret agent just as other boys wanted to be cowboys, firemen or train drivers.

A psychiatrist who examined him just before he returned to New Orleans noted, 'Lee has a vivid fantasy life, turning around the topics of omnipotence and power.'

After he returned to New Orleans Lee joined the Civil Air Patrol, a semi-military version of the 'Air Scouts', and went camping and learning about the United States military. Here he fell under the influence of the officer running the local Civil Air Patrol branch, airline pilot David Ferrie. At about this time Lee apparently became interested in Marx and Communism as well. He tried to join the Young Communists and spouted Marxist diatribes to the fury of at least one of his friends' parents. He tried to enlist in the US Marines even though he was under age. The USMC rejected him first time round, but a few days after his 17th birthday, Lee Harvey Oswald joined the US Marines.

Basic training for any US Marine grunt was never going to be easy, but Lee survived 10 weeks of boot camp at San Diego and was selected for Radar and Air Traffic Control duties in the spring of 1957. He finally passed as a qualified USMC Aviation Electronics Operator, which was only open to the top 10% of USMC recruits. From there he was posted to Japan, to Marine Air Control Squadron 1 based at Atsugi. This was the unit responsible for the CIA's U2 secret over-flights into the USSR and China. It was a highly sensitive and secret appointment and, although the US government has grudgingly admitted that Oswald 'may have held a limited clearance for Secret', the truth is that this kind of sensitive task needs a SECRET-CRYPTO-GRAPHIC security clearance. Lee Harvey Oswald was in fact a highly qualified radar operator helping to guide and plot the USA's top-secret over-flights of the Soviet Union.

The U2's official ceiling was 68,000 feet: nearly 13 miles. This made the U2 a difficult challenge for the PVO Strany – the Soviet Air Defence Forces. The result was that the U2 was virtually invulnerable to the Soviet air defences. 'The Black Lady' was a constant American provocation to the Kremlin by the 1960s. Whatever Washington may subsequently have said, Lee Harvey Oswald was operating at the cutting edge of American Intelligence against the USSR when he was at Atsugi AFB in Japan. Lee appears to have been good at his job. His rating officer wrote that Oswald was 'very competent' and 'brighter than most people'.

It was at this time that he began to develop his second, secret life. He would disappear on a weekend pass to

Tokyo and hang out in the Queen Bee nightclub. The Queen Bee was no place for Marine Corps privates. A good evening would set a customer back $70: a month's pay for a Marine pfc. In spite of this, Oswald took to spending his 48-hour passes in Tokyo and picking up a beautiful Eurasian woman with Russian connections. Some time in Japan the shy kid who fantasised about being a spy achieved his boyhood dream and became a real 'US secret agent'.

Oswald was always a creature of the Office of Naval Intelligence (ONI) and later the Defense Intelligence Agency (DIA). The ONI took particular interest in the Queen Bee Nightclub, as did the local Tokyo CIA station. The KGB were neither blind nor stupid and knew that Atsugi was both home to strange aeroplanes and housed some kind of CIA facility. In 1957, Atsugi Base was a 'Category 1' intelligence priority for the KGB and its military intelligence counterpart, the GRU; and Lee Harvey Oswald was at the heart of it, working in the joint CIA-military Air Traffic Control Centre.

The idea that Oswald with his access may not have been of great interest to the Soviets is ridiculous. So is any idea that the US Base Counter Intelligence and Security officials equally didn't keep a close eye on their off-duty personnel. When Oswald was back in the USA in 1959, he confided to a fellow marine that a bargirl at the Queen Bee had begun asking questions about his work at the base. Oswald reported the approach to the base security officer, and was briefed by a civilian intelligence officer who told him he could do his country a great service. The woman was a known KGB informant and Lee could pass on false information to her. Oswald agreed – it was perhaps the moment he had been waiting for ever since his first youthful enthusiasm for undercover work – and he became a 'low-level directed source' for the ONI and CIA with an allowance for expenses. That these duties were not without an element of risk became clear later in his service. In 1958, he contracted gonorrhoea, although his records show that it was, 'in the line of duty ... not due to his own misconduct.'

It was in Japan that Lee began the strange series of incidents that follow him thereafter. On 27 October 1957, a small .22 Derringer pistol supposedly fell out of his locker and went off, causing a small graze to his elbow. Despite the trivial nature of his injury, he spent 3 weeks in hospital, away from his unit. Six months later Corporal Oswald was court-martialled for possession of an illegal firearm. He was given 20 days hard labour, a $50 fine and broken back to the rank of private.

On 21 June 1958, Oswald tried to pick a fight with the sergeant, then poured his drink over him. Sergeant Rodriguez charged Oswald, who was hauled in front of a court martial. This time the court sentenced him to 28 days in the 'Brig' – and threw in the previously suspended sentence for good measure. Oswald disappeared into the Navy's detention centre for 45 days, until 13 August 1958. Or did he?

Only one other US Marine saw Oswald during his supposed incarceration and Lee was walking free and wearing civilian clothes. Oswald returned to his unit 'cold and withdrawn' and 'kept himself to himself', according to his colleagues. While no one has proved it, a reasonable supposition would be that he received some intelligence training during this time.

In October his unit was ordered to Formosa (Taiwan). It was there that the next odd incident in the Lee Harvey Oswald story took place. While on guard duty one night, he loosed off a volley of shots into the woods. By the time the Duty Officer found him, Oswald was 'shaking and crying'. Oswald was diagnosed with psychiatric trauma and shipped back to Japan for another inexplicable absence from his unit. This time he was attached to a US Air Base in Iwakuni, where he ran into an old marine buddy, Owen Dejanovich. To Dejanovich's surprise, Lee cold-shouldered him. Owen was astonished to hear Lee spouting off against the evils of Capitalism, the virtues of the Communist system and the glorious achievements of the USSR. He was also learning Russian.

In the narrow-minded society of the US Marine Corps in 1958, at the height of the Cold War, this was a very remarkable thing indeed. However, Lee Harvey Oswald's officers do not seem to have taken his alleged communist views very seriously. There is no record of a worried company commander informing the battalion security officer that his US Marine unit, especially one with a 'Secret – CRYPTO' security clearance, was nurturing a budding communist. Once again we are confronted not just by the absence of the normal but by the presence of the abnormal in the case of Lee Harvey Oswald.

What followed next is bizarre. In December 1959, Oswald was posted Stateside and took up his duties with MACS 9, based at El Toro Airbase near Santa Anna, California. There he quite openly flaunted his alleged interest in Communism. His fellow Marines joked about it, calling him 'Oswaldski' and accepting his habit of calling his fellow marines 'comrade' and answering questions with *'nyet'* and *'da'*. While at El Toro, Lee, with several others, was approached and briefed by a 'civilian in intelligence', and later Oswald told a Marine called Bucknall that this was his case officer and handler at Atsugi, adding that 'he was being sent to Russia by American intelligence and would return to America in 1961 as a hero.'

Oswald's service record supports this. He was discreetly admitted to the Defense Language School at Monterey, California, for a crash course. Communist sympathisers applying for their early discharge from the US Marines do not normally get expensive language courses, courtesy of the US taxpayer. Oswald learned his Russian at Monterey, courtesy of American Intelligence.

On 17 August 1959, Oswald formally applied for a hardship discharge because of an injury sustained by his mother. To the astonishment of his fellow Marines, within two weeks his request was approved and arrangements made for his discharge from the service. The next week he applied for a US passport and got one back in the post within 7 days. The very next day, 11 September 1959, Lee Harvey Oswald was discharged from active duty.

By 17 September Lee returned to New Orleans, where he drew $203 from the bank. He gave $100 of it to his mother and sailed for France. On 8 October, he disembarked at Le Havre and somehow arrived at Southampton. Oswald then got to London Heathrow airport where he flew on to Finland.

Despite the fact that there were no London-Helsinki flights that day, he surfaced at the smart – and very expensive – Helsinki-Torni Hotel the next day, 10 October 1959, ready for his first encounter with the realities of life in the USSR.

***

Lee Harvey Oswald was the first US Marine to defect to the Soviet Union – ever. He was supposedly disgruntled with America and the capitalist system; he carried a treasure trove of highly classified electronic secrets in his head; and he could confirm or deny a great deal of what went on inside the American's top secret air base at Atsugi. Ignoring this cornucopia of secrets, the Soviets treated Oswald with the deepest suspicion when he eventually pitched up at his Intourist Hotel in Moscow and announced to his courier guide that, notwithstanding his sixday visa, he wanted to defect.

The problem was that in the autumn of 1959 defectors were two-a-penny. The news that Oswald wanted to stay impressed no one, particularly not the USSR's MVD, internal police. They ordered him deported. Oswald now resorted to desperate measures. He slashed his wrist and was admitted to the local psychiatric ward, where he stayed in hospital for eleven days. The Soviet authorities still didn't want him, so Lee stormed into the US Embassy, threw his passport down melodramatically on the desk of Richard Snyder, the Consul, and 'renounced his US citizenship'. In one of those curious coincidences that hover over Lee Harvey Oswald, just by pure fluke, Consul Snyder (who also doubled as a CIA officer) had written to the State Department Legal Office shortly before, asking 'for guidance on an attempted renunciation of US citizenship.' It was a weekend and he told Oswald to come back on Monday. Snyder signalled

Washington with the serious news that an ex-Marine with a SECRET CRYPTO clearance was 'about to defect to the Russians, threatening to tell them all that he knew.'

Washington's reaction to their traitorous Marine was remarkably relaxed, to say the least. The fact was that they already knew. Their ONI attaché had already warned them a week before about Oswald. Unfortunately over 40 lines of his cable back to the USA have been blacked out so, even now, we cannot read all of what he said. The ONI and the Pentagon were equally restrained. They noted the event and merely asked to be 'kept informed of significant developments'. This is not the normal reaction of a Service Security Agency confronting the disaster of a traitor threatening to betray his own country and pass on details of highly secret intelligence operations. Normally such news would cause senior intelligence officials and security bureaucrats to scurry around like a disturbed ant's nest. Like so many things involving Lee Oswald, it just didn't happen.

The Soviet authorities then dragged Oswald off and from 16 November to 29 December 1959, Lee Harvey Oswald disappeared. He must have pleased his new masters, because when he next surfaced, he had been granted 5,000 roubles and given a luxury (by Soviet standards) apartment in Minsk, where he was greeted personally on his arrival by the city's Mayor. He was given a Mickey Mouse job in the local electronic plant. A tantalising snippet does throw some light on this blank period in his life. On May Day 1960, the PVO Strany finally got lucky and managed to shoot down a U2 spy plane deep inside the USSR. Oswald's detailed knowledge of the aeroplane's IFF transponder's frequencies could easily have turned it into a homing beacon for a suitably configured surface to air missile.

Apart from this incident, Oswald appears to have led a privileged life in Minsk; travelling, taking photographs and even receiving a firearms license for hunting. He had girlfriends, hobnobbed with the local senior Party officials and generally lived well beyond his means.

Defection, it appeared, paid handsomely.

26

THE SPY WHO CAME IN FROM THE COLD – THE CURIOUS CAREER OF LEE HARVEY OSWALD

'TELL ME,' CONTROL CONTINUED, 'ARE YOU TIRED OF SPYING?'
JOHN LE CARRÉ

Lee Harvey Oswald was not the only ONI 'defector' sent to the Soviet Union at the end of the 1950s. A disillusioned ex-CIA officer, Victor Marchetti, confirmed that the ONI had just such a programme:

[It] involved three dozen, maybe 40, young men who were made to appear disenchanted, poor American youths who had been turned off and wanted to see what Communism was all about. They were sent into the Soviet Union or Eastern Europe with the specific intention the Soviets would pick them up and 'double' them if they suspected them of being US agents, or recruit them as KGB agents. They were trained at various naval installations both here and abroad, but the operation was run out of Nag's Head, North Carolina.

Lee Harvey Oswald turns out to have been an American intelligence agent sent to the USSR posing as a defector. Senators Schweiker and Hartz reported to the Senate Intelligence Committee that, 'Lee Harvey Oswald was a product of, and interacting with, the intelligence community.' We even have confirmation of his real role from his time in Japan from Jim Wilcott, the Tokyo CIA Station financial controller at the time.

Oswald was originally under the control of the Tokyo station's Soviet Russian branch. He was trained at Atsugi Naval air station, the secret base for CIA Tokyo special operations. When Oswald returned from the USSR, he was brought back to Japan for debriefing. They were having some kind of difficulty with Oswald. The Soviets were on to him from the start. That apparently made him very angry and difficult to handle.

The problem appears to have been that the KGB suspected him of being a plant. The CIA-ONI were receiving nothing worth-while in the way of intelligence from 'their man in Minsk'. So when Oswald's mother asked after his welfare and Oswald decided he wanted to return to the USA in the spring of 1961, everyone jumped at the chance. If Oswald went back to the States, everyone benefited. The Russians got rid of an expensive burden, the CIA-ONI got their boy back and could debrief him, then watch to see if the KGB made an approach to Oswald in the USA. And Oswald got to come back home. There was just one snag: Lee Harvey Oswald was a self-confessed traitor who had betrayed his country and sold its secrets, and who faced arrest, trial and jail if he returned to his homeland. The penalties for treason are severe.

Everyone appears to have ignored this important legal fact. Oswald was readmitted to the US without any of the normal penalties greeting a traitor. Before his return, however, Lee had one last bit of business in the USSR. On 30 April 1961, after a whirlwind romance, he married Marina Nikolayevna Prusakova. This was standard procedure for the KGB – she had an uncle who was a Colonel in the Ministry of Internal Affairs. Oswald married Marina and the Russians now had their girl on the inside.

There was another little complication along the way, too, as the Oswalds awaited their exit visa. On 15 February 1962, Marina gave birth to a baby girl. Finally, after a year's delay, they got permission to leave the USSR. The returning 'traitor' was given his passport back by the US Embassy and, remarkably, a government loan to ease the financial burden of his journey home. The American State Department loaned Oswald $435, and on 1 June 1962 the little family boarded a train in Moscow to begin their journey back to the United States. The train took them via Warsaw and Berlin to the border crossing from East to West Germany at Helmstedt, where Marina had her passport stamped.

Oswald entered West Germany separately. The probability is that he got off at Berlin and travelled by US Diplomatic car through the corridor to the West having been met by the CIA Station in Berlin. By the end of the day the family was reunited in a CIA safe house in Amsterdam, where Oswald was debriefed for at least two days before they boarded the SS *Maasdam,* finally arriving at Hoboken, New Jersey on 13 June 1962.

The returning traitor was not met by a hostile deputation of the New Jersey police and the FBI brandishing an arrest warrant. On the contrary, they were met instead by an obliging member of the US Travellers' Aid Society who loaned them money, helped them with the baby and their seven or eight suitcases, and escorted them to a New York hotel before eventually putting them on an aeroplane for their final destination, Fort Worth in Texas. For some strange reason the Oswalds took an indirect flight through Atlanta, Georgia where they dropped off five suitcases. They then flew on to Dallas. Finally, on 15 June 1962, the Oswald family arrived at their new home in Texas. After many adventures and false lives, Lee Harvey Oswald had at last come home.

***

One of the enduring mysteries of Oswald's case is the almost complete lack of official interest shown in him by the US authorities. Normally when a CRYPTO-cleared technician working on top secret projects defects, there are case conferences, panic damage assessments, followed by lengthy analyses of possible related compromises of intelligence related activity by the other side. None of this happened. Even odder was the reaction of the security authorities on his return. Here he was, a defector and betrayer of his country's secrets, and nobody gave a damn. Apart from a desultory follow-up FBI interview when he reached Dallas (at which Lee was decidedly uncooperative) there is no record of any further interest in the 'traitor' who had returned from two years in the heartland of America's Cold War enemy. It didn't ring true then, and doesn't ring true now.

Yet Oswald was still a very active case and he was being run and controlled by joint DIA-FBI officers from the moment he got back from the Soviet Union. The key intelligence requirement was, would the KGB try and contact Oswald or Marina to try and run him now he was in the USA? To bait the hook the local CIA office allocated him a minder, an ex-Russian nobleman called George de Mohrenschildt. His task was to befriend the Russian-speaking Oswalds and keep them plugged into the local Russian community. As Marina didn't speak any English, this was the natural place for the Oswalds to socialise and relax, and allowed the local CIA to keep an eye on them.

George de Mohrenschildt was a long-term CIA asset and in theory the rich, aristocratic businessman was an unlikely handler for the ex-US Marine private. But as so often happens in the case with agent handlers, he took it upon himself to assume the role of father figure to his charge. The urbane, sophisticated, four times married, well-travelled oil man who spoke five languages and who knew Jackie Kennedy's family was an unlikely foil to Lee's relatively youthful but rough cut personality.

De Mohrenschildt found Lee a post with Jaggars-Chiles-Storall, a company with a contract to produce highly classified maps for the US Army, and even plotted U2 mission maps. This was the mouth-watering bait to which Oswald suddenly had access in Jaggars' notoriously insecure plant. As far as we know, the KGB wasn't tempted.

He worked diligently, sometimes doing suspiciously extra overtime in the evenings. With the failure of the mousetrap ploy, and as an experienced undercover field agent, Lee naturally looked for his next mission from his intelligence handlers. As ever, the problem was the money trail. Somehow Lee cleared his government debt. Someone was feeding Lee money because, in addition to paying off his loan, he acquired a complete and expensive spy kit consisting of a Minox camera with all the extras. Taken with the suspicious ease and speed of acquiring a new passport, there can be little doubt that Lee was preparing for another intelligence mission.

The problem was, however, that by spring 1963 Lee had a shadow: someone was impersonating him. After his arrest Oswald insisted that he had never owned a rifle. And yet on 12 March 1963, as we have seen (see section "THE VOICE OF THE GUNS"), 'A.J. Hidell' ordered a rifle and pistol by mail order from Kleist's Sporting Goods in Chicago. Assuming that Oswald was not lying, then who?

Oswald or someone calling himself Oswald opened a post office box in Dallas as 'A.J. Hidell' and US Army Intelligence held a file on him in that name; a file which they later destroyed with suspicious haste. The most likely explanation is, however, that someone was impersonating Oswald from the spring of 1963 onwards and using the 'Hidell' alias as well.

Another curious incident was Lee Harvey Oswald's supposed attack on

Major General Edwin Walker. General Walker was a classic Cold War warrior who genuinely appears to have believed that the United States was facing a Communist takeover. As commander of the 24th Division in Germany he had briefed his assembled officers and soldiers against the policies of his Commander in Chief and had also made some strident anti-Kennedy statements to his troops; he was quite clearly guilty of political indoctrination of his soldiers.

As a result the US Army swiftly removed Major General Walker from his command and quietly retired him. Walker was far from happy about this turn of events; in retirement he embarked on a series of lecture tours and publicly aired his views. Walker blamed the 'gutless, pinko-liberal conspiracy' of Communism in general, and John F. Kennedy in particular. On 12 April 1963 someone took a pot shot at General Walker in his home. Walker was unharmed. His two aides saw cars drive away and after Kennedy's death Marina Oswald told the FBI that it had been Lee. She said 'he had come in late in a panic and told her that he had buried a rifle.'

Marina was testifying under FBI control at the time. The Dallas police dug the bullet out of the wall and identified it as a 30.06 round. By the time the Warren Commission investigated it over a year later it had changed into a completely different Mannlicher–Carcano 6.5mm bullet, one that just happened to fit nicely with Lee and his supposed rifle. The point about the Walker shooting was that it showed that Lee had a Mannlicher–Carcano rifle and that he was prepared to use it. But the evidence of the whole affair is clear: Lee, the dangerous Lefty, was either really 'hunting Fascists' with his trusty Mannlicher Carcano – or someone was setting up a false story that suggested he was.

The key may lie in Oswald's next mission. De Mohrenschildt and the CIA still held him under 'tight surveillance', which in Oswald's case meant surrounding the Oswalds with a network or web of close personal contacts. These included Michael and Ruth Paine and other members of the local

Russian-speaking community who were helping the CIA. A CIA Office of Security file dated 29 April 1963 asks for a check on de Mohrenschildt. Before his death, de Mohrenschildt admitted that he had been directed to 'baby-sit' the Oswalds for the CIA and the new Defense Intelligence Agency. When De Mohrenschildt left in mid-1963 to carry out a mission in Haiti, Oswald began to re-house his family in preparation for his next assignment: Cuba.

His new interest in Cuba began abruptly in May 1963. At the height of the USA's problems with Castro, Lee Harvey Oswald suddenly moved to New Orleans and started up a one-man branch of the Fair Play for Cuba Committee (FPCC). He stood on street corners with a placard warning 'HANDS OFF CUBA!' and wrote to the national chairman of the FPCC, asking for more leaflets. The slightly puzzled chairman wrote back advising caution and suggesting that Lee should keep a low profile and not draw attention to himself. Lee did the complete opposite. In June he leafleted the crew of the aircraft carrier USS *Wasp* as she docked, handing out 'Support Castro' pamphlets to the baffled sailors, until an irritated New Orleans cop told him to move along.

From then on, Oswald seems to have ignored Cuba for two months. In fact Lee was very busy at this time. His new base was on the third floor of ex-FBI agent Guy Banister's offices, where Banister was working closely with Dave Atlee Phillips of the CIA and the two Marcello associates, Clay Shaw and David Ferrie, to penetrate the FPCC and any other dissident organisations on behalf of the FBI and CIA. Banister's company was a front for the US intelligence community and Oswald was the perfect front man for them. He was an ex-Communist, he had defected to the Soviet Union (and returned home supposedly because he didn't think it worked) and was now backing the left wing revolutionaries in Cuba. The Oswald jigsaw makes absolute sense: in 1963 he was building a 'legend' to support his next mission as an undercover agent in Cuba.

There were, inevitably, slip-ups. The pro-Castro pamphlets being passed out by Lee on the streets of New Orleans were all provided by the CIA. The second problem, as always in these affairs, was money. Oswald's two-bit jobs at Reily's [sic] Coffee Company could never have supported his level of spending. He was clearly getting extra money from somewhere (see section "THE ROAD TO DALLAS").

Part of Lee's problem in establishing the legend for his 'next mission' was that he was of considerable interest to another undercover organisation – Carlos Marcello's New Orleans Mafia. When Lee moved to New Orleans in the late spring of 1963, he stayed for a while with his Uncle Dutz, who just happened to be one of Carlos Marcello's stable of illegal local bookmakers. There is clear evidence to suggest that Lee supplemented his income in New Orleans that summer by working as a runner for Marcello's local business and at least one eyewitness saw him getting 'a wad of money ... passed under the table' in the restaurant in the Marcello organisation's building.

By summer 1963, Lee's base at 544 Camp Street had become a centre for all sorts of local anti-Castro groups, whether government, under contract to the government, or the Cuban Exiles themselves. The house at Camp Street was effectively a US intelligence clearing house and Banister was running a number of officially sanctioned operations, from spying on students across the South to setting up anti-Castro forays into Cuba.

To add to this roll call of dubious characters hanging around Camp Street was the bizarre figure of David Ferrie. He hated John Kennedy – whom he regarded as a weak-kneed liberal of the worst kind, soft on Communism and a gutless traitor over Cuba – with a deep and vocal passion. In one rant at a conference of the 'Military Order of World Wars', his attack on the US President was so offensive that the chairman insisted he step down from the podium. This was the company with whom Lee Harvey Oswald was now mixing. It was not their first encounter, either. They already knew each other because 'Captain' David Ferrie had inducted Lee Oswald into his Civilian Air Patrol in 1955, and had doubtless made a deep impact on the impressionable young 16 year old.

Lee was certainly busy with Cuba. He had gone into a store managed by an anti-Castro activist called Carlos Bringuier and expressed sympathy for the Cuban Exiles. He talked a good talk and as an ex-Marine offered to help train them. We can only imagine Bringuier's surprise a few days later when a friend told him that the same man was now handing out *pro*-Castro leaflets in the street outside the Trade Mart. Bringuier confronted Oswald and a scuffle ensued.

Purely by chance the incident was filmed by a local press and TV reporter who just happened to be passing. Oswald spent the night in jail, was arraigned two days later where he pleaded 'guilty' to a charge of disturbing the peace and was bound over and sentenced to a $10 fine. It was all most odd, especially as Bringuier had caused the punch-up. He said that he felt that the whole event was 'staged' and that Oswald 'was in control all the time'. Even odder was Oswald's discreet request to see an FBI official once he was locked up. Sure enough, an FBI agent spent over an hour with him that night in his cell.

The incident spawned a flood of publicity. Oswald became a minor celebrity on the radio. Later, during a free talk debate on TV, *Conversation Carte Blanche,* Lee made a spirited defence of his progressive views for half an hour against Bringuier. What he didn't know when he went on air was that someone had briefed the TV station and his interviewers on his FBI file and record in Russia. The whole affair smacks of a set-up; designed to get as much publicity as possible for 'Oswald, champion of Castro.' As Dave Atlee Philips was primarily a propaganda specialist, as well as being the coordinator of the CIA's operation to penetrate the Fair Play for Cuba Committee, it is safe to deduce that the altercation outside the Trade Mart and the fortunate proximity of TV cameras was a well-organised piece of CIA news management.

The whole affair was designed to build up Oswald's credentials for his next mission, to send Oswald to Cuba.

Lee was now on dangerous territory. He was pretending to be pro-Castro while working for a group of men with ties to the CIA and to the Mafia, both of which were determined to get rid of the Cuban dictator. The problem for Lee was that the CIA and the Cuban Exiles also wanted Kennedy removed one way or another; and the Mafia had a blood contract out on the American President. Lee was caught smack in the middle of all this: and he was in deep.

***

The months leading up to Oswald's arrest on 22 November 1963 are confusing and contain a number of gaps. On 17 September he obtained a visa from the Mexican Consulate in New Orleans. His tourist card was FM824085. The man who got the visa immediately before him (FM824084) just happened to be CIA officer William Gauntlet, who also just happened to have been an eyewitness to the punch-up with Bringuier outside the Trade Mart. If ever proof were needed that the CIA were keeping tight surveillance on Oswald, it is this incident. Lee would have company – in every sense – with him when he went to Mexico City to prepare for his journey to Cuba.

The Mexico trip is perhaps the most baffling piece of the jigsaw of evidence and events. Its timing, however, does make sense when tied in with the top secret White House plan to foment a coup in Cuba on 1 December 1963. What the CIA called Operation Amworld was a very pressing problem for the Kennedys and its cover plan was well documented.

The outgoing (and disgruntled) CIA Director of Assassinations and Anti-Castro Operations at the start of 1963 was William Harvey. Before he was sacked by Bobby Kennedy, Harvey had warned that there must be no trail of evidence leading back to the USA. At the request of the Joint Chiefs he drafted a memo to say that 'some pro-Castro US asset should be slipped into Cuba.' Lee Harvey Oswald was the perfect choice for such a task and met the CIA's specifications perfectly. Lee was overtly pro-Castro, pro-Russian, had defected to the USSR and had a communist background: theoretically getting him into Cuba should have been possible. Once there, he could serve two roles for the White House and CIA. He could report on and support the coup and, if the Cubela assassination against Castro failed, the CIA could abandon him to take all the blame from an infuriated Castro.

There seems little doubt that Lee, or someone very like him, did go to Mexico City and did stay at the Hotel Commercio on 26 September. However, there is something definitely odd about the man calling himself Lee Oswald who turned up at the Cuban Consul's office on Tuesday, 27 September and visited it over the next few days. The clerk who dealt with him was called Silvia Duran and she remembered 'Oswald' very well. Duran described 'her' Oswald as being a short 5'4" and with 'dark-blondish hair' and different features to the man arrested after Kennedy's death. When he was told that he could not have a transit visa to Cuba, 'Oswald' went round to the Soviet Embassy and returned that afternoon, claiming that the Russians were prepared to give him an immediate visa.

Duran thought this odd and telephoned the Soviet Embassy who told her that 'Oswald' was lying.

When 'Oswald' was finally told that he could not get travel documentation to Cuba he had a blazing row with the Cuban Consul himself and stormed round to the Soviet Embassy where he got short shrift. Later when he telephoned the Embassy, the CIA bugged the call. This 'Oswald' couldn't even speak proper Russian. The surveillance photograph grudgingly provided later by the CIA is emphatically *not* Lee Harvey Oswald. When later confronted with this allegation, the CIA changed their story, even claiming that their camera covering the Soviet Embassy had been 'out of order for that period'.

Someone was also building a legend for the real Lee Harvey Oswald back in Texas. That someone was almost certainly a man called William Seymour, from Phoenix, Arizona, who was an Oswald lookalike. Seymour just happened to be the same size and weight as Lee Harvey Oswald and, more important, could easily pass as Oswald's twin. Seymour took the name 'Leon Oswald' in the summer of 1963 and acquired a set of false identification papers in that name. But Billy Seymour may not have been the only fake 'Lee Oswald' planting a false trail of evidence in Mexico, New Orleans, Montreal and Dallas. Witnesses saw an angry Jack Ruby throwing another man 'who could pass for Oswald' out of his nightclub in the autumn of 1963 and shouting, 'I told you never to come in here!'

A private detective called David L. Lewis actually saw 'Leon Oswald' in 1963 and identified him as Seymour. Bannister's secretary remembers Carlos Quiroga, one of the anti-Castro Cubans, introducing a person resembling Lee Harvey Oswald as 'Leon Oswald' to Lewis and herself. On another occasion when Lewis was leaving Bannister's office he bumped into 'Leon Oswald', alias William Seymour, and some days later walked in on a meeting in Bannister's office between Bannister, Quiroga, David Ferrie, and Seymour ('Leon Oswald'). Lewis was quite clear that this was not Lee Harvey Oswald but 'someone who looked very much like him.' Someone was using Oswald's identity to set up a story.

***

Sightings of the fake Lee Harvey Oswald continued throughout October and November 1963. He even pops up as far away as Atlanta, Georgia in October on his way to Chicago, where he was also reportedly seen a long way north at the University of Illinois in the company of Guy Banister just before President Kennedy came to the Windy City. Just to make sure there was a solid record of his movements, the Oswald in Atlanta helpfully left a pistol in his hotel room on checking out and the hotel had to track him down to return it, an action so blatantly indiscreet that it would be bound to be remembered. David Ferrie's telephone records support this visit; someone called him long distance collect from both Atlanta and Chicago at that time.

The question was, then, who were they? And who was responsible for setting up the American low-level intelligence operator for a fall? And why? It wasn't the KGB. It couldn't be

Castro, and the Mafia didn't have those kinds of resources. But the CIA did.

As he sat in his cell in Dallas Police Station on the evening of 22 November 1963, nursing his black eye and a murder charge, 'the man who lived three lives' must have wondered what the hell was going on. His despairing words to the police after his arrest give the game away: 'Now everyone will know who I am.' Lee Harvey Oswald's boyhood dream of being a James Bond spy and his career as an undercover operator and secret agent was finished.

Now he waited to see what fate had in store for him.

27

FROM A VIEW TO A KILL – JACK RUBY AND OSWALD'S MURDER

TO GRIM NECESSITY; AND HE AND I WILL KEEP A LEAGUE UNTO DEATH
SHAKESPEARE, *RICHARD II*

What fate had in store for him was a small time Jewish gangster called Jacob Rubenstein, better known as 'Jack Ruby'.

A typical product of the mean streets of Chicago in the early years of the twentieth century, Ruby fitted the mobster profile, having been schooled in the hard world of the Chicago underworld. He was quick with his fists, even quicker to anger – hence his nickname 'Sparky' – and treated violence and crime as part of his trade. Whether he was a 'made' Mafia member (that is, someone who had 'made his bones' by killing someone to order) is unclear, but unlikely.

What is clear is that the Chicago family trusted him and in 1947/48 Ruby was moved to Dallas to help establish and run the new Mafia 'chapter' in Texas. The Mob only got the chance to move in because the local Dallas thieves had fallen out. Having made sure that they had permission from Carlos Marcello, the Louisiana and New Orleans Godfather, the Chicago boys moved quietly into Dallas. In crime, as in everything else, nature abhors a vacuum.

One of Jack Ruby's other Mob duties was to 'square' the Dallas Police Department. The American Mafia survived, and thrived, only when the cops were not too diligent, or when intelligent policemen saw the benefits of the totally unregulated, selfadjusting market in specialised – but much in demand – goods and services. Jack Ruby appears to have oiled the wheels with the authorities very well. His stocky, cheerful face was well known to patrolmen and police chiefs alike, down at the Dallas Police HQ. His night club offered free drinks and engaging female company to the bored off-duty members of 'Dallas's Finest', and the occasional brown envelope went some way to ensuring that even the lowest paid patrolman had something to put into his kids' Christmas stockings. Jack Ruby was nothing less than organised crime's 'liaison officer' to the Dallas Police Force. In the 16 years from 1947 to 1963, he was arrested no fewer than nine times for offences from running a bawdy house to hitting an off-duty cop. Despite numerous run-ins with the Dallas Liquor Licensing Board, his only conviction was a $35 fine for failing to pay a parking ticket.

As well as his drugs, gambling, and bribing police officers, Jack Ruby had another profitable sideline. He was a gun-runner. As Castro's revolutionaries gradually came down from the hills in Cuba and began to close in on the Batista regime, they needed arms. The Mafia, obliging as ever, moved to fill this gap in the market. Shrewd racketeering brains like Meyer Lansky and Santo Trafficante reasoned that if they supported Castro discreetly behind the scenes, if (or when) he ever managed to overthrow Batista, the bearded Revolutionary would be suitably grateful and look favourably on the Mob's glittering casinos, drug parlours and prostitutes in downtown Havana. They were to be disappointed, because within a year he moved to close them down and throw the Mobsters in jail.

At that point the Mafia decided that it was time to find some new customers. Having supplied Castro with arms and ammunition, they now offered their lethal wares to his enemies, the Cuban Exiles. Moreover, on this occasion they did it with the approval and connivance of the United States government itself. Jack Ruby was at the heart of it all, even storing large shipments of arms and ammunition in a house near the coast in Texas. Even the US government got in on the act. There is evidence to suggest that the CIA may have orchestrated a fake 'break-in' to a Federal armoury aimed at passing the latest US arms to the anti-Castro rebels while being able to deny any official involvement. The gun-running business also attracted big names: Frank Fiorini, better known as Frank Sturgis, CIA contract agent; Santo Trafficante; Loran Hall of the International Anti-Communist Brigade (whose members included David Ferrie); and a French-Canadian called Lucien Rivard, whose base in Toronto and Montreal was the Canadian end of the 'French Connection' drugsmuggling racket. They were all involved. Jack Ruby worked with, and sometimes for, them all. He was no small-time Damon Runyonesque nightclub owner, as the Warren Report tried to claim. Ruby was a paid-up soldier of the Mafia. Just to be on the safe side, he was also acting as an FBI informer, reporting to an Agent Charles Flynn.

In the weeks and days before the assassination, Jack had been busier than usual. He had renewed contact with his fellow gangster and role model, a suave Las Vegas hood called Lewis McWillie, and made contact with a number of other heavyweight underworld players. Ruby's phone calls increased exponentially. In the first three weeks of November alone he made over 100 out-ofstate long distance calls.

He was also a very worried man. Ruby owed the IRS over $40,000 in unpaid taxes and the Feds were after him for his arrears. However, in the weeks before the assassination Jack Ruby suddenly came into money. A British businessman witnessed him being handed 'a one inch thick envelope full of money' at a Chicago Coffee house on 27/28 October 1963, and on the afternoon of the assassination he was in his Dallas bank clutching $7,000 in notes. What is curious is that his only recorded bank transaction that day was a $31 cash withdrawal. We can even work out where Ruby stored the money he received in Chicago. In the first week of November he had a brand new safe installed in his office. To further support the evidence that Ruby had suddenly acquired big money, he was heard talking about going on a Caribbean cruise and moving to a new apartment at double the rent. For a notoriously cash-strapped owner of a failing nightclub this was unusual behaviour.

We will never know for sure what the money was for, but Ruby's actions over that fateful weekend give us a pretty good idea. This sudden largesse points to a pay-off. Ruby was given a job he couldn't refuse – kill Oswald – and the money came from Jimmy Hoffa and the Mafia. Once the money was received, Ruby packed his gun into his waist and went out to begin stalking 'the man who had shot the President', now languishing as a prisoner in the Dallas Police headquarters.

The prisoner in question was having an unusual time at the hands of the police. For 12 of the total of 48 hours he was in custody, Lee Harvey Oswald was questioned by Captain Will Fritz, Chief of Homicide. Fritz was an experienced and patient interrogator. If we are to believe the DPD and the Warren Report, there was no stenographer present, no tape recording and no notes were taken at any of the Oswald interviews. This is clearly nonsense. The Assassinations Records Review Board found some reconstructed notes by Fritz in 1999 and Oswald himself said petulantly at one point to

Fritz, 'look it up for yourself. You took notes, didn't you?' Another possible reason for the lack of documentation is that Oswald may have said that he was an undercover DIA/FBI agent and asked for no record until his credentials had been checked. If so, he was to be sorely disappointed. His secret masters had disowned him and hung him out to dry.

Captain Fritz talked to Lee from 14.25 to 16.04 on the day he was arrested. Oswald seems to have been reasonably honest, although he denied ever having been in Mexico City. However, if he was still trying to maintain his cover, that would make sense. He denied owning a rifle and was quite open about his time in the USSR. Oddly, he claimed that he had received an award for marksmanship in the USMC.

Lee was then dragged out to take part in a line-up for Mrs Markham, the woman who had seen the Tippit shooting in Oak Cliff. Also among the crowded corridors of Dallas Police HQ was Jack Ruby who even tried to get in to the room where Oswald was being questioned but was stopped by two cops who said 'You can't go in there, Jack.' Thwarted, Ruby then went off to his synagogue where a memorial service was being held for the murdered President. According to witnesses he seemed 'depressed, down'. This seems reasonable, as any order to pull a pistol and gun down a prime suspect in a police station in front of wellarmed Texas cops was always going to be a high-risk enterprise.

Lee meanwhile was complaining bitterly about being railroaded by a manifestly rigged identity parade and continued his complaints in Capt. Fritz's office. He asked for a New York lawyer, Mr Abt of the ACLU, and strongly denied that he had ever ordered any guns by mail order. At this time, Sheriff Roger recorded that Lee said despondently, 'Everyone will know who I am now.' At 18.30 he was taken out for another line-up and took the opportunity to yell to reporters, 'I didn't shoot anyone ... I never killed anybody.' At 19.10 he was arraigned and charged with the Tippit murder.

By 20.00, after yet another line-up, Lee was getting fractious. He had every reason to be. He had still not had access to a lawyer or a telephone, and the police identification parades had descended into farce. Bill Whaley, the taxi driver who had driven Lee home from the depository on the Friday, gives us a good flavour of the atmosphere in the DPD headquarters building that evening.

> You could have picked Oswald out without identifying him just by listening to him, because he was bawling at the policemen, he showed no respect for the policeman, he told them what he thought of them ... how they were trying to railroad him and he wanted his lawyer ... Anybody who wasn't sure could have picked out the right one just for that.

Once out of the line up, Lee again demanded a lawyer and said he didn't care to talk anymore. He was then fingerprinted and given the gunshot residue paraffin test. He reacted to this with scorn, telling the police 'I never fired any gun.' At 22.45 he was finally allowed to make his phone call. He elected to call a number in Raleigh, North Carolina, 919 834 7430. The telephone operator in the Dallas Police HQ was a Mrs Swinney and she logged the number person-to-person with a Mr Hurt.

Two federal agents then came into the telephone exchange and instructed Mrs Swinney to pull the plug and tell Oswald that there was no answer from the number he had requested. Mrs Swinney did so and threw the note with the number into the trashcan. Her colleague was a Mrs Troon who later retrieved Mrs Sinney's crumpled note from the waste bin. Many years later it surfaced in a Freedom of Information case; but Lee never got his phone call that night. When the number was eventually checked out it turned out to be one Lt Col (Retd) Hurt, an ex-military intelligence officer. Raleigh in Carolina just happened to be the centre for the secret ONI programme to send defectors to the USSR. It seems that Lee was trying – unsuccessfully – to call home to his handlers at Nag's

Head. But Lee was now an intelligence leper.

Later that evening Jack Ruby was back at the police station, looking for another chance to get close to Oswald. He had brought sandwiches for the officers on duty for what looked like a long night and he appears to have been given the run of the place. He even managed to get into the press conference by saying that he was writing for a Jewish periodical. It was at this gathering that he corrected District Attorney Henry Wade who had announced that Oswald was a member of the 'Free Cuba Committee'. Jack corrected him, saying 'No, that's the Fair Play for Cuba Committee.' Having confirmed that he got his black eye from the police, Lee denied shooting the President.

He was then led to a cell, only to be hauled out again at 1.35 to be arraigned for the murder of President John F. Kennedy. Captain Fritz later claimed privately to colleagues that the new President, Lyndon Baines Johnson, had actually telephoned him personally to say, 'You've got your man; the investigation is over.' A stunned Lee Harvey Oswald was then led back to his cell, still demanding to see a lawyer and locked up for the night.

Next morning Lee was re-examined. He admitted using the name 'Alik Hidell' as part of his FPCC role, but staunchly denied owning a rifle. He confirmed that he had 'a lot' of personal belongings stored in sea-bags in the Paines' garage. Later he was visited by his mother Marguerite and his brother, and took part in yet another rigged ID parade. Finally at about 17.30 the accused assassin got a lawyer of sorts. He received a brief official visit from H. Louis Nichols, President of the Dallas Bar. By 1800 he was back in Fritz's office, where he was confronted with the famous back-yard photographs.

For once Lee seems to have been jolted out of his composure. He denied that the picture was of him. His exact words echo his reaction to the image in front of him.

> This picture is not mine but the face is mine. The picture has been made by superimposing my face. The other part of the picture is not

me at all and I have never seen this picture before ... I will be able to show you that is not my picture and has been made by someone else ... It is entirely possible that the Police Department has superimposed this part of the photograph over the body of someone else.

Lee had every right to be startled by the notorious photographs. They were obviously faked. Moreover, the discovery many years later in the Dallas police archives of a master copy of a photograph of his famous 'back-yard' picture with a blank cut out silhouette superimposed on it gives the game away.

Jack Ruby was dashing all over Dallas that Saturday. He went to Police HQ at least three times, always asking the same question: did anyone know when Oswald was being transferred to the County Jail? In the early hours of Sunday 24 November, he made an anonymous telephone call to the Dallas FBI and the Police warning them that 'a committee had decided to kill the man who killed the President,' and ended up by saying, 'you're going to have to make some other plans or we're going to kill Oswald there in the basement.' The officer who took the call (and reported it) thought at the time that the voice was vaguely familiar. Next morning – too late – he remembered. It was Jack Ruby.

The only logical explanation for this curious behaviour is that Ruby was trying to make his Mafia mission impossible. Whoever tried to shoot Oswald stood a good chance of being gunned down himself by a number of enraged and trigger-happy Texas law enforcement officers. Ruby may well have reasoned also that if he had been bribed to silence Oswald, then maybe one of Dallas's Finest may have been paid to shoot and silence him in his turn. However, Ruby may have calculated that if he couldn't get close enough to Oswald because of tight security, then he couldn't reasonably be blamed for failing in his mission. Unfortunately for Ruby, and for Oswald, the Dallas Police failed to make any security changes. Ruby went back to his apartment and waited for the morning. It would be his last chance to earn his money and it would be extremely dangerous.

On the day Jack Ruby had some help. It was none other than Sam Bloom, the Dallas Citizens' PR man who suggested that the Dallas Police make Oswald accessible to the press. He also suggested – against the explicit advice of the local FBI – that they move the alleged assassin from the Dallas police station to the Dallas County Jail in order to give the newsmen a good story and pictures. Dallas FBI agent James Hosty always believed that Bloom and Ruby were in cahoots; when the police later searched Ruby's home, they found a slip of paper with Bloom's name, address and telephone number on it.

***

At 9.30a.m. on Sunday 24 November, Lee was handcuffed to an officer and taken by elevator down to the basement. Ruby turned up twice – once at 10.00, the scheduled move time, and again at 11.20, the real move time. He slipped down a side alley, let himself in by a supposedly unlocked fire door on the ground floor, and then mingled with the throng of reporters waiting to film the transfer of the 'man who shot the President' to the County Jail.

At 11.20 the elevator door slid open and Oswald was led out between Officers Groves and Leavelles of the Homicide Squad. Someone shouted 'Here he comes' and the press pack surged forward into action, firing flashlight bulbs and shouting questions. As Oswald emerged dazzled by the TV lights, a car horn sounded a single short blast. Jack Ruby pulled out his .38 special, stepped forward from behind the cover of Officer Harrison – who, like so many of the Dallas Police, knew Ruby well – and rammed the pistol at Lee's stomach. Detective Leavelles jerked the handcuffs to try and save his prisoner but only succeeded in turning him before the revolver boomed out in the basement in front of a horrified worldwide TV audience. Oswald's face contorted in shock and agony. The wound was mortal.

In the ambulance the frantic medics asked the dying Oswald if he had anything to say. The 'man who lived three lives' just shook his head and slipped into unconsciousness.

The key witness in the whole Kennedy conspiracy had been silenced forever. Jack Ruby had done his job.

PART 5

THE GREAT COVER-UP

28

COVERING THE TRACKS

EVIL IS FOSTERED AND DEVELOPED BY CONCEALMENT
VIRGIL

Despite the fact that he was now facing a death sentence, the first person to sigh with relief on being told that Lee Harvey Oswald had died was Jack Ruby. Once he heard the news that his target was silenced for ever, Ruby relaxed visibly. When an officer reminded him that he now faced the electric chair for firstdegree homicide, he even smiled.

In South Carolina, Joseph Milteer, the man who had predicted that Kennedy would be shot by a sniper from a tall building, heard the news and turned to Somersett, the FBI informer, saying, 'that makes it work perfect, now we have no worry.' Milteer also told Somersett the day after the assassination, that 'a big Jew' had been responsible for the conspiracy. The FBI transcript of his statement recorded, 'there is a Communist conspiracy by Jews to overthrow the United States,' and later in the same field report, 'the Zionist Jews killed Christ 2000 years ago and on 22 November 1963 they killed the President of the United States.'

This might normally be discounted as the ravings of some right-wing militant white supremacist, but Milteer proved his reliability by being one of the very few people who had predicted in advance that Kennedy was going to be killed and how. His words must therefore be weighed carefully. He genuinely believed that there was some kind of Jewish influence at work.

While Oswald was still alive and beginning to realise that he was being set up, he was an extremely serious threat. If he lived to go to trial, the whole story would come out. Although he would not have known about the Kennedys' secret plot to support a Cuban coup, Oswald probably knew that something big was being planned in Cuba soon. Given his background as a secret agent and his links with Guy Banister and 544 Camp Street, there is every reason to believe that he may have been given orders by his CIA/FBI controllers to 'penetrate and report on a plot to assassinate the President.' This would be ideal cover to infiltrate the plot – but it would also make it easy to set him up as a patsy.

One obvious ploy would have been to place him at the scene for the attempt, telling him 'he could take the story with him to Cuba to boost his legend or cover story', and that the whole assassination attempt was all being faked for his benefit. He may have even been told that the gunmen would shoot to miss, or that it was some test of 'presidential security'.

He carried the identities of his CIA and Mafia contacts in his head. On no account could Lee be allowed to live and talk. That is almost certainly the real story behind the mysterious killing of Officer Tippit. Lee was trying to make contact with someone when he went to the Texas Theatre and an aeroplane was definitely revving up at Redbird airstrip that afternoon, waiting for a passenger who failed to turn up.

There is hard evidence that Lee Harvey Oswald was planning to fly out on the afternoon of 22 November. According to Wayne January, a partner in a light aviation business based at Redbird airstrip, someone tried to hire him on 20 November. Wayne was officially listed by the CIA as 'a reliable contact'. On the Wednesday before the assassination 'a hippie-looking' couple approached him asking for a flight on the 20th. Wayne was suspicious. He refused and advised them to ask a neighbouring company in the next hangar. There was a third member of the group who stayed in the car. Wayne got a close look at the young man. Two days later when the television pictures flashed round the world, he realised that he had seen someone who looked very like Lee Harvey Oswald. Was Officer Tippit's role to take Lee to Redbird? Was he meant to set up the killing of Oswald 'on the run'?

Someone else who took an unusually close interest in Oswald's death was Lyndon Baines Johnson. According to Dr Crenshaw, while he was working unsuccessfully in the Dallas Parkland Hospital to save the life of Lee Harvey Oswald that Sunday morning, he was summoned to the telephone to take a call from the White House. The new President pestered him to know if Oswald was still alive and had he made a deathbed confession?

There is no reason for Dr Crenshaw to have invented the story and he stuck to it until the day he died. If true, it is a curious thing for a President to do, particularly one who grumbled that 'the White House couldn't get involved in every two-bit shooting in Texas.' A number of other people were very anxious indeed to know if Oswald was dead because if there was evidence of more than one gunman being involved and working across a state line, it also became a federal matter for the Attorney General.

The notion of a vengeful Bobby Kennedy giving direct orders to the FBI and vigorously pursuing the investigation into his dead brother's murder sent chills down a number of spines, not least that of J. Edgar Hoover. The murder had to be made to look like the work of a single gunman, at all costs. The problem was that there was no concrete evidence that Oswald had actually killed anyone. The eyewitness evidence was dubious, despite the FBI's novel 'witness direction programme'. For example, in one notorious incident with Dick Carr the FBI told him, 'if you didn't see Lee Harvey Oswald in the school book depository with a rifle, you didn't witness it.'

Carr was just about to testify at Jim Garrison's 1969 indictment of Clay Shaw in New Orleans when someone took a shot at him. Later, in Atlanta, Carr was attacked again. He was stabbed in the arm and back but managed to pull out his pistol and kill one of his assailants. Mr Carr would have made a very disconcerting eyewitness had he ever gone on the stand at any trial. Even Dallas Police Chief Curry had said that he 'couldn't place Oswald with a rifle in the depository' and had not ruled out a second gunman until the new President and J. Edgar Hoover telephoned him personally to give him a little advice on attitude adjustment.

If there was no evidence, then the answer was simple: create some. On 25 November, the day following his death, an FBI fingerprint team, with a camera and a crime lab kit, spent a long time in the morgue. One FBI agent even confessed to smuggling the disassembled rifle barrel into the funeral parlour and pressing the dead man's hand around it.

It will come as no surprise, therefore, that the Mannlicher-Carcano rifle had by the 26th suddenly acquired a clearly identifiable Oswald palm print on the metal part of the rifle barrel. The fingerprints linked him directly to the rifle. The DA announced this important news in response at press conference. Oswald was guilty: case closed.

***

Now, with Oswald silenced, the real work of the cover-up operation could begin. It has been a massive and well-planned deception plan, remarkable for both its longevity and the resources dedicated to it, from eminent scientists and academics parroting the Government line, to some neighbourhood muscle putting the heat on witnesses either by intimidation, disappearance or murder.

The damage control began the moment the guns stopped firing. Fake Secret Service agents blocked any swift followup by flashing forged credentials and stopping pursuers rushing up the grassy knoll for a few vital seconds. Fake IDs, fake Secret Servicemen and knowledge of genuine procedures all helped the getaway of the gunmen and their accomplices. As time stood still for the onlookers, every second counted for the conspirators.

However, one group in particular appears to have been caught by surprise by the events in Dealey Plaza. There is evidence of a sudden panic in in the Office of Naval Intelligence. On the night of 22 November officers were called back to their offices and spent a frantic two hours destroying their files on Lee Harvey Oswald and his activities since returning from the USSR. For any Washington-led cover-up to work, all the evidence about Lee had to be 'sanitised'.

One piece of evidence eluded them initially. Abe Zapruder's film could have been extremely damaging. Fortunately with the purchase and suppression of the film by the notoriously anti-Kennedy and pro-CIA mouthpiece, *Life* magazine, the next two phases of the operation could begin: planting false evidence and pumping out the false line for the media to publish.

Planting the evidence was not difficult. All it required were three empty 6.5 Mannlicher-Carcano cases on the sixth floor of the depository and then the Mannlicher-Carcano rifle itself. Unfortunately for the plotters, it was the wrong type of Mannlicher-Carcano and it didn't work – but none of that came out until years later. What did emerge fairly quickly was that the rifle found in the 'sniper's nest' was not the gun being held by Oswald in the notorious back yard photographs published by *Life* magazine in February 1964. The Mannlicher-Carcano proudly held aloft for the Press by Lt Day of the Dallas Police on 23 November 1963 had a clear groove along its wooden stock. The rifle on the *Life* cover, 'the weapon used to kill President John F. Kennedy', did not. But that error was three months in the future. The real task for the cover-up plan on 22 November was to get the plotters' version of events into the press quickly and to plant the idea that there was only one gunman involved and he was a 'lone nut'.

One foreign newspaper had solved the case already – and suspiciously early, too. The paper was the *Christchurch Star* based in New Zealand. JFK was hit at 12.30p.m. on Nov 22, Dallas time, which was 7.30a.m. on the 23rd in New Zealand, across the International Date Line. But the *Christchurch Star* was on the streets in New Zealand by about 13.00 NZ time, carrying a highly detailed front page spread all about Lee Harvey Oswald and the President's death.

According to the *Star* story, Oswald had been arrested initially as a suspect in the killing of a Dallas policeman. He had been brought to the Police HQ in Dallas at about 14.00 US – 9.00 NZ. But Oswald's story only *started* to break to the newsrooms at about 15.30 US, which was about 10.30 in NZ: only three hours after the first news of the shooting. Somehow this newspaper on the far side of the world, which went to the final presses between 10.30 and 11.00 NZ, had assembled a complete front page news and feature spread from scratch in less than an hour. The newspaper had to have assembled and typed their basic story from fragmentary wire services and telephone, then collected, collated and written the full story and got it to the compositors and then onto the presses – this was in the days before word processors and computers – by not much later than 11.00 NZ time. Either the New Zealand newspaper story had benefited from some pre-briefing, or the *Christchurch Star* had assembled an incredibly high-powered newsroom of phenomenally prescient and accurate reporters in the days long before e-mails, Google and the internet.

The New Zealand story stated that Lee Harvey Oswald was the 'prime suspect in the assassination of the President'. It seems that the *Christchurch Star* already had a good picture of Oswald, a picture of the depository with an arrow pointing to the sixth-floor window, plus a very detailed biography of the alleged perpetrator, including his discharge from the US Marines, his defection and stay in Russia, his marriage to Marina, and his 'chairmanship' of the FPCC. And the *Christchurch Star* had done all this within three hours of Oswald's arrest on the far side of the world and *before he had even been charged with the murder of Officer Tippit.* It is clear that someone had been giving the publication a helping hand. The question is, who?

This egregious piece of investigative journalism was swiftly followed by a barrage of heavyweight reports in the serious US press, all pushing the same line: the President had been shot by lone assassin, Lee Harvey Oswald. The *New York Times* headline on the 23rd set the scene: **KENNEDY IS KILLED BY SNIPER.** The rest of the world's press followed suit without query. There had clearly been a prepared press 'line'. The same picture of Oswald appears in nearly all the papers. Where did they all get it from? The biographical detail on Oswald could only have come for one single source. Someone had prepared a briefing package and had it ready to use before the shooting took place.

Another story in the *New York Times* is even more revealing. At a time when even Captain Fritz of the Dallas Police was convinced that the prisoner sitting in front of him was perfectly sane and normal, the *New York Times* published a feature article that Oswald was a disturbed and violent individual. There is no way that the newspaper could have known about the suspect's mental condition, but the 'crazed lone nut' story would be trumpeted over and over again. It was a propaganda triumph. The American press compliantly printed the story the government wanted told and virtually nothing else.

The source of all these stories was originally J. Edgar Hoover. He and his FBI were briefing and leaking 'Oswald the lone nut gunman' to anyone who would listen from 15.30 on the afternoon of Kennedy's murder onwards. Even on the plane bringing Kennedy's Vietnam Policy Group back from Hawaii on the afternoon of the 22nd they were being briefed on 'Oswald the Lone Assassin'. The individual leading the Kennedy case in the FBI was Alan Belmont, Director of the FBI's Domestic Intelligence Division. Two days later on the day of Oswald's death he minuted his boss to stitch up the case once and for all.

> We are sending [two investigators] to Dallas ... for the purpose of going carefully over written interview and investigative findings of our agents in the Oswald matter so that we can prepare a memorandum ... attaching exhibits such as photographs etc. to set out the evidence showing that Oswald is responsible for the shooting ...

we will show that Oswald was an avowed Marxist, a former defector to the Soviet Union and an active member of the FPCC, which has been financed by Castro ... and the story of what happened when the President was shot and subsequently until Oswald was picked up at the theatre. We will set forth the items of evidence which make it clear that Oswald is the man who killed the President.

Apart from blowing a huge hole in the statement that 'no notes were ever taken of any of the interviews with Oswald,' this memo exposed the official news spin. The CIA-penetrated US media cooperated enthusiastically and parroted this story exactly from 25 November onwards. The CIA's Operation Mockingbird had planted over 400 journalists working directly for the CIA by 1963. Those who were not already working for the Feds found that their bosses and proprietors were only too happy to help the boys at Langley.

***

The problem of manipulating the dead President's wounds to match the story was trickier. The doctors and trauma team at Dallas's Parkland Hospital knew that the President had been shot by a small calibre bullet in the throat and by an 'exploding' bullet in the right temple, which had blown a hand sized hole out of the back of his head. Governor Connally had been shot from behind through the chest and in the right wrist and left thigh. The medical evidence pointed to a hail of bullets from at least two gunmen, if not more.

To cover this up required a criminal act of such breathtaking audacity as to rival the murder itself. The plotters stole the body and cut it to match the story that had been sold to the press. In order for the 'lone gunman' story to stick, its success hinged on two key factors: firstly, altering the existing wounds to fit the bullet holes 'from behind' theory; secondly, convincing the medical staff at Parklands that they had not seen everything. David S. Lifton's detailed researches and findings were published in 1980 and led to one inescapable conclusion: someone did tamper with John Fitzgerald Kennedy's body between it leaving Parkland Hospital in Dallas and it arriving at the Bethesda Naval Hospital in Washington.

Someone switched the coffins. The body that arrived at Bethesda arrived in a different coffin to the one that left Dallas. It could only have been switched in three places: on the way to Love Field in Dallas, where the bronze casket had been loaded onto Air Force One in the full view of the world's TV cameras; in flight to Washington; or on arrival in Washington. During the flight, the senior military aide in the party had radioed ahead to demand an ambulance to Walter Reed Army Hospital.

But the presidential party was greeted by *two* ambulances. A grey Navy ambulance accompanied Jacqueline Kennedy and the bronze casket to the front door of the Bethesda. There was, however, another black civilian hearse-ambulance which had already unloaded a coffin containing the dead body at the back door of the hospital, at least 20 minutes earlier. The Chief Naval NCO on duty that night saw it all and is adamant in his version, as are the all the Washington medical corpsmen who received the body. It all supports the theory that the body was cut and altered somewhere *en route* because, in a bizarre tale of two hospitals, the wounds on the body on the slab at Bethesda do not match the wounds on the body that left Parkland in Dallas.

The head in Dallas had apparently been shot from the front; and the head in Washington appeared to have been shot from behind. In the chaotic bear garden of the Washington autopsy, someone – probably Dr Humes – shouted, 'Who's in charge here?' to which Admiral Berkley, the President's tame physician, snapped, 'I am!' and proceeded to direct the doctors as they worked on the body. Dr Finck even admitted on oath at the Garrison trial of Clay Shaw in 1969 that he had not fully investigated or probed the President's wounds, on the direct orders of an unidentified senior officer, adding, 'When you are a Lt Col in the Army, you just follow orders, and at the end of the autopsy we were specifically told

... as I recall it by Admiral Kenney, the Surgeon General of the Navy, not to discuss the case.'

According to the Bethesda autopsy report, the President had been shot from behind in the right shoulder where it joins the neck – in fact nearly 6" above the real back wound which was in the shoulder blade, and he had an 'entrance wound' at the *back* of his skull and an '*exit* wound' high on the right skull above the ear. The throat wound suddenly became an 'exit wound' for the bullet in the back of the neck. Afterwards Dr Humes burned all his original autopsy notes and substituted a more 'acceptable' set, as he later admitted on oath in his testimony to the Warren Commission (1964), the House Select Committee on Assassinations (1976) and finally, in more detail, at the Assassinations Records Review Board (1996).

He also admitted that he had destroyed the draft *report* of the autopsy as well, because it 'was blood stained'. This was, unfortunately for posterity, also the copy that included his medical colleagues' detailed contemporary notes.

When questioned about this on oath at the ARRB in 1996, a clearly uneasy Commander Humes denied any pressure from his superiors or the Secret Service to alter his preliminary report, despite clear evidence to the contrary from the sworn testimony of other ARRB witnesses. He claimed that he burned his notes because 'they had bloodstains on them' and admitted that the final autopsy report differed from his burned preliminary autopsy report. Finally, he claimed said that he 'couldn't recollect across the years'.

David Lifton investigated the detailed history of the autopsy, interviewing all those involved and uncovering a string of anomalies and contradictory statements. He concludes that there has been a blatant and orchestrated alteration of the wounds and their true evidence. He believes that the body was switched to the cheap transit coffin probably during the public swearing-in of LBJ then quietly taken out of the right rear door of Air Force One at Washington, while the TV cameras were filming the stately removal of the now empty bronze coffin on the left-hand side of the aircraft. This would have allowed at least 20 minutes to make the necessary 'adjustments' to the corpse en route to the Bethesda. It would also explain the fresh bleeding discovered when the body was unwrapped in the hospital. The botched autopsy (described by the President of the American Academy of Forensic Medicine as 'extremely superficial and sloppy, inept, incomplete ... and incompetent') did however unearth one valuable clue. The three harassed doctors discovered a 'small bullet' in Jack Kennedy's lung, obviously the small calibre bullet that had punctured his throat and then disappeared. They handed it to the FBI Agents present as evidence, and even got a receipt from the FBI 'for a missile removed during examination of the body.' It has never been seen again.

But one person was forgotten by the plotters. The embalmer's notes give the game away. Thomas Robinson, one of JFK's embalmers, was adamant that the President's wounds were indicative of a

headshot from the front. His verbatim embalming notes state:
- **Large gaping hole in back of head**
- **Smaller wound right temple, crescent shape, flapped down (3")**
- **(Approx. 2) small shrapnel wounds in face**
- **Wound in back (5 to 6 inches) below shoulder to the right of backbone**
- **Adrenalin gland and brain removed**
- **Other organs removed and then put back**
- **No swelling or discolouration to face (died instantly)**

The second problem for the cover-up was getting the Parkland medical staff to change their story. They all agreed that JFK was shot in the right temple. Even the presidential press spokesman pointed to his right temple during that first hasty press conference in Dallas. Now the doctors had to be made to cast doubt on that version.

Dr Perry was the man who had worked on and had the best view of the wound in the President's throat. His statements that it was an entrance wound were unequivocal. Dr Perry was in a curious position. He had seen the throat entrance wound very clearly but had also effectively 'destroyed the evidence' when he cut it open to turn it into a tracheotomy. Dr Perry grudgingly acceded to the government line. One sharp reporter on the *St Louis Post-Dispatch* spotted the change and identified where the pressure had come from. On 18 December, his story was:

AFTER VISIT BY AGENTS, DOCTORS SAY SHOT WAS FROM REAR

The doctors' dilemma was apparently resolved by showing them the 'official' autopsy report. Coupled with the fact that the Dallas doctors had been working under great pressure for only 22 minutes with Kennedy, their memories of events were inevitably fragmentary. They must have felt a twinge of professional unease when they learned that they had completely missed the President's back wound. Had they actually been giving out misleading information to the press? The Dallas doctors backed off; leaving the official medical evidence to the Washington team and Commander Humes.

There remained just one more area that needed to be covered up: the scene of the crime. The 'STEMMONS' sign with its incriminating bullet hole was taken down never to be seen again. The chipped kerbstone near James Tague was replaced; the bullets found in the grass were quietly slipped into the pocket of Federal Agents, real or impostors. Only one more area had to be cleared up: the presidential limousine itself. The car was a crucial source of evidence. So it is with some surprise that we discover that the Secret Service wasted no time in destroying that evidence of the crime scene too.

When the stretch Ford Lincoln Continental made it to the Parkland it was carrying at least three vital pieces of information. There were both blood and brains in the car; there were bullet fragments on the floor; and there was a bullet hole in the windscreen. Sgt. Ellis of the Dallas Police who escorted the car to Parkland was quite clear:

'you could have put a pencil through it.' Photographs confirm this, but there was pressure on Ellis to ignore the evidence: 'some Secret Service agent ran up [and] said, "That's no bullet hole. That's a fragment!" It wasn't a damn fragment. It was a hole.' The Secret Service ordered a policeman to stand guard on the limo and forbade any more photography. They then began to wash the blood off the car with a bucket of water, thus destroying vital evidence. For professional law enforcement and security officers this was suspicious behaviour.

By 13.09 the Secret Service quickly drove the car back to Love Field where they loaded 100-X onto the waiting C-130 Hercules, which took off, landing in Washington at 20.05, from where the car was driven to the White House garage on 22nd Street, escorted all the way. At the garage, agent Charles Taylor reported 'a small hole just left of centre in the windshield.' However, nothing was left by the time the FBI forensic team appeared. The crime scene had been effectively sanitised. On 26 November the damaged windshield was removed and replaced by the Arlington Glass Company. By the time the case of the presidential limo reached the Warren Commission months later, Secret Service Chief Rowley's submission contained no mention of the bullet hole seen by four witnesses at the scene and reported by Agent Taylor.

For once the various agencies had failed to synchronise their stories, because Secret Service Chief Rowley's formal letter to the Warren Commission maintained, '...there is no hole or crack through the windshield...' But there had been. People had seen it.

***

The cover-up plan immediately after the assassination was the classic Big Lie, told on several fronts simultaneously, ignoring any other possibilities and with a lot of help from highly placed government officials. The credulity and sometimes overt cooperation of the gullible American media helped to frame and shape the news agenda and hammer home one simple truth: Lee Harvey Oswald, acting alone, shot and killed the President of the United States. But first the conspirators had to prove that for public consumption.

They turned to the Chief Justice of the US Supreme Court, Earl Warren.

29

WARREN – AND A WHITEWASH

IT IS WISER TO ARRIVE AT A THEORY BY WAY OF THE EVIDENCE RATHER THAN THE OTHER WAY AROUND.
BARBARA TUCHMAN

Earl Warren was Chief Justice of the Supreme Court of the United States. In 1963 he was 72 years old. He had risen to the senior post in Washington more by politics than by law.

Initially Warren wanted nothing to do with the commission that bore his name. He felt that any investigation of the President's murder was properly a matter for the Justice Department. However, Bobby Kennedy appeared so genuinely grief-stricken and incapable of focussing for several weeks that he virtually abandoned his duties as Attorney General and let things drift.

Neither LBJ, Hoover, nor the acting Attorney General, Nicholas Katzenbach, wanted a presidential commission at first but the pressure of public disquiet and the dangers of an uncontrollable Texan or Congressional enquiry forced the Washington politicallegal establishment's hand. It was essential that someone, and someone very authoritative, 'proved' Lee Harvey Oswald's guilt in a very public way and scotched the dark rumours of conspiracies that were beginning to surface – and do it quickly.

During the last week of November 1963 it became clear that if Washington didn't take a firm grip of the situation and set the agenda, then the Texas courts probably would – and legally could. The Dean of Yale's Law Faculty suddenly came up with a proposal that received swift official support, calling for 'a presidential Commission be appointed of very distinguished citizens ... Bi-partisan and above politics,' and adding oddly, 'no Supreme Court Justices.'

Within hours of Oswald's death an alarmed Hoover had seen the danger too, and weighed in heavily behind Rostow's suggestion and for one clearly stated reason: 'The thing I am so concerned about Oswald having something issued so that we can convince the public that Oswald is the REAL assassin.'

Hoover's remark about 'the REAL assassin' unwittingly gives the game away. The Warren Commission's real job was to publish the government's version of the facts on Washington's terms, in order to keep the real truth buried as deeply as possible, as a worried Hoover was saying quite openly. From the start, the Warren Commission was going to be a hanging jury.

This theme was taken up and echoed by the Deputy Attorney General's minute to LBJ's senior aide, Bill Moyers, the day after Lee's murder by Ruby:

> The public must be satisfied that Oswald was the assassin; that he did not have confederates at large; and that the evidence was such that he would have been convicted at trial ... We need something to head off public speculation or Congressional hearings of the wrong sort.

Warren was aware of the constitutional dangers from the start. LBJ wanted the *imprimatur* of the Chief Justice of the United States Supreme Court to bestow a legitimacy and a spurious semi-legal status to his presidential whitewash that few critics would dare to question. The Texan 'Court of Inquiry' and the other investigations being proposed needed to be stopped, and quickly too. LBJ moved to convince Earl Warren that he should lead the commission.

Earl Warren refused – twice. Johnson had a reputation on Capitol Hill as a political bully and blackmailer: not for nothing was he a long-standing personal friend of J. Edgar Hoover and the FBI Director's secret cache of compromising 'Official and Confidential' file records. Earl Warren emerged from an interview with LBJ in tears, saying that he would do the new President's bidding, if only to 'prevent a nuclear war with the Soviets and stop up to 40 million people being killed.' Either because of the threat of a nuclear war with the USSR or, more likely, because of some deep and dirty secret in his past, the old man caved in. LBJ quite openly admitted as much on the telephone next day to an old Senatorial friend, Richard B. Russell. Johnson said:

> Warren told me he wouldn't do it under any circumstances ... I called him and ordered him down here, he told me 'no' twice, so I just pulled out what Hoover told me about some little incident in Mexico City. And then he started crying and said, 'well, I won't turn you down ... I'll do whatever you say.'

After this promising start to the highest legal affairs of the Union, the Warren Commissioners came on board. They were:
- Congressman Gerald Ford, Chairman of the House Republican conference
- Former World Bank President John McCloy (The very man whom Ike had thought was the voice of the 'military-industrial complex')
- Senator Richard B. Russell, D. Georgia, LBJ's great friend and mentor
- Senator John S. Cooper, R. Kentucky, and an Establishment man to his fingertips

- Congressman Thomas Hale Boggs, D. Louisiana, Majority Leader
- Alan Dulles, the ex-CIA Director sacked by JFK after the debacle of the Bay of Pigs

Between them Dulles and McCloy could be relied on to do everything in their power to toe the Establishment line. Ford was in the pocket of FBI Director Hoover, and could be relied on to report everything back to him. Dulles in particular was there to guide the Commission from within, with a Machiavellian subtlety. He, McCoy and Hoover made sure that the Commission did exactly what the CIA and FBI wanted. Richard Russell, like Earl Warren, did not want to be a member of the Commission but in yet another memorable piece of LBJ arm-twisting, Johnson blackmailed him as well, reminding him on the telephone of some dark secret from his past.

The Commission's official mandate was promulgated by Executive Order 11,130 on 29 November. Its task, in the words of Lyndon B. Johnson, was:

> to examine the evidence developed by the Federal Bureau of

Investigation and any additional evidence that may come to light or be uncovered by federal or state authorities; to make such further investigation as the Commission finds desirable; to evaluate all the facts and circumstances surrounding [the] assassination, including the violent death of the man charged with the assassination, and to report to me

This mandate awarded the Commission extremely wide powers and, with permission from Congress to subpoena witnesses, it was capable of interviewing anyone about anything. It could, almost certainly, have probed deeply into the murky depths of the CIA, the Agency's support for freebooting bands of renegade murderous Cubans, and its cosy links with organised crime. It could have explained Lee Harvey Oswald's real background as an intelligence agent for the US government. It chose to do none of these things, thanks mainly to the machinations of John McCloy and Alan Dulles. These two men, with the assistance of Hoover's FBI, ensured that the Warren Commission did what it was set up to do – find Oswald guilty, all on his own.

They soon demonstrated their power. They proposed Lee Rankin, former Solicitor General, as Chief Counsel for the Commission; a man who was in the FBI's pocket. A puzzled Warren (who nominated another candidate) accepted. A raft of supporting lawyers was selected, no less than nine from the American Jewish community – which in all fairness may have been inevitable, given the large number of Jews in the American legal profession – and on 16 December 1963 the Commission got down to business.

Its cover-up agenda had already been cunningly shaped by John McCloy and Alan Dulles. At the first executive meeting on 5 December, McCloy had openly touted his views of the Commission's role and purpose; 'to lay the dust, dust not only in the United States but all over the world.' On 16 December Alan Dulles personally distributed copies of a 1953 book called *The Assassins* to his colleagues. The book's main premise was that assassinations of US Presidents were the speciality of lone gunmen with psychiatric disorders. The Commission was impressed at this short cut to a solution for them all, and just before the Christmas holidays too, so gratefully took the hint. Crazy lone nuts shot Presidents. Within just three weeks the agenda for the cover-up was firmly in place: Oswald shot the President; he did it all alone; and he was crazy.

McCloy and Dulles then proposed an action plan to bolster their case. They set the agenda. The main areas for investigation were:
1. The facts of the assassination.
2. Confirmation of the assassin's identity.
3. Oswald's background, history and motivation.
4. The possibility that Oswald conspired with others.

By 11 January 1964 the Commission's investigators had a plan of work that supported those four goals and only those four. It relied almost entirely on an FBI report that named Oswald as solely responsible for the murders of Kennedy and Tippit. The

Commission's work plan relegated 'Possible conspiracy' to 'Refutation of allegations' to dispose of any notion of conspiracy. The official investigation had actually become a skilfully contrived and tightly controlled whitewash.

The men who shaped that investigation, or cover-up, were all linked and were all members of the American Establishment. Alan Dulles was not just an ex-Director of the CIA, fired by Kennedy for the Bay of Pigs fiasco, but a rich man, well connected in his own right. He and Banker John McCloy had been friends for years. They were both members of the same elite New York and Washington clubs and both had financial connections to the Rockefeller and Morgan Banks. McCloy was on the boards of United Fruit, AT&T and Metropolitan Life and had been chairman of Chase Manhattan and then the World Bank. Both knew Alan Belmont, who was handling the FBI's input to the Commission and J. Edgar Hoover. Belmont and Dulles served on the same Washington committees.

The personal links went even further. General Charles Cabell (who had also been fired by Kennedy for his role in the Bay of Pigs) had been Alan Dulles' military aide at the CIA and it was his brother, Earle Cabell, who was Mayor of Dallas. Dulles and McCloy knew Henry Luce, the owner of Time-Life, well. It was Luce's *Life* magazine that had bought and locked away Abe Zapruder's film of the assassination. All these senior officials, rich bankers and Wall Street men knew each other well and were working together hard to prove it was Oswald and no one else. All of them had influence and control over large chunks of the American media, the American government, American business, and the American Establishment. Every single member of the Commission bar one was a senior Freemason, as were LBJ, J. Edgar Hoover and Arlen Specter, the senior counsel. The Warren Commission was an American Establishment cover-up from the word go.

***

With its verdict already agreed, the Warren whitewash proceeded at a less than incisive pace. The idea that the Commission sat and solemnly took evidence like a court is false: Of the 266 known witnesses, the Commission questioned only 126. Of those, 51 thought that the shots came from the grassy knoll; 31 thought from the depository. The final Warren Report not only does not reflect this fact; it studiously ignores it.

Questioning of witnesses was selective, and only sparked when someone began to say something that was clearly not in the script. Dangerous questions were avoided and knowledgeable witnesses simply ignored.

Thus Mrs Markham, the hysterical woman who couldn't identify Oswald at the ID parade until she was helped, became a 'credible witness' and strong witnesses like Sam Holland, who swore blind that he saw a gun fired on the grassy knoll, were ignored. Only four of the 13 witnesses on the railway overpass bridge were questioned. Bethesda Surgeon Commander Humes was never asked to explain exactly *why* he burned his original draft notes or admit that Kennedy's back wound was low down and didn't even pierce the chest cavity, let alone go on to half-kill John Connally, as the magic bullet 'Exhibit CE 399' was supposed to have done.

That 'Single Bullet Theory' was the keystone of the whole Warren argument. Everything depended on that one key finding: that there were only three shots fired. That meant that one bullet had to have inflicted seven wounds, changed direction four times and remain unscathed. It was Warren's ultimate lie.

Not everyone on the Commission was deceived. Commissioners Hale Boggs, John Cooper and Dick Russell all had serious doubts. In one secret exchange Boggs agonises about the FBI's input and later told an aide, 'Hoover lied his eyes out to us – on Oswald, on Ruby, and on their friends, the bullets – you name it, he lied.'

More worrying was the potential bombshell that Oswald had been working as an undercover FBI informant in Texas. As Congressman Boggs put it, 'The implications are fantastic.' Alan Dulles agreed but typically suggested the solution was that 'the record should be destroyed'. In the end the Commission insisted that there is not the slightest hint of potential FBI links with Oswald. It failed even to interview at least 20 material witnesses, including Richard Carr (see section "DALLAS ON THE DAY") and James Chaney, the nearest motorcycle patrolman who saw Kennedy 'struck in the face' by the final, fatal shot. Some witnesses even discovered that their testimony was altered in print in the final report, from the Dallas City surveyors to James Tague. Julia Mercer (the woman who saw Jack Ruby in a stalled van in Dealey Plaza before the shooting) complained that someone had altered her statements to the FBI and even forged her signature on fake police forms. No one paid the slightest attention.

Some witnesses had a much more alarming experience. Jean Hill had seen at least one gunman on the grassy knoll. As she ran across the road to see whether there was anything she could do, a man detained her near the Pergola, flashing Secret Service credentials. At this point a second man appeared and searched her, confiscating the Polaroid pictures in her pockets before arresting her and forcibly frogmarching her to the Records building. There she 'interviewed by two men sitting overlooking the Plaza and Elm Street.' They asked her how many shots she had heard. Mrs Hill said 'four to six', to which her mysterious captors said 'No, you didn't. You heard three shots. We have three bullets and that's all.' When Mrs Hill insisted that there were more, she says the man growled, 'You heard echoes, lady. Echoes. You'd be wise to keep your mouth shut.'

Jean Hill later flatly refused to go to Washington and give evidence to the Commission. Arlen Specter, one of the Commission's lawyers (and the man who dreamed up the magic bullet idea) then asked the FBI to bring her in for an interview in Dallas. Specter kept trying to shake her story, and eventually became exasperated when she insisted she had heard up to six shots, adding 'I'm not going to lie for you.' What happened next – considering that it came from an officer of the court and a federal counsel on a presidential commission – was extraordinary. According to Hill, Specter then started threatening her, saying that he could make her 'look as crazy as old Marguerite Oswald' and see she was 'locked up in a mental institution' if she didn't cooperate. Later when she saw her supposed testimony when the report was published, she 'knew it was a fabrication from the very first line.'

Behind the scenes the CIA and FBI were working hand in hand to make sure that their stories tallied. An FBI internal memorandum of 13 May 1964 is particularly damning. It warned the Director of the FBI about their joint CIA/FBI line at the Warren Commission's questioning, and its source was none other than James Jesus Angleton, who was managing the 'Warren problem' for the CIA. In it he quite openly coordinates the FBI and CIA responses to various questions.

Angleton said it occurred to him that it would be well for both McCone and Mr Hoover to be aware that the Commission might ask the same questions wondering whether they would get different replies from the heads of the two agencies.

One question will be 'Was Lee Harvey Oswald ever an agent of CIA?'

The (CIA) answer will be no.

A second question will be 'Does CIA have any evidence showing that a conspiracy existed to assassinate President Kennedy?'

The answer to this question will also be no.

Finally, on 24 September 1964, the Commission reported. Its findings are now widely acknowledged as a whitewash, and a bad one at that. The Warren Commission concluded:

1. That the shots that killed President Kennedy and wounded Governor Connally came from the sixth floor window of the depository.
2. Only three shots were fired in Dealey Plaza.
3. There was persuasive evidence that one single bullet pierced the President's throat and caused all of Governor Connally's wounds.

4. Those shots were fired by Lee Harvey Oswald acting alone.
5. Oswald later shot and killed police officer Tippit.
6. Oswald resisted arrest and tried to shoot another Dallas Police Officer at the Texas Theatre.
7. There was no evidence that Oswald or Ruby were part of any conspiracy or knew each other.
8. The investigation found no evidence of conspiracy, subversion or disloyalty to the US Government by any federal, state or local official.

The Commission finally concluded decisively that 'Oswald acted alone'.

The Report was publicly acclaimed at the time as 'thorough' by a beaming President Johnson. In fact it was anything but thorough. For example, Wesley Liebeler, one of the Warren Commission staff members, was highly critical of the evidence about the Mannlicher-Carcano rifle. In an internal complaint at the time he warned that the Commission's claims about Oswald's supposed skill with a rifle were demonstrably false. His long-secret memo is worth quoting:

> You can't leave a rifle and scope laying around in a garage underfoot for almost three months, just having brought it back from New Orleans in the back of a station wagon, and expect to hit anything with it, unless you take the trouble to fire it and sight the scope in. The present draft leaves the Commission open to severe criticism ... it is simply dishonest.

The Warren Commission dealt with such objections, even from its own staff, by simply ignoring them. The big guns of the American Establishment swung into line to spin the story and to back the Commission.

The ever helpful owners of *Life* magazine – no friends of the dead President – gave Warren front cover endorsement, and two months later, while the applause of a grateful nation was still ringing in the commission members' ears, all 26 massive supporting volumes of the Commission's statements and testimony were quietly slipped onto the street just before

Christmas – *but completely unindexed.* That achieved its effect, too: it took years of work to track down and catalogue all the omissions and misrepresentations contained in Warren.

In 1967 one Sylvia Meagher finally produced 'a meticulous dissection of the Commission and its conclusions'. She demonstrated very plainly that the report contained numerous lies and inaccuracies: misrepresentation of testimony; omissions of counter-arguments; suppression of evidence backing Oswald; incomplete investigation of suspicious facts; a failure to question material witnesses; and, finally, drawing conclusions completely at odds with the evidence it had been given. However, she was three years too late.

The groundswell of complaints, however, could not be denied forever. In 1976 the Senate Select Commission slammed the Warren Report as 'misleading', charging that, 'Senior officials in both agencies (CIA and FBI) made conscious decisions not to disclose potentially important information.'

President Nixon also gave the game away, chortling on his notorious White House tapes that 'the Warren Report was the biggest hoax.' Senator Schweiker of the Senate Intelligence Commission delivered the final nail in the Commission's coffin in his damning criticism of the Report in 1976, when he reported officially to the US Senate:

> The Warren Commission has collapsed like a house of cards. And I believe that the Warren Commission was set up at the time to feed pablum to the American people for reasons not yet known, and that one of the biggest cover-ups in the history of our country occurred at that time.

When the House Select Committee on Assassinations reinvestigated the Kennedy shooting in 1977-1979 its criticism of the Warren Commission was damning. For example, it said that the Warren Commission failed to adequately investigate the possibility of conspiracy: 'The Warren Commission failed to investigate adequately the possibility of a conspiracy to assassinate the President. This deficiency was attributable in part to the failure of the commission to receive all the relevant information that was in the possession of other agencies and departments of the Government.'

When the Congressional Assassinations Records Review Board finally got underway in 1994 it declassified a few million pages of documents that reopened many of the subjects avoided by Warren and with them many of the unanswered questions about the assassination. The ARRB's final report claimed, 'a great many unresolved issues relating to the assassination of President Kennedy will have to be addressed in the years to come.'

Back in the autumn of 1964 none of this mattered, however. The Warren Report had 'proved' Lee Harvey Oswald did the killing all on his own and effectively put the lid on the assassination at that time and either gave false explanations for – or just ignored – the hard evidence that there really was a conspiracy of some sort. It never explained how Oswald's description was on the police radio net within 20 minutes of the assassination, or why there were no records of Oswald's interrogation. It blatantly distorted the testimony of the witnesses. It explained away the obviously faked photographs of Oswald supposedly clutching a rifle and the other planted evidence. It skipped over the fact that the President's body left Dallas in a bronze casket with one set of head wounds, but arrived at Bethesda in a plain coffin with a new set of injuries. It hid the fact that Kennedy's back wound was so shallow that the missile never made it to his chest cavity, let alone go through Governor Connally's chest cavity, wrist and thigh, six feet and five other wounds away. The Commission's description of the life and travels of CE399, the magic bullet was, in fact, a complete fairy story. Much of the critical evidence surrounding the assassination (such as the autopsy X-ray films and the remains of the President's brain) was either substituted or disappeared from the archives.

 Warren's official version was firmly intended as the only true explanation of the President's murder. Anyone who could not accept this, or who knew differently, would have to keep their mouth shut in future. Because to suggest any other interpretation of events could be very hazardous to one's health.

It could even get you killed...

30

DEAD SILENT?

THIS PENALTY HIS CHATTERING TONGUE HAS PAID.
OVID

John Kennedy's assassination was followed by a wave of unexplained deaths of important witnesses in the years immediately afterwards. These are often dismissed as mere coincidence or as examples of the natural statistics of life and death. But some of the murdered witnesses had openly spoken of the threats they had received specifically as a result of their knowledge of the Kennedy assassination.

The graph of the various deaths peaks at least three times (see graph below) and all are just before or around the investigations into the Kennedy killing. Such a statistical anomaly cannot be explained away glibly as a 'natural trend of mortality'. Mortality rates are statistically consistent and do not go up and down except in plague, famine or war.

It is normal for researchers into the dead witnesses to approach the topic chronologically, starting with the murder of Lee Harvey Oswald. This method is vulnerable to criticism as it mixes some genuine deaths from natural causes with highly suspicious suicides and convenient murders. A more revealing method is to single out those who we know specifically warned friends that they were frightened, threatened or felt at risk, because of what they knew or had seen concerning the assassination of JFK. Even this limited list is surprisingly long and very clearly linked to some knowledge of the events in Dallas.

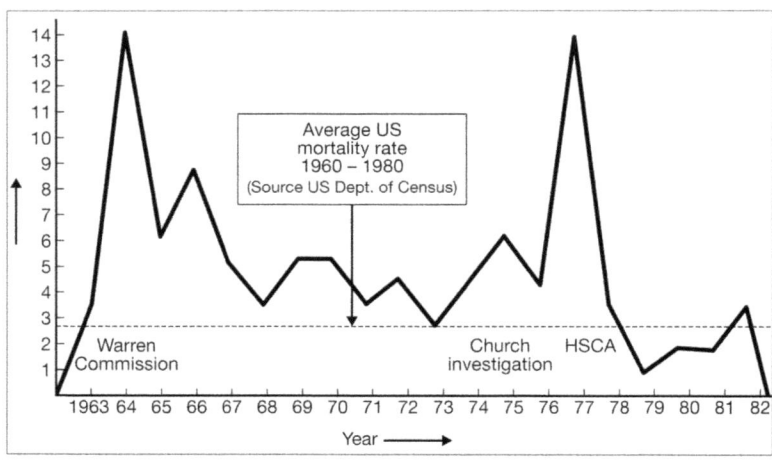

Statistical anomalies – the strange increases in deaths of those linked to the assassination.

One of the most suspicious is the demise of Gary Underhill, one of the many 'media assets' controlled by the CIA. Underhill's time with the OSS and CIA is a matter of record.

On the night of the assassination Gary Underhill fled to New York because he was scared for his life. According to his friend Charlene Fitzsimmons he said that he 'he knew too much about the people behind the Kennedy assassination' and that he 'knew about Oswald being set up as a patsy.' He told her that his problem was that he 'knew who had planned and executed the murder and that they knew he knew.' Six months later he was dead with a bullet hole in the left side of his skull. The coroner ruled that the cause of death was suicide. His friends pointed out that he had said he was specifically afraid for his life because of what he knew about the murder of JFK. Moreover, Gary Underhill was right-handed.

Another shooting was a clear case of murder. Jack Zangretti was closely associated with the Mafia. He ran a casino nightclub called the Red Lobster and on the night of Saturday 23 November Zangretti openly told his friends that 'three other men – not Lee Harvey Oswald – shot the President' and that 'a man named Jack Ruby will kill Oswald tomorrow and in a few days a member of the Frank Sinatra family will be kidnapped just to take some of the attention away from the assassination.'

All his predictions came true, but a week later someone killed Jack Zangretti and dumped his body in a nearby lake.

The death of a man called Hank Killam was directly linked to his knowledge of the JFK assassination.

Killam knew Oswald in Dallas, and his wife had worked in Ruby's nightclub. Between them they could identify any Ruby-Oswald links. After he had been questioned by the FBI he was clearly unnerved and lost jobs because federal agents harassed him repeatedly at work. Just before Christmas 1963 he fled to Florida. On 17 March 1964 someone cut Killam's throat and pushed him through the plate glass window of a department store. The police said it was suicide. The Florida Coroner ruled it was an accident. Killam's brother snorted that it was a very odd suicide: 'Did you ever hear of a man committing suicide by jumping through a plate glass window?'

In February 1967 a Florida County Solicitor named Carl Harper began to investigate Killam's death and discovered that Killam even told his brother, 'I'm a dead man. I've run as far as I'm going to run.' To this day key FBI and CIA documents on the case have been withheld from public release.

The dangers to witnesses seem to be linked directly to what they were or were not prepared to testify in public. We have already looked at the cases of

Domingo Benavides and Warren Reynolds (see section "OFFICER TIPPIT"), both of whom witnessed the events surrounding the murder of Officer Tippit.

Benavides's father-in-law J.W. Jackson was unimpressed by the Dallas police's handling of the murder of Benavides's brother and started to make his own enquiries, much to the consternation of the Dallas policemen. They warned Jackson that he should 'lay off this business' and 'don't go asking questions. That's our job.' Someone took a shot at him in his home and a passing police patrol car made no effort to apprehend the fleeing gunman. The incident confirmed the suspicion that Domingo the witness had been the intended victim, not his brother, and all because he swore that the man whom he had seen shoot Officer Tippit did not look like Lee Harvey Oswald.

These unnatural deaths were all single witnesses. But on the night of 24 November 1963 five men met in Jack Ruby's apartment. They had all visited Jack Ruby in jail and listened to what he had to say. Two were Ruby's attorneys, Tom Howard and Jim Martin; two were journalists, Jim Koethe of the *Dallas Times-Herald* and a visitor from the Californian *Long-Beach Press Telegram,* Bill Hunter. The fifth member was Ruby's room-mate, George Senator. We have no record of what was discussed that night because George Senator disappeared, not to be seen or heard from again. According to Martin, Senator had been 'overwhelmed with fear' at the meeting and, believing that he was going to be next to die, had begged to spend the night at Martin's house.

    Martin, the only one of the five to survive later told the Warren Commission and a Texas reporter that 'he couldn't remember what they all talked about.' On 24 April 1964 Bill Hunter was shot and killed (ironically in the Long Beach 'Public Safety Building'). Hunter was on duty and sitting down when a police officer came in and shot him clean through the heart at 'a range of no more than three feet'. The detective said that 'he had dropped his gun and it had gone off' but the angle of the bullet suggested otherwise. His colleague had already testified that 'he hadn't seen the incident because he had his back turned at the time.' It was all very odd, especially coming the day after George Senator had told the Warren Commission everything he knew, which turned out to be very little indeed.

Next to go from the unlucky five was Jim Koethe, just three days before the Warren Commission reported. On 21 September 1964 Koethe was getting out of his shower when an unknown assailant allegedly delivered a lethal karate chop to his throat. The only items stolen were Koethe's notes for a book on the Kennedy assassination. However, according to a counter view, Koethe had in fact been strangled by a man he had picked up. Why that anonymous murderer should then choose to disappear with the JFK manuscript, and nothing else, is not explained.

Tom Howard was next. The attorney, who had been present in the Dallas Police basement at the moment Oswald was moved and who had fortunately been on hand to act for Jack Ruby the second he was arrested (with his client's bail bond already typed out), died of a sudden heart attack. According to friends he had been 'acting strange' for two days and was taken to hospital by a stranger whom no one could identify or trace. There was no autopsy and the body was cremated unusually quickly.

With Hunter, Koethe and Howard dead, George Senator fled and has long since disappeared. Jim Martin was the only survivor; and he claimed that he couldn't remember what the little group in Ruby's apartment had discussed the night that Oswald was shot by Ruby. The small group had suffered one murder, one accidental shooting and one heart attack in the 18 months after their friend Jack silenced Oswald for ever. Knowing Jack Ruby was as hazardous as knowing Lee Harvey Oswald.

One person who could have testified to that was the newspaper columnist Dorothy Kilgallen. Although she was best known as a popular radio and TV personality, Kilgallen was a serious investigative journalist. In March 1964 she managed to secure a personal interview with Jack Ruby during his trial.

Over the next few months she began investigating further in the New Orleans and Dallas areas and confided to a society friend, one Mrs Smith, that she had a big scoop and was on to information that could 'blow the whole Kennedy assassination story wide open.'

A year later, on the morning of 9 November 1965, Dorothy Kilgallen was found dead in bed. Her autopsy took eight days and she was officially declared to have died from 'an ingestion of alcohol and barbiturates'. What makes her case odd is that the friend she had told about Ruby and the assassination, and to whom she had given some notes, died just three days later and may well have been murdered, too. Mrs Earl T. Smith, Kilgallen's best friend had what appeared to be an unexplained and sudden cerebral haemorrhage, collapsed and died.

The link between knowing secrets and revealing secrets was eventually made clear by Warren Reynolds, the man who had followed the killer of Officer Tippit down the Jefferson

Boulevard in Dallas. He had initially denied that the man he chased looked anything like Lee Harvey Oswald, and had been shot in the head for his pains. Eventually after being shot, harassed and his family threatened, he faced the Warren Commission and testified that the man he had followed after the Tippit shooting was Lee Harvey Oswald after all. He cheerfully confided to his wife, 'I don't think they're going to bother me any more.' But he never did explain who 'they' were.

Grant Stockdale was a friend of John Kennedy and LBJ and four days after the assassination he had flown to Washington to talk to Robert and Edward Kennedy. He came back 'a deeply troubled man'. His lawyer said, 'It didn't make much sense. He said something about "those guys" trying to get him. Then all about the assassination.' Next day Stockdale fell – or was pushed – out if his office window on the 13th floor of the Miami DuPont Building. His involvement with the assassination has never been clear, but he was a partner in the Serve-U Corporation and deeply implicated in the Bobby Baker-LBJ scandal. Stockdale may well have known more than was healthy about a number of things. Yet again the death is clearly connected with the assassination and some group frightening – or even killing – witnesses or those who held some damaging information.

Al Bogard was the car salesman at Downtown Lincoln Mercury in Dallas who was visited by 'Lee Oswald' on 9 November 1963. Bogard's mistake was probably his evidence to the Warren Commission that the would-be car buyer 'took a new Mercury for a test run up the Stemmons Freeway at 60 or 70 miles an hour ... he said he'd be coming into money in a couple of weeks ... and that he might have to go back to Russia to buy a car' and wrote the name 'Lee Oswald' on the back of one of Bogard's business cards.

The problem was that it could not have been Oswald. Lee couldn't drive and was recorded somewhere else at that time on that date. The FBI insisted on a polygraph (lie detector) test, which Bogard passed with flying colours. Two years later a work colleague explained,

'I'm afraid to talk ... Bogard was beaten by some men so badly that he was in hospital for some time, and that was after he'd testified.' Following his release from hospital, Bogard quit his job and fled to Hallsville in Louisiana, saying he was scared for his life. He was found dead in a car on 14 February 1966 with a hosepipe running to the car's exhaust. The coroner ruled it was suicide.

One of Bogard's colleagues at Downtown Lincoln had been Jack Lawrence, who was a regular at Ruby's Carousel Club and who also knew George Senator, Ruby's room-mate. Lawrence had only joined the car sales company a few weeks before the JFK murder. On the day of the assassination Lawrence didn't appear for work until about half an hour after the events in Dealey Plaza, when he came running into the dealership, 'muddy and sweating profusely' and rushed into the lavatory, where he promptly vomited. The dealership car that he had borrowed the night before was later found abandoned behind the wooden fence on the grassy knoll in Dealey Plaza. Lawrence's co-workers were suspicious and called the police. Lawrence was arrested and then released. Next day he quit his job and disappeared. Only later did it emerge that Lawrence had been hired on phoney references from New Orleans, was closely associated with extreme right-wing politics and had been an expert shot in the USAF.

Less mysterious than the Lawrence case was the story of Lee Bower, the signalman in the railroad control tower in the railyards behind the grassy knoll. When Bowers tried to testify to the Warren Commission about the flash and smoke he had noticed on the grassy knoll, one of the lawyers cut him off. After his appearance at the Warren Commission, Bowers began to receive death threats.

In 1966 Bowers, now vice president of a construction company, drove his brand new company car into a bridge at Midlothian, near Dallas. The doctor who treated him at the hospital noticed that the injured man was suffering from 'some strange kind of shock ... A different kind of shock than the accident victim experiences, I can't explain it. I've never seen anything like it.' Lee

Bowers died in hospital. When Penn Jones, the researcher who has investigated the string of curious Kennedy-related deaths, talked to Bowers' widow, she became flustered, saying, 'They told me not to talk...' Yet again, the ubiquitous 'they' were involved.

Not all the deaths have been of bystanders and civilians.

One of the medical officers present at the Bethesda Naval autopsy on JFK was Lt Cdr Bill Pitzer, USN. He was a senior X-ray specialist and took the official JFK autopsy record. Afterwards he told friends that he had been debriefed by security officers and threatened with dire consequences if he ever spoke out about what he had seen. He described the experience at the hands of the unidentified federal agents as 'intimidating' and 'horrifying'. On 29 October 1966, a few days before he was due to retire, he was discovered with a bullet in his head and a .45 calibre pistol in his right hand. The coroner's verdict of suicide was hotly disputed by his wife and his friends. Bill Pitzer was *left*-handed. Another troubling fact was someone had crushed his left hand so severely before he died that the mortuary technician couldn't remove his wedding ring. Despite being renowned as a meticulous note-taker, Pitzer left no suicide note. Odder still, he had just been offered a plum job at $45,000 a year, suggesting little motive for suicide. Pitzer's name has since been removed from the official US record of those involved in Kennedy's autopsy.

Roger Craig was one of the deputy sheriffs on duty on 22 November. He had been Dallas Traffic Commission's 'Policeman of the Year' for 1960 and had been looking forward to a promising career. About 15 minutes after the shooting Craig noticed a man running down the grass slope in front of the depository and leap into a pale Nash station wagon with a 'dark or Latino' driver. Craig said it was Oswald – or someone who looked just like him.

The Warren Commission made 14 unauthorised and inaccurate changes to his testimony. In one telling example, the Commission refused to accept the fact of Craig's presence in Captain Fritz's office when Oswald was being interviewed. However, there exists a crystal clear photograph of Craig standing in the glass-fronted office of the Dallas Captain of Homicide, with Oswald in the chair before him.

Craig's stubborn refusal to lie made him a problem for the DPD. He was harassed at work, belittled and ordered not to talk to the press. In 1967 he was summarily fired by Sheriff Decker. He was criticised in the media after giving evidence for Jim Garrison's prosecution of Clay Shaw in 1969, and physically attacked on three other occasions. On 15 May 1975 Roger Craig was found dead at his father's house, this time the victim of what appears to have been a genuine suicide.

***

The next wave of deaths cluster around the time of the House Select Committee on Assassinations in 1975/6. Sam Giancana was killed Mafia-style, a neat circle of bullet holes round his mouth to emphasise exactly why he had been executed. Johnny Rosselli was found in an oil drum off Miami, dead from multiple stab-wounds. 'Now there are only two people left who know the truth about the Kennedy killing,' was Mafia Don Santo Trafficante's response.

Bill Harvey of the CIA, his old anti-Castro boss, succumbed in 1976 to one of the many sudden heart attacks to afflict the Kennedy witnesses, while Bill Pawley of *Life* magazine and the CIA, who had helped to build the CIA's anti-Castro efforts in the 1960s, was found dead the following year, having apparently shot himself in the chest. All were to be prime witnesses for the 1978 House Select Committee on Assassinations, the HSCA, as were the Chicago Mob's trigger man Charlie Nicoletti and Oswald's CIA 'babysitter', Baron George de Mohrenschildt. Nicoletti was shot in the head and his car set alight. De Mohrenschildt had his head blown apart by a close-range shotgun blast the very day that the HSCA asked him to testify on the JFK killing. The local Sheriff's office thought the death suspicious; the local coroner ruled it as suicide.

There was a curious cluster of sudden deaths around the time of the HSCA hearings in 1978. Three deaths were timely for any cover-up: Regis Kennedy, the FBI agent in New Orleans who always insisted that Carlos Marcello was nothing more than a small time tomato salesman; David Morales, the CIA counterinsurgency specialist who admitted that 'they had taken care of that son of a bitch [JFK]'; plus William Sullivan, Hoover's number three at the FBI, who had resigned after becoming disenchanted with the senile old man's corrupt and dictatorial ways and was due to tell all to the HSCA. If ever a man knew the inside secrets of J. Edgar Hoover's FBI, it was Bill Sullivan. He was shot and killed by a high-powered rifle while out hunting, shortly before he was due to give evidence.

Individually the Kennedy witnesses' deaths might not be significant, although some are highly suspect and others downright odd. But taken together and put on a timeline they look like more than mere coincidence (see graph in chapter 30). Whatever the cause, the Garrison investigation team never got a deposition from their two key witnesses. The alleged suicide of the bizarre David Ferrie on 22

February 1967, just before he was due to give evidence to the Garrison indictment of Clay Shaw for the Kennedy murder, and after he told a friend that he 'was going to be a dead man for agreeing to open his mouth,' remains a mystery. The brutal murder of his boyfriend Eladio del Valle in Miami at exactly the same time is beyond coincidence.

Another curious death was the taxi driver who picked Oswald up and took him to his lodgings after the assassination. William Whaley was killed in a head-on collision on 18 December 1965; his passenger was critically injured. Whaley had been with the City Transportation Company since 1936 and had a perfect driving record. He was the first Dallas cabbie to be killed on duty since 1937. When JFK researcher Penn Jones Jr went to interview the manager of the cab company about Whaley's death, he was hustled out of the office and told, 'If you're smart, you won't be coming around here asking questions.'

Of all the witnesses' deaths Jack Ruby's was perhaps the most significant.

Of all the surviving witnesses he knew more than anyone about the facts surrounding the murder in Dealey Plaza and the events in Dallas that weekend. When he was interviewed by Earl Warren himself in Dallas, Ruby begged to be interrogated in Washington. He hinted quite openly at a conspiracy.

He said that he didn't feel safe in Texas and that 'I want to tell the truth but I can't tell it here ... Does that make sense?' Justice Warren refused to allow Ruby to come to Washington, pretending he didn't have the power to order the move. The truth was that no one wanted to hear what Jack Ruby had to say.

Ruby was tried and sentenced to death in March 1964. The sentence and conviction was quashed on appeal in 1966 and a fresh trial ordered. However, on 3 January 1967 the key surviving witness to any investigation of Jack Kennedy's murder died after a brief illness and before any new trial could convene. He had been suffering from a highly unusual and fast breeding form of lung cancer. Although Ruby claimed that he had been injected with live cancer cells by a strange doctor, as he had been diagnosed as a paranoiac depressive by then, his claim that he was being 'systematically murdered' must be treated with caution.

In the 30 years from 1963 to 1993, 21 witnesses with first hand knowledge of the Kennedy assassination were murdered. Fifteen more apparently committed suicide, 20 died from various accidents and five from car crashes: 25% of the known witnesses. It is a long and morbid list: coincidence, happenstance or just bad luck? But no life insurance actuary would have predicted such a high mortality rate for such a random group, even in the gunhappy USA.

We are, once again, as so often with the strange tale of JFK's murder, in the presence of the abnormal and the absence of the normal.

31

THE STORY UNRAVELS AND THE TRUTH EMERGES

OH WHAT A TANGLED WEB WE WEAVE, WHEN FIRST WE PRACTISE TO DECEIVE!
SIR WALTER SCOTT

No sooner had Warren hit the streets than the doubts began.

In Britain Lord Bertrand Russell had already formed an unofficial British committee to try and get behind the obvious lies and obfuscations of the Warren Commission. But the story had started to unravel on the very night of the assassination. After an evening's boozing, Guy Banister, Lee's controller at 544 Camp Street, pistol whipped his associate Jack Martin for shouting in a drunken argument, 'What? Are y'all gonna try and kill me the way you killed Kennedy?' Martin was taken to the hospital where the story eventually came out, although he refused to press charges.

But what Martin did give away when the police interviewed him in his hospital bed was that Banister's associate David Ferrie had disappeared and that he might be implicated in the assassination of the President. Ferrie told investigators that he had been in New Orleans until 21.00 on the night of the assassination, celebrating with his Mafia boss Carlos Marcello who had that morning beaten JFK's federal court rap to deport the Louisiana Don.

Then Ferrie drove through the night with two others to Houston, where he went to an ice rink. The manager remembers him hanging around a pay phone there for a long time 'making and receiving calls' with a handful of quarters. Ferrie then drove off to Galveston and checked into another motel there. With his background he may have been moving into position ready to act as a get-away pilot should he be needed.

Author Mark Lane was suspicious from the start. He had applied to the

Warren Commission to act as the legal representative of Lee Harvey Oswald and been brusquely rejected. Apparently the dead Oswald didn't need anyone to tell his side of the story. Lane eventually did manage to testify to the Warren Commission and handed over his tapes of an interview with Mrs Markham. Warren was unconvinced. In 1965 Lane produced *Rush to Judgement,* a highly critical book on the Commission's report that opened the floodgates of suspicion and claims of cover-up over the assassination. In 1966 Louisiana Senator Russell Long said to New Orleans DA Jim Garrison, 'those fellows on the Warren Commission were dead wrong, you know. There's no way in the world that one man could have shot up John Kennedy that way.'

The politically ambitious Garrison – who was convinced many of the conspirators lived on or near his patch – began the investigation that bore his name. It was not a popular move either in Washington or with the various federal agencies. Garrison ignored the slurs and doggedly pursued his suspects, trying to bring an indictment that would show that the Kennedy assassination was orchestrated from 544 Camp Street by Guy Banister and his associates: Clay Shaw, David Ferrie and their shadowy friends and backers.

Oswald's close associate Banister could not be interviewed because he was dead. He had suffered one of those timely heart attacks so prevalent among the unfortunate Kennedy witnesses. His alcoholic friend Jack Martin on the other hand was still very much alive and sang like a canary, revealing the existence of a joint Mafia-CIA supply route across the Deep South to run drugs, guns and money.

News of the investigation eventually caught the eye of the press and on 17 February 1967 the *New Orleans States-Item* published a full story under the headline, **D.A. LAUNCHES FULL JFK DEATH PROBE.** Garrison felt that he had now amassed enough evidence to haul Ferrie before a Grand Jury. But a terrified Ferrie warned Garrison that 'he was now a dead man'. On 22 February 1967, just one week after the newspaper story broke, both Ferrie and his boyfriend Eladio del Valle were murdered on the same day, 600 miles apart.

Garrison then turned to his next suspect, Clay Shaw, the rich and well-connected director of the International Trade Centre and Mart in New Orleans, a man who had close links with Permindex and Louis Bloomfield in Canada and with the CIA. To make sure that Shaw didn't suffer the same fate as Ferrie and del Valle, the DA had him arrested 'for his own protection'. Garrison got an indictment from the Grand Jury and on 29 January 1969 Clay Shaw went on trial charged with 'wilfully conspiring with David Ferrie and Lee Harvey Oswald to murder John F. Kennedy.'

Garrison's case was in serious trouble from the start. He used 'truth drugs' to get a statement from Perry Russo, a 25 year old insurance salesman who testified that he had attended an 'assassination party' at David Ferrie's apartment, where Shaw, Ferrie, and Lee Harvey Oswald had discussed killing President Kennedy. But Big Jim ran into a lot more trouble. His investigation team was infiltrated by federal agents who stole his files; an ex-FBI man tried to set him up in a homosexual compromise; an underworld contract was offered for his murder; and allegations that he was being paid off by the Mob were leaked to the press.

Despite all this, Garrison succeeded in finally getting his case to court, where he showed the Zapruder film to a shocked jury. Even then Garrison had had to fight *Life* magazine all the way to the Supreme Court in order to get his hands on this startling real time evidence.

During the trial nothing went right for Jim Garrison. Witnesses disappeared or didn't turn up; the Judge ruled that the officer who finger-printed Shaw/Bertrand was lying; and it turned out that another key witness, Gordon Novel, was a plant working for a CIA front organisation whose sole purpose was to wreck Garrison's evidence. One witness, a lawyer, openly lied on the stand (for which he later went to jail). And Shaw blatantly perjured himself, denying he had even met Ferrie, let alone Oswald. In Garrison's own words,

'Clay Shaw made a mockery of the law against lying under oath.' In the end the New Orleans DA lost his case. The jury accepted that there had indeed probably been a conspiracy, but found that Garrison had not proved that Shaw was personally involved in it.

But Garrison's 1969 case helped to open the floodgates of criticism and questioning. Books with titles like, *They've Killed the President, The Day Kennedy was Shot* and *The Secret World of Lee Harvey Oswald* bounded off the presses. Academics and researchers hurled themselves into the fray with plot and counterplot, claim and counterclaim. As the academic bar fight developed, a truth began to emerge. Someone was pulling the strings behind the scenes.

One of the curiosities of the Kennedy case is the way that someone, somewhere immediately rushes to challenge any new revelation or to plug any embarrassing leak in the wall of secrecy. Every crack in the edifice of the official government version, 'that Oswald did it, on his own and only fired three shots,' was promptly challenged, disputed or 'rubbished', often by a compliant media who should have known better. To the objective observer this all looks remarkably like damage control springing into action. Indeed, there exists a CIA letter to all Heads of Station confirming this, and which gives precise instructions on a 'media line' and clear steps to follow should the CIA ever be challenged over its involvement with the assassination or Warren. (See Appendix.)

That there was a deliberate attempt to block embarrassing revelations is not in doubt. For example, we know that Warren failed to file a major reservation about the single bullet theory in the final report. Even John McCone privately admitted to a CIA source that he was going to find it difficult to justify that it was Lee Harvey Oswald, acting alone, who had killed JFK. Warren also allowed the report to completely misrepresent the location of the wound in Kennedy's back thanks to Gerald Ford, the FBI's stoolpigeon on the Commission, who later confessed that he had personally changed the wording on the final report to read: A bullet had entered the base *of the back of his neck* slightly to the right of his spine.'

The doubts were shared all along by one member of the Warren Commission itself. By 1971, Congressman Hale Boggs had seen enough of Hoover and spoke out, telling Congress;

> Over the post war years we have granted to the elite and secret police within our system vast new powers over the lives and liberties of the people. At the request of the trusted and respected heads of those forces, we have exempted those grants of power and their appeal to the necessities of national security, from due accounting and surveillance.

He was not alone in his views. By the end of the first decade of the 21st century the balance had shifted. Polls show that 80 per cent of the American people now believe that President John F. Kennedy was killed as a result of a conspiracy; a sizable minority now believe that Lee Harvey Oswald was innocent and was, as he claimed plaintively to the press pack that night in Dallas Police Headquarters, 'just a patsy'.

Fletcher Prouty, CIA insider and acerbic critic of the Warren Report, spelled it out very clearly. 'The Warren Commission Report is trash. Because it is. The Warren Commission either was part of the conspiracy and as part of that conspiracy they used their report to cover and obfuscate the crime, or they too had been under the control of that powerful cabal.'

He went on to add, 'I prefer to believe the latter. There was not an ignorant or stupid man on that Commission. So they may have been persuaded that the better part of discretion was to put out the report "to soothe the public".'

***

The fact is that Warren has been long-exposed as a fraud, as at least one American President and even Robert Kennedy, the dead man's brother, have admitted. However, Warren served its purpose at the time, which was to soothe the American taxpayers and voters, and to 'lay the dust' of the

Kennedy affair by blaming the whole thing on Oswald, the 'lone nut' gunman.

So we are left with the biggest questions of all.

Who really did it? And how?

32

WHO KILLED JFK?

CRIME GOES UNPUNISHED WHEN IT IS THE WORK OF MANY.
MAXIMEUS LUCANUS

Unravelling the true story of the assassination of JFK is a tough challenge. Too much time has passed, too many people are involved and too much disinformation has been scattered into the story along the way.

On one key point, however, we can be clear from the start. The Dallas Police, the Head of the FBI, the new President and the testimony of eyewitnesses all agreed at the time that there was more than one gunman in Dealey Plaza on the day as a fact. When combined with the evidence of the bullet wounds, the acoustic record, the ballistics and the photographic evidence, it is beyond doubt that Lee Harvey Oswald – or whoever else had their finger on the trigger – could not have acted alone. We have the official verdicts of the House Select Committee on Assassinations (despite the undercover work of a CIA officer called Ioannides seconded to manipulate the HSAC's findings), the Assassinations Records Review Board, and the Schweiker Senate Report, all of which *officially* demolished the conclusions of the Warren Report. We are therefore looking for more than one gunman.

And if there was more than one gunman then, by definition, we are dealing with a conspiracy.

Perhaps the easiest question to begin any investigation is to identify exactly who wanted the President out of the way – permanently? The list is a long one and included the Mafia; the Cuban Exiles; the cartel of arms manufacturers; disaffected elements in the CIA and the military; the rich bankers of Wall Street who owned the Federal Reserve; the oil barons; the antisegregationists in the Deep South, plus the Israelis and their American supporters. Add to this list the Head of the FBI and the Vice President and the roll call of Jack Kennedy's enemies is impressive, to say the least.

However motive by itself does not necessarily imply the deed. To will the action and to strike a man down in broad daylight are two quite different things. This shortens our list. We know that the Mafia Godfathers hired gunmen to murder the President. This is backed up by a number of confessions from some of those who have been directly involved in the shooting, or claim to have been. All their claims can be tested and weighed in the balance to see if they are true. But, in order to reach a conclusion, we need answers to the following questions:

1. What actions did Kennedy take that invited dire retribution?
2. Who said that they intended to kill the President?
3. Who else had a motive to remove him?
4. Who warned of the killing in advance?
5. Who had the opportunity to kill the President?
6. Who confessed to being involved?
7. Who was present in Dallas on the day?
8. Who claimed credit for the killing?

9. Who behaved suspiciously both before and after the murder?
10. Who covered up the true facts of the murder?
11. Who benefited most from the killing of the President?

From the answers to these questions, the most likely killer – or killers – slowly emerge and take shape, like figures in the fog.

***

The first three questions are easily answered.

Jack Kennedy's White House had hounded and lied to the Mafia and their friends; he had also alienated the Cuban Exiles, who felt they had been betrayed over the Bay of Pigs. Both groups had openly sworn to 'get Kennedy'. The Mafia had even taken out a contract, a fact known to many. In doing so they joined a remarkable constituency of organisations that were only too glad to see the back of Jack Kennedy, from the bankers and moguls of the eastern Establishment to the hard-nosed oil barons of Texas.

Kennedy had even inspired bitter enmity within his own administration. Vice President LBJ and the FBI's J. Edgar Hoover both had strong motives for seeing Kennedy dead: the former to stay out of jail, and Hoover to hang on to his job.

Kennedy had also acquired two other personal enemies, both capable of violent retribution and both with a serious grievance against him for his attacks on them: the family of the murdered South Vietnamese premier Ngo Dinh Diem and Cuba's Fidel Castro. Diem's family wanted revenge for his death, while *El Jefe Maximo* was only too well aware of the White House's openly expressed intention to remove him from power by any means. The Cuban leader had specifically warned the United States that any more attempts to kill him would be repaid in kind. On 7 September he told a Brazilian journalist: 'If the US leaders are aiding terrorist plans to eliminate Cuban leaders, then they themselves will not be safe. Let Kennedy and his brother Robert take good care of themselves, since they too can be the victims of an attempt which will cause their death.'

There was also clear warning of the assassination. Leaving aside the Cassandra-like croaks from the hospital bed of the drug-addict Rose Charamie, the clearest alarm bells that something was going to happen to the President are the three genuine advance warnings from Richard Nagell, Joseph Milteer, and even the FBI. According to Nagell, the plan to kill Kennedy had been devised by anti-Kennedy Cuban exiles whose ranks had been penetrated by Lee Harvey Oswald on behalf of the FBI or CIA. Nagell swore blind that he had posted a registered letter, marked 'Personal to the Director of the FBI' on 13 September 1963, warning of the plot to murder the President. Hoover denied ever receiving such a letter.

Nagell had no reasons to lie and the FBI's Director had many. If nothing else, Nagell's extraordinary story implicates the Cuban Exiles, especially the CIA-backed Alpha 66, and also points the finger of suspicion directly at Hoover for both allowing the assassination to happen and also for helping to cover it up afterwards. Taken with all the other evidence, Nagell's testimony effectively accuses the FBI Director of being an accomplice to murder, both before and after the fact.

The FBI also received another unambiguous warning in good time from the White Supremacist Joseph Milteer. What makes Milteer such an important witness is that he correctly predicted not just the intention to kill the President but also the people involved and the precise method they would use – and well in advance, too.

We know that the police in Florida passed on the information to the national domestic security agency, the FBI, and they in their turn should have alerted both the Secret Service and the Dallas Police. The FBI failed to do so, either through bureaucratic incompetence or, more likely, on the orders of J. Edgar Hoover, who appears to have sat on this vital piece of intelligence.

But the FBI received other intelligence of the plot. On 19 August 1963, one Garrett Trapnell alerted the FBI that a group of Cubans had considered an assassination attempt earlier in the spring but 'felt that there had been a leak, that the authorities knew of the plot so they decided to postpone the attempt until late August or September 1963.' This intelligence needed to be taken with a pinch of salt – Trapnell had form as a con man – but 10 days later his wife confirmed his story. Trapnell then revealed that the real plan was to kill *John* Kennedy, not his brother.

The FBI did nothing. They seem to have treated Trapnell's warning as coolly as the FBI's own warning signal to the Secret Service on 15 November, informing them of a threat from 'militant groups ... to assassinate the President'. However, the FBI report then downplays the risk, adding that there was 'no information that would indicate any danger to the President in the near future or during his trip to Texas.'

Another clear indication of a threat came from the Army signals operator Private Eugene Dinkin who had gone AWOL from France, claiming that he had learned of a military/CIA plan to kill the President. There is evidence that

Dinkin's allegations were passed to the CIA, the White House and the Justice Department – which of course included Hoover at the FBI. Dinkin was locked up for his pains. (See section "THE ROAD TO DALLAS".)

From this wide selection of intelligence and warnings comes one inescapable conclusion – that the FBI and its Director J. Edgar Hoover had been given plenty of warning that something was in the wind to put the President's life in danger. The testimony of William S. Walter, the FBI New Orleans duty operator for the night of 16/17 November, gives final confirmation of this. Walter later swore under oath that he received an AirTel alert from FBI headquarters in Washington about 'a threat to assassinate President Kennedy November 22/23 in Dallas by a militant revolutionary group,' and 'immediately contacted the SAIC [who] instructed me to call the agents that had responsibility and informants. I noted the names and times of the agents that I called.'

There can be no doubt, when reviewing the threat and the warnings, that by November 1963 the FBI had more than enough intelligence indicators that an attempt was going to be made on President Kennedy's life around the time of his Dallas trip. J. Edgar Hoover suppressed nearly all of this vital information and didn't pass it on to the Secret Service, who were responsible for guarding the President. Or, if he did, then the Secret Service seems to have been either remarkably complacent, incompetent – or something much worse.

While there can be little argument about the accuracy and timelines of the various warnings, the question of exactly who had an *opportunity* to kill the President is nothing like so clear cut.

'Opportunity' implies access to Dealey Plaza on the day and therefore, by extension, to the buildings in the vicinity, the plans for the presidential visit plus any security arrangements. Closest in was the presidential security detail who were actually in and around the presidential limo: beyond that was the Secret Service back-up; then the Dallas Police; Sam Bloom, the Zionist owner of the Dal-Tex building, together with oil millionaire 'Dry Hole' Byrd, the owner of the depository; the Mafia and their friends; and finally anyone in the crowd who had seen the motorcade's planned route as printed in the *Dallas Morning News.*

The fact was that there were an awful lot of people who had the opportunity to take a pot shot at Jack Kennedy on 22 November in Dallas.

Not surprisingly, the list of those who actually confessed to the President's murder is much smaller. The clearest admission of involvement and foreknowledge came from Marita Lorenz, the CIA and FBI undercover agent and the mistress of CIA contract officer Frank Sturgis who reported seeing E. Howard Hunt, Jack Ruby and Lee Harvey Oswald – or his double – in the Dallas Hotel the night before the shooting discussing how they would shoot the President. After the assassination she said that Sturgis had boasted to her about the shooting in Dealey Plaza and said that she 'had really missed the big one.'

Lorenz's claims are important, because *they have been accepted as legal testimony.* They were made on oath in 1985 at the civil trial of the CIA's E. Howard Hunt during a defamation case against a magazine which had insisted that CIA man Hunt had been involved in the assassination in Dallas on the day. The jury believed Lorenz's version of events and accepted that the CIA officer had been present in Dealey Plaza with Sturgis and his Cuban gunmen on 22 November 1963.

As to the gunmen themselves, the likely suspects come down to eight potential gunmen and possibly even more. Chief of these is a confessed professional hit man named Charles Harrelson, who died in prison in 2007 while serving a life sentence for the murder of US District Court Judge John H. Wood Jr. Harrelson made a partial confession to the Kennedy murder and admitted that he was present in Dallas. However, following his death in jail, we will never know for certain.

The most compelling claim to have actually fired the shot that killed President Kennedy comes from James

Files, a.k.a. James Sutton. Files, apparently under pressure, confessed to firing a Fireball .222 rifle from the Grassy Knoll. Needless to say, Files's story has been vigorously rubbished by others who have studied the assassination, some of whom have links with the CIA, and others who have their own theories to sell; but, on the information to hand, Jim Files does appear to be a prime suspect, as does his partner Charles Nicoletti.

We know that Nicoletti was a notorious killer for the Chicago mob and there is no shortage of proof that he was a recognised Mafia gunman. Files claimed that both he and Nicoletti were in Dealey Plaza on the day with a contract to 'whack Kennedy', and produced – albeit reluctantly – a stack of evidence to support his claim.

Another known gunman identified in Dallas on 22 November was LBJ and Ed Clark's 'tame' hitman, Mac Wallace. Fingerprint evidence places Wallace in the depository on the day and, with his record as a murderer and his links with LBJ and Ed Clark, Mac Wallace is a natural suspect for any assassination team on LBJ's home turf.

Perhaps less clear is the role of a Corsican hit man named Lucien Sarti. Sarti was a known killer and a member of the French underworld based in Marseilles. He had previous links with Meyer Lansky as part of the 'French Connection' drug trafficking organisation and appears to have been hired by Louis Bloomfield of Permindex. Sarti was named as a possible Kennedy gunman in 1990 by two other Corsican gangsters, Michel Nicoli and Christian David. Sarti competes with Files as the best candidate for the man who fired the fatal shot from the Grassy Knoll, and is believed by many to have been the 'Badge Man'; the man in the police uniform on the grassy knoll.

One French gunman who was definitely in Dallas around the time of the shooting was the Frenchman Michel Mertz, using the alias of his criminal rival 'Jean le Souetre' and working out of Canada. We can be certain of the presence of this known killer because, thanks to the Freedom of Information Act, we have the FBI/CIA and

Immigration Service records of his detention and deportation from the United States two days after the shooting. Significantly, Mertz appears to have left the US for Paris via Toronto or Montreal, Permindex's base, and in 1977 the French Secret Service admitted the presence of a French national in Dallas on 22 November.

This small army of gunmen and their supporters in or around Dealey Plaza is augmented by at least two others, both with track records linking them either to the Mafia or the CIA: Operation Hemming and 'Jim' Eugene Brading. Hemming was an ex-Marine and Marita Lorenz's sworn testimony places him in the CIA 'Operation 40' convoy that journeyed to Dallas on the eve of the assassination.

At a 1996 conference on the JFK assassination Hemming was recorded as saying:

> Prior to, probably, March or April '62, it had always been Fidel, Fidel. The money's available. The first time the conversation shifted, was gonna 'do the guy that has to be done' [a euphemism for Kennedy]

was at that point in time. But that conversation was killed, very quick. The first big one, with someone that was persistent, was with Banister, at [unintelligible] house ... I stepped off to one side. Banister wanted to yak on this JFK business.'

Lorenz also names Hemming as a member of the CIA's 'Interpen' anti-Communist brigade of US soldiers of fortune. The 'Inter Continental Penetration Force' also provides a significant link to a number of others suspected of involvement in the assassination, because Frank Sturgis of the CIA, Dave Morales, David Ferrie, Carlos Marcello's employee, and Loran Hall of the Cuban Exiles logistic team were all closely linked with Hemming and with the CIA's Cuban attack groups of one sort or another – and all were vehemently anti-Kennedy.

The second gunman with known CIA-Mafia links who happened to be in Dealey Plaza at 12.30 on 22 November 1963 was Eugene Hale ('Jim') Brading. Brading was an ex-convict on licence with close links to Carlos Marcello and David Ferrie. Carrying false documentation and calling himself 'Jim Braden' he had broken the terms of his parole and travelled out of state from California to Dallas to meet oil millionaire Lamar Hunt on 21 November, ostensibly to discuss the oil business. Jack Ruby was present at that meeting. Brading booked into the Cabana Motel that night and we know that Jack Ruby later visited him there as well. Next day Brading was arrested coming out of the Dal-Tex Building immediately after the shooting. The DPD had nothing on 'Braden' and so let him go.

Contemplating this roll call of up to eight possible assassins and the evidence of their presence in and around Dealey Plaza on the day Kennedy was shot, it is hard to see how anyone can still claim that the President's death was the work of a single deranged gunman, acting alone.

When we combine this list of known gunmen or their associates with the list of those who acted strangely before or after the assassination, then the case for a well-organised conspiracy becomes even more compelling. Suspicious activity comes from four quarters: the

Mafia; the CIA and their Cuban friends; the Texas oil men; and the Secret Service. The curious actions of the CIA and the Cuban Exiles are also far from innocent. Someone quite blatantly impersonated Lee Harvey Oswald on at least five occasions, if not more. While the Mafia may have been able to achieve much, only the CIA could control the Cuban Exiles and build a false legend.

The Texas oil men in their turn behaved in a way that invites closer investigation. LBJ's Mr Fixit lawyer Ed Clark seems to have been responsible for a number of meetings with people and organisations with a vested interest in the President's removal. At least two of the oil barons he dealt with were personally linked to the events in Dealey Plaza; Lamar Hunt met Ruby and Brading the day before the shooting, and 'Dry Hole' Byrd actually owned the depository building.

Perhaps even more significantly, two of the principal characters allegedly involved with the events surrounding JFK's death fled from Texas immediately after the assassination. The oil millionaire H.L. Hunt was taken into 'protective custody' by Federal agents on 22 November and flown to Washington on Delta Flight 44, where he spent a week in a secure hotel in New York under 'FBI protection'. Chauncey Holt, Carlos Marcello's 'accountant', CIA contract operator and apparently one of the 'three tramps', was whisked off to Mexico on 23 November and stayed there surrounded by a small army of security bodyguards for three months. These apparently precautionary moves are extremely odd to say the least. Why would these two individuals need to run and hide? Who organised and paid for their official boltholes?

Perhaps the most curious activity of all was the behaviour of the Secret Service. Charged with the solemn duty of protecting the President of the USA, they appear to have committed a series of remarkable security blunders around the President's visit to Dallas, and were rightly censured by the HSCA for what appears to be gross incompetence. The Secret Service's cumulative failures are highly suspicious. While the drinks escapade the night before might be overlooked as merely the laddish, good ol' boy culture of the time, the presidential security detail cannot escape their culpability for permitting a motorcade diversion through Dealey Plaza that was completely contrary to their own standard operating procedures.

Added to the bizarre episode of stripping the close cover bodyguards off the presidential limo at Love Field, and then reducing the number of police motorcycle outriders and moving them to the rear, the Secret Service's role appears extremely odd.

Agent Greer's unprofessional lapse in virtually halting the presidential limo when it came under fire is yet another curious breach of standard operating procedure (he should have accelerated, not stopped) and has never been explained. It had the effect of making the President a virtually static target and it was the precise moment that the fatal 'volley of shots' ripped into the car. When combined with switching the coffins and tampering with the President's body whilst under Secret

Service guard between Dallas and Washington, plus their unseemly haste in 'cleaning up' the evidence in the presidential limousine after the shooting, the Secret Service's behaviour is more than suspicious; it is positively damning. Someone in their number stands accused of gross negligence at the very least – or something much, much worse. The finger of suspicion certainly points at their complicity in the events at Dallas.

There are two other curious events in Dealey Plaza that require explanation, and both involve Lyndon Baines Johnson. The night before the Dallas visit, LBJ called on the President in his Houston hotel and asked if Governor Connally – LBJ's close friend – could ride with him in the Vice President's car instead of Senator Yarborough. Kennedy refused; Connally's place as State Governor of Texas was to ride up with the President in the presidential limousine. LBJ insisted, then begged, and a violent row ensued between the two men that was heard by many. In the end LBJ stormed out.

Next morning at Love Field Governor Connally actually tried to climb into LBJ's car and had to be politely but forcefully taken by White House aides to the head of the motorcade and into the President's car. To further raise eyebrows, as the motorcade entered Dealey Plaza, LBJ was reported 'hunkered down' in the corner of his limo and listening carefully to a handheld police radio, tuned to the security channel.

In the circumstances, Governor Connally's anguished cry, 'My God! They are trying to kill us all!' as the bullets ripped into the car becomes an extremely curious *cri de coeur.* Why that plural, *'they'*? And why assume in the heat of the moment with a bullet through the chest and another in the forearm, that the bullets were really intended for someone else? The truth is that, like so many of the events connected with the assassination of John Kennedy we are once again in the presence of the abnormal: taken with LBJ's attempts to get Connally moved from the President's car to the Vice President's, it all adds up to something highly suspicious. LBJ and Connally seem to have known that someone was going to take a shot at the President.

The cover-up that followed the assassination reinforces these suspicions. It is obvious from the evidence that the events in Dealey Plaza were planned. Lee Harvey Oswald was clearly being set up and used by unknown forces long before 22 November 1963. To do that required a plan and a plan moreover that was deliberately laying a paper trail of false evidence which could be swiftly brought to public attention once the assassination attempt was over. Only those with access to federal agencies – or those malcontent elements within the agencies – could have put together the resources and coordinated the whole affair. Such actions were way beyond the competence of the mobsters of the Mafia.

The impossibly swift 'outing' of Oswald in the press and the obviously prepared 'press packs' speak loudly of news management. This area of expertise just happened to be the specialist province of two of the CIA's top black ops and propaganda experts: Cord Meyer and Dave Atlee Phillips. The Warren Commission's highly selective whitewash and their deliberate suppression of vital evidence is also indicative of an attempt to cover up by sweeping a lot of unpalatable truths under the carpet.

So too are the early deaths of an unusually large number of key witnesses, many of whom openly warned their friends that they were at risk because of what they knew about the assassination or the participants. That the new President connived at the cover-up is not in doubt. LBJ, J. Edgar Hoover and the CIA stand condemned by their own words and deeds. The supplementary question must therefore be not only 'who covered up and how?' but also, 'who benefited from covering-up the truth behind the assassination of JFK?'

The final question, 'who benefited most from the murder of President Kennedy?' leads us straight back into motive and the beneficiaries. Two suspects, however, stood to gain more than any other: Lyndon Baines Johnson and the state of Israel.

While the Mafia felt the heavy boot of the Federal Justice Department removed from their necks, and the Federal Reserve Bankers and the oil barons could carry on making money undisturbed, both LBJ and Israel were now able to *survive.* JFK's death removed a mortal threat to them both. If Kennedy had lived, LBJ would eventually have gone to prison in disgrace. Now as the new President he could demand any government file and make sure that it did not see the light of day for as long as he liked. And for the Government of Israel, Kennedy's demise not only removed an implacable roadblock from Israel's route to nuclear weapons, but also, thanks to LBJ, 'Israel's Texan friend', now guaranteed the continuation of the flow of American financial support and weapons without which Israel could not survive.

Israel also gained an added benefit, overlooked by many, from Jack Kennedy's death. By replacing JFK with LBJ in the White House, the Zionist dream of a 'Jewish President' was effectively now fulfilled. Not for nothing did LBJ make the opening of a new Synagogue in Texas one of his first official public trips, the first President ever to do such a thing. This highly symbolic gesture sealed LBJ's secret pact with Israel. During his term as President, LBJ would emerge as Israel's agent and benefactor. He would open the floodgates of American arms and money to Israel, he would turn a blind eye to Israel's nuclear ambitions and he would even overlook the deliberate murder of 37 American sailors by Israel's attack on the USS *Liberty* during the 1967 war. LBJ was not just sympathetic towards Israel: as President he acted as Israel's trusted man in the White House, ever ready to consider Israel's interests above America's.

With Kennedy dead, LBJ and Israel were saved from potential disaster; and J. Edgar Hoover could heave a sigh of relief at keeping his job.

33

HOW THE DEED WAS DONE

FALSE FACE MUST HIDE WHAT THE FALSE HEART DOTH KNOW.
SHAKESPEARE, *MACBETH*

It is clear from the evidence that there were at least three distinct conspiracies.

The first was the long-term operation to set up an unsuspecting patsy as the scapegoat to take the blame.

The second was the assassination itself.

Last, there was the prepared operation to cover the whole thing up afterwards.

With good planning and command and control, all three operations could be independent of each other, without knowledge of the other two. If nothing else, that would account for the large numbers of people who seem to have been involved. It also points to control by an individual or a group at the highest level and one who could influence or direct government agencies, the media and the Mafia.

By the middle of 1963, Jack Kennedy had effectively signed his own death warrant. In addition to his other policies by then he was preaching a reduction in the Cold War, planning to pull out of Vietnam, squeezing the Federal Reserve and signing a nuclear test ban treaty, whilst at the same time closing down support for the Cuban Exiles and threatening the government of Israel.

From July 1963 onwards the plot accelerated. Financial support came from Texas millionaires who hated Kennedy: Sid Richardson, Clint Murchison, and Jean DeMenil (of the Schlumberger Corporation), and probably H.L. Hunt, augmented by secret subscriptions raised by their friends such as 'Dry Hole' Byrd.

As Israel had decided that as a matter of national policy Kennedy would have to be removed from office, Louis Bloomfield's Zionist network based on

Permindex and Canada mobilised its supporters throughout the United States, aided by Permindex employee Clay Shaw and Carlos Marcello's aide, David Ferrie. Their task was to act as the links between Marcello and Guy Banister at the New Orleans end.

Mossad was kept well informed through Bloomfield and Lansky of what was going on. The enterprise was by then being helped by disgruntled CIA officers like James Angleton, Cord Meyer and Bill Harvey, who were allowing their anti-Kennedy junior officers and the vengeful Cubans a free rein. Carlos Marcello and Santo Trafficante allowed their own Mafia gunmen to be recruited and, somehow, at least two key members of the Secret Service presidential security detail were suborned, probably by a few wellplaced bribes distributed by Clark on behalf of LBJ.

Secret planning meetings were held under the auspices of Ed Clark and members of the 8F Group in Texas, New Orleans and Mexico City. In Washington and New York the Establishment and the men of power would be aware that the 'problem of JFK' was being dealt with. For the club men of Manhattan, a nod was as good as a wink. That was all they needed to know. They were *certainly* not plotting to murder their President; but if someone else was, they knew – and approved.

In Mexico, the planning was coordinated by E. Howard Hunt and Dave Philips, under the command of the long serving Mexico CIA Head of Station, Win Scott, who worked direct to James Jesus Angleton at CIA headquarters in Langley. Scott was an outstanding CIA operator, who at various times had had three Mexican presidents on the CIA's payroll. Mexico City at the time resembled Cold War Berlin. The City was a 'hotbed of spies, revolutionaries, and assassins' and has been described as 'the Casablanca of the Cold War'. What Win Scott probably didn't know was exactly *why* Langley wanted him to set up a fake legend for Oswald.

Scott retired in 1969 and wrote a book about his time in the FBI, OSS and CIA. He completed the manuscript,

It Came Too Late, and made plans to discuss the book with CIA director Richard Helms in Washington on 30 April 1971. However, four days before the meeting Scott died of a sudden heart attack. No autopsy was performed. Angleton personally came to Mexico and took away his manuscript as well as three large cartons of files, including a tape-recording of the voice of Lee Harvey Oswald. When Michael Scott eventually got his father's manuscript back from the CIA, 150 pages were missing, chapters 13 to 16 were deleted in their entirety and everything about his life after 1947 had been removed on grounds of 'national security'.

Other key players such as Richard Nagell, Jim Brading, Billy Seymour and Emilio Santana all appear to have been involved at this stage. Some time in the summer of 1963, Lee Harvey Oswald joined the group as an undercover operator preparing for his next assignment in Cuba – or so he thought. Ex-FBI and CIA asset Guy Banister with FBI agent Jim Hosty were his day-to-day handlers and case officers. We will never know, but the odds are that Oswald was being gulled with some story that he was under deep cover to report to the FBI on a plot to assassinate the President. That would explain his clandestine links, the Hidell alias and the $200 FBI dollars a month pay packet.

By the autumn of 1963 it is unthinkable that J. Edgar Hoover was unaware of the growing plan. He did nothing. And if Hoover knew that something was being planned, then LBJ did too – the two men were too close and too exposed to the problem of what to do about JFK not to have communicated their concerns and their knowledge.

Attempts to kill JFK in Chicago on 2 November and in Tampa on 18 November had to be aborted but gave valuable experience to the plotters. They also provide us with hard evidence of two other 'patsies' in the towns, with suspiciously similar stories to Lee Harvey Oswald's. As the political pressure grew on the Kennedys to launch their secret coup in Cuba, so did the pressure on the plotters to make their move, and in Dallas on the 22nd they had their chance, aided by Israel's local sympathisers and some cooperation from elements in the US Secret Service.

The Israeli/Mossad link helped local Zionist collaborators to fix the motorcade route through Dallas and make sure that it was published in the press using Sam Bloom's PR company. Someone encouraged the Dallas Police to leave Dealey Plaza unsecured and someone arranged for Bloom's Dal-Tex Building to become the nerve centre of a well-arranged ambush. Local military intelligence protection teams had been warned off by someone in the Pentagon. The Secret Service stripped away the President's close-in protection at the last moment.

On 22 November, using Jack Ruby as their local coordinator and bagman, the four kill teams moved into place; three to Dealey Plaza and a back-up team of Cubans covering the Trade Centre in case the main ambush failed or was aborted. They may well not have known of the existence of the other teams; each gun group was a self-contained unit with at least one, and in some cases two, marksmen. Behind them in the gun teams was a protection man, with a radio, disguised as Secret Service or police to watch their backs; a disposal man to grab the rifle and hide it; and one getaway car for each team. All teams had fake Secret Service credentials and badges thanks to LBJ, Ed Clark and Chauncey Holt.

With three teams covering Dealey Plaza – one firing from the depository, a second from the Dal-Tex Building and the third from the Grassy Knoll – the triangulated crossfire on the kill zone was almost perfect. A close-in spotting team used an umbrella as a signalling device to trigger the ambush. To cover the snipers' final move into position, one of the plotters created a noisy diversion in front of the depository by faking an epileptic fit and drawing an ambulance to the scene at the crucial moment.

The principal marksmen appear to have been Mac Wallace and Seymour in the depository, Lawrence, Sarti or Files firing from the Grassy Knoll, and Nicoletti and Santana from the Dal-Tex

Building. Harrelson, Brading and Lawrence were the back-up men and co-ordinators. The whole operation was controlled from the Dal-Tex building by radioman Jim Hicks using small walkietalkies. Meanwhile the Cubans were waiting to get Kennedy at the Trade Centre in case the Elm Street ambush didn't come off.

The moment the shots were fired, the gunmen dispersed as calmly as possible. The individual escape plans worked well. The grassy knoll team split up; half along the fence and half behind the pergola. A white car left from behind the pergola and drove off about one minute after the shooting and disappeared under the triple underpass. Jack Lawrence rushed back to his job at the Lincoln Auto Agency and promptly was sick in the lavatory from shock and tension. Ten minutes later, the depository team came down the grass bank to their pale-coloured station wagon briefly stopped in Elm Street (which is where Deputy Craig saw Oswald look-alike Seymour running down the grassy bank) while the Dal-Tex group left out of the back of the building to be picked up by the driver. After 30 minutes a freight train started to roll out of the marshalling yards but was stopped by the police and the 'three tramps' discovered and detained.

The small plane at Redbird Airfield waited for hours, engine running (to the irritation of nearby residents), for either Oswald or the man ordered to shoot him. Tosh Plumlee flew the remains of what he believed was his CIA 'abort' team out later that afternoon. Clay Shaw was in California on the telephone the whole time. David Ferrie drove like a madman through the night to get to Houston in case anyone needed his services as a getaway pilot. At least one of the gun teams returned to the Fort Worth safe house, run by one of Ruby's dancing girls calling herself 'Tammy True', and stayed there in hiding for nearly a week.

Oswald himself appears to have been unaware of the magnitude of the plot. His brief, which he probably believed was a joint ONI/FBI attempt to penetrate and report on a plot to kill the President and then to use his inside knowledge and carefully constructed legend to get into Cuba, left him wide open as a fall guy. The irony is that Oswald didn't even fire a rifle that day. By the time he had gone to Oak Cliff to meet the contact who was due to take him to the airport that afternoon, the plot had started to come unglued. The plan was for Oswald to be shot on the run after gunning down the President, possibly by Officer Tippit. A dead assassin 'shot by the police while resisting arrest' would have stitched the whole story up nicely, leaving no loose ends and no one to talk. But something went wrong and the plan unravelled.

Dallas policeman Roscoe White is the most likely candidate for the murder of Officer Tippit, whose role seems to have been to act as taxi driver to get Oswald to the waiting plane at Redbird and shoot him on the way. Something went wrong. No one killed Oswald, who fled. Tippit himself was shot, almost certainly because he lost his nerve at the last moment. He knew too much and couldn't be allowed to talk. White deliberately scattered .38 revolver bullets – and possibly a billfold/wallet

– on the ground to incriminate Oswald, then ran off, leaving Oswald adrift to get to his fallback rendezvous at the Texas Theatre and meet his contact there. Instead he was betrayed and arrested – alive. Once in the hands of the Dallas police, a bewildered Oswald was doomed. He knew far too much and Jack Ruby was ordered to eliminate him, which he did with the help of his well-bribed friends in the DPD.

***

The inescapable conclusion in all this must be that J. Edgar Hoover of the FBI knew about the whole thing. Conclusion crystallises into likely fact: for Hoover to be on the telephone over 2000 miles away within less than 90 minutes of Oswald's arrest, briefing people in detail about Lee Harvey Oswald, is literally unbelievable: unless he was prepared for such an event. At best Oswald was supposedly only a low level ($200 a month) provincial FBI informer. For the chief of a continent-wide secret police force to have Oswald's detailed file to hand so conveniently that afternoon stretches credulity beyond belief. Hoover must have been ready and primed. And if Hoover knew what was in the wind, then the implications are profound.

Hoover would undoubtedly have told his good friend LBJ what was going on – and all the evidence indicates that LBJ was very much in the know. There can be little doubt that LBJ knew what was being planned. According to his mistress, Madeleine Brown, Johnson admitted as much to her quite openly on 31 December 1963. She claims that he said:

> Hell, that Irish Kennedy Mafia ... they came out with suicidal cuts in the Oil Depletion Allowance ... over $280 million! He [JFK] stopped half a dozen mergers under the Antitrust Act ... the market dropped 137 million dollars, steel fell 50% ... This was war to some rich fat cats we know ... He made plans to close 52 military bases in 25 states and was getting ready to quit in South East Asia. And he sent in the FBI to dismember another agency, CIA. America just couldn't have this!

Even assuming that Brown was writing many years later, the level of detail in these accusations is beyond any mere mistress's invention.

LBJ's Jewish friends would certainly have alerted him, as would J. Edgar Hoover and his Texas colleagues in the Suite 8F Group, especially his lawyer and partner in crime, Ed Clark. He is further implicated by Milteer's boast to Somersett, that the plot had been arranged by 'The Big Jew'. That can only be a reference to either LBJ or Louis Bloomfield. As Milteer had never met Bloomfield, it almost certainly refers to the tall and lanky Texan; in which case there is an even stronger reason to believe that LBJ knew all about the plan from the start and encouraged it.

He certainly cooperated quickly and enthusiastically in the cover-up afterwards, along with his close friend and ally J. Edgar Hoover and other key anti-Kennedy figures in the Washington Establishment such as *Life's* owners, the Luces, and Jock Whitney. However, a cover-up of that complexity required more than a presidential blessing to ensure its success. Someone at a lower level had to manage and control the whole affair for the media as well as the various federal agencies on a day-to-day basis. This was well beyond the capabilities of the Mafia and organised crime.

It seems no coincidence that the most likely CIA officers involved in the assassination are known to be experts in 'black ops' and media specialists. Jim Angleton, Cord Meyer, Dave Atlee Phillips and E. Howard Hunt were all men who had made their names on either black propaganda or 'news management'. All were implicated in the events surrounding the assassination. And all three were united in their dislike of the Kennedy boys.

The chain of command and the organisation of those principally involved in the murder of JFK can be best summarised by the diagram above.

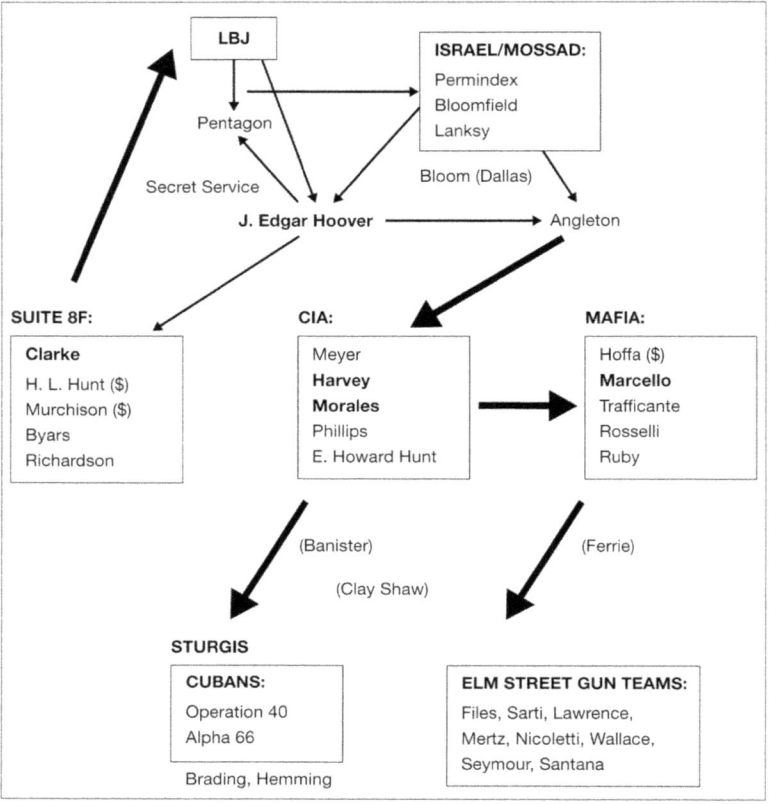

Who knew? The likely links of the assassins and their backers.

Such a complex operation is, by definition, difficult to plan, harder to manage and extremely difficult to keep secure. To have three separate stand-alone operations makes a lot of sense and fits the pattern of events. Such 'compartmentalisation' is also the obvious way to handle the problem of leaks and compromise, and there is some evidence that the various gun teams may have been unaware of the others' existence.

Equally, such a complex operation needs a good controlling brain, secure reliable communications and ample funds. This was well beyond the Mafia's capabilities. Instead it points directly to the coordinating role of Ed Clark, Louis Bloomfield's Permindex, and the disaffected rogue elements in the CIA as the behind the scenes puppet masters. They held the plot together and acted as its command and control element in Texas, Mexico, Florida, Chicago and Washington; which in turn points to CIA Counter-Intelligence Chief Angleton.

Even the American government now concedes that Lee Harvey Oswald could not have acted alone. In 1979 the House Select Committee on Assassinations (HSCA) reluctantly agreed that there must have been at least *four* gunshots in Dealey Plaza, not three. By confirming that there were at least four gunshots, the HSCA was admitting, officially, that there was more than one gunman in Dealey Plaza.

We have a considerable body of hard evidence that the organisation shown above is on the right lines. The conclusions that we can draw from the facts are even confirmed in some cases from the conspirators themselves. Despite the long held belief by some that there was no conspiracy because 'someone would have talked', several of those involved *have* talked over the years: there are at least eight confessions by individuals claiming to have inside knowledge of the plot.

In 1985 Carlos Marcello inadvertently confessed to his involvement in the plot to murder Jack Kennedy. He was not alone. Shortly before he died, in what amounted to a deathbed confession, CIA man E. Howard Hunt named Meyer, Morales, Harvey and Philips as conspirators in JFK's death and linked them all directly to LBJ – as had Jack Ruby. The confessions all point to and confirm the same thing: a joint CIA-Mafia-Cuban plot to kill the President. Further confirmation came in an explosive revelation in 2009 when a secret informant told the FBI that Carlos Marcello once told him during a prison yard conversation, 'I had the little bastard [JFK] killed. He was a thorn in my shoe.'

Van Laningham, who was at the Texarkana Federal Prison for bank robbery at the time, ratted out Marcello for the FBI in a deal that sprang the FBI informant from prison early. Marcello explained that Oswald had visited him in New Orleans and that 'he was my man. He did what the hell I told him to do.'

As for Jack Ruby, Marcello told his cellmate that Ruby, the Dallas strip club owner, was under his thumb, deeply in debt, and that he owed the Mafia Don 'big'. So Marcello, according to Van Laningham, ordered Ruby to pay off the debt by rubbing out Oswald. Thomas Kimmel, the FBI agent who supervised the informant, says he has no reason to doubt Van Laningham's story. Technology supported him. Van Laningham subsequently passed a polygraph test.

It is one of at least seven other confessions and admissions over the years:

1. Carlos Marcello's confession while delirious in prison hospital.
2. E. Howard Hunt of the CIA on his deathbed.
3. An inmate of a federal prison called Jim Files, a professional gunman.
4. LBJ's admissions to his mistress.
5. Dallas policeman Roscoe White's deathbed confession.
6. Mafia lawyer Frank Ragano's 1992 admission that in 1963 he took a message from Hoffa to Trafficante and Marcello: 'You won't believe what Hoffa wants me to tell you. Jimmy wants you to kill the President.'
7. Ragano added in 1994 that after Kennedy was killed, Hoffa said: 'I'll never forget what Carlos and Santos did for me.' Marcello later told Ragano: 'When you see Jimmy, you tell him he owes me – and he owes me big.'

These were not isolated revelations. For example, shortly after David Morales' death in 1978, HSCA investigator Gaeton Fonzi talked to his lifelong friend Ruben Carbajal and a business associate of Morales' named Bob Walton. Walton told Fonzi of an evening when Morales, after some hard drinking, went into a tirade about Kennedy and his failure to support the Bay of Pigs. Morales concluded with a satisfied grin, 'Well, we took care of that son of a bitch, didn't we?' Carbajal corroborated the story. Morales was also named by Howard Hunt as a participant in the JFK assassination.

With all these confessions, plus the supporting evidence, the structure of the conspiracy – indeed, several neatly interlocking conspiracies – slot into place like pieces in a jigsaw. The Mafia, the CIA and the Cuban Exiles all had motive, method and opportunity to kill the President of the USA. Texas oil billionaires, arms manufacturers, Wall Street and the state of Israel would all benefit if they did.

And, with Jack Kennedy dead, LBJ and J. Edgar Hoover would survive.

34

CONCLUSION

Looking back over 40 years to that historic day in Dallas we can see that the plot to assassinate John F. Kennedy was much more than a simple shooting. It was a high level, sophisticated and well-planned ambush that was cleanly executed and had a sound exfiltration plan, plus a complex and well prepared national-level cover-up afterwards. It was an assassination, but it was also effectively a *coup d'état* to place a different man in the White House.

At least two people suspected this from the start. Immediately he heard of his brother's murder, Robert Kennedy suspected that the Mafia – as well as the CIA and their tame Cuban exiles – were responsible. After all, what had happened was exactly what he himself was planning to do to Castro in his plan for a coup in Cuba a week later on 1 December. On the very afternoon of the assassination in Dallas:

(Bobby) frantically worked the phones at Hickory Hill – his Civil War-era mansion in McLean, Va. – and summoned aides and government officials to his home. Lit up with the clarity of shock, the electricity of adrenaline, Bobby Kennedy constructed the outlines of the crime that day – a crime, he immediately concluded, that went far beyond Lee Harvey Oswald, the 24-year-old ex-Marine arrested shortly after the assassination. Robert Kennedy was America's first assassination conspiracy theorist.

In public, Robert Kennedy was consumed with grief. However the reality is that, with his brother dead and his arch-enemy LBJ now sitting in the White House and commandeering all the relevant files, he was powerless. To family members, however, Bobby admitted, 'JFK had been killed by a powerful plot that grew out of one of the government's secret anti-Castro operations.' There was nothing they could do at that point, Bobby added, since they were facing a formidable enemy and they no longer controlled the government.

His sister-in-law, Jackie Kennedy, agreed with him. In 2011 the tapes of her private thoughts at the time were released by her daughter. The President's widow was unequivocal back in 1963 and 1964. She blamed Lyndon Johnson for the assassination and believed that was the work was a plot by a cabal of millionaire Texas businessmen. 'Jack said it to me sometimes. He said, 'Oh, God, can you ever imagine what would happen to the country if Lyndon were president?'

To the public at large, however, it looked at first like a communist plot. The finger of suspicion promptly pointed at Castro's Cuba. After all, was not Lee Harvey Oswald a known communist, a defector to the USSR and a friend of Cuba? America's new rulers knew full well that it was nothing to do with the Soviets but were only too happy to let Lee Harvey Oswald be demonised as the 'lone nut gunman' and a Communist returned from Russia to boot. Let him take the blame. Such a solution suited everyone nicely.

The Kremlin and its volatile leader Nikita Khrushchev had serious concerns with this version of events, however. In the tense atmosphere of the Cold War, loose accusations of Soviet complicity in the murder of the American President were dangerous and could lead to trouble. Having swiftly assured Washington and the trigger-happy Pentagon that it was nothing to do with them, the Soviet leadership ordered their own secret KGB investigation to find out what had really gone on.

The Kremlin inquest was masterminded by the KGB's most experienced investigator, and was a comprehensive review of all the Soviets' records and sources in the US, both open and classified. In America itself the investigation was led by Colonel Boris Ivanov, chief of the KGB residency in New York City, who mobilised all KGB resources in the US 'to solve the problem of who exactly had been responsible for Kennedy's death,' as he put it to a closed meeting of KGB and GRU staff on 25 November 1963. He also advised the assembled Soviet spooks that the assassination of

President Kennedy had been 'the work of an organised group, rather than the act of one individual assassin,' a view shared by Police Chief Curry of Dallas, J. Edgar Hoover, and the British Secret Intelligence Service.

Nearly two years later, by the middle of September 1965, the Kremlin had their answer. The KGB American *rezidentura* received orders from Moscow to open an in-depth investigation into all the 'existing personal relationship' between President Johnson and the Kennedy family, as 'data now indicated' that 'President Johnson had been responsible for the assassination of the late President Kennedy.' This Soviet bombshell was not shared with either the American public or the American government for obvious reasons. When an FBI source finally reported the information, it was unsurprisingly classified as 'Sensitive' and disappeared into J. Edgar Hoover's personal cache of 'Official and Confidential' files behind his private office.

In September 1965, the KGB finally briefed the Kremlin on the findings of their investigations into the assassination of the late President Kennedy. They told Khrushchev and the assembled Praesidium that 'the murder of President Kennedy in Dallas was not an isolated act; it was nothing less than a *coup d'état,* carried out by rogue elements in the US administration, backed by rich businessmen.'

***

The KGB was right. The murder of Jack Kennedy was no isolated act by a crazed individual. Charles de Gaulle's derisive laughter at the Warren Commission Report's far-fetched tale of some crazed lone gunman playing 'Cowboys and Indians in Texas' was well justified.

The assassination of President John F. Kennedy was a political assassination committed with a clear political aim, and one that had major political consequences. Above all else, the killing in Dallas removed a head of state who was determined to take the United States down a political path that was unacceptable to the invisible power brokers who really ran America at the time. Jack Kennedy's long-term mistress, Mary Meyer, realised immediately what had happened when she heard the news of her lover's murder. According to Timothy Leary, she telephoned him the very afternoon Kennedy was assassinated, 'very scared' and saying, 'they couldn't control him any more; he was going too fast.' That intimate insider's knowledge was to cost Meyer her life.

The assassination of John Fitzgerald Kennedy stands in stark contradiction to the ringing phrases, a century before, of his murdered predecessor Abraham Lincoln. On 19 November 1863 in his Gettysburg address, Lincoln, in words that have come to be accepted as one of the bedrocks of America's democratic ideals, told his listeners that those who died in the cause of preserving America's core values 'shall not have died in vain – that this nation, under God, shall have a new birth of freedom – and that the government of the people, by the people, for the people, shall not perish from this earth.'

The conspiracy to murder their own President in Dallas by a power-hungry clique of his rich and powerful fellow countrymen, determined to seize power for their own selfish ends, makes a complete mockery of any high-minded rhetoric about 'government of the people, by the people, for the people'.

John Fitzgerald Kennedy's untimely death in Dallas and removal from power was most certainly not democracy in action. And his assassination in what was effectively a *coup d'état* on 22 November 1963 – a conspiracy which has, ever since, been kept as a closely guarded secret by those responsible – was most definitely not America's finest hour.

APPENDIX

CIA Instructions to Media Assets

This CIA instruction dated 4/1/67 (US dating) to its field officers demonstrates just how defensive the agency was about the whole subject of the JFK assassination. That it was a sensitive document is clear from the fact that it was marked 'DESTROY WHEN NO LONGER NEEDED'.

CIA Document #1035-960, marked 'PSYCH', presumably for Psychological Warfare Operations, in the division 'CS', the Clandestine Services, sometimes known as the 'dirty tricks' department.

RE: Concerning Criticism of the Warren Report

1. Our Concern. From the day of President Kennedy's assassination on, there has been speculation about the responsibility for his murder. Although this was stemmed for a time by the Warren Commission report, (which appeared at the end of September 1964), various writers have now had time to scan the Commission's published report and documents for new pretexts for questioning, and there has been a new wave of books and articles criticizing the Commission's findings. In most cases the critics have speculated as to the existence of some kind of conspiracy, and often they have implied that the Commission itself was involved. Presumably as a result of the increasing challenge to the Warren Commission's report, a public opinion poll recently indicated that 46% of the American public did not think that Oswald acted alone, while more than half of those polled thought that the Commission had left some questions unresolved. Doubtless polls abroad would show similar, or possibly more adverse results.

2. This trend of opinion is a matter of concern to the U.S. government, including our organization. The members of the Warren Commission were naturally chosen for their integrity, experience and prominence. They represented both major parties, and they and their staff were deliberately drawn from all sections of the country. Just because of the standing of the Commissioners, efforts to impugn their rectitude and wisdom tend to cast doubt on the whole leadership of American society. Moreover, there seems to be an increasing tendency to hint that President Johnson himself, as the one person who might be said to have benefited, was in some way responsible for the assassination. Innuendo of such seriousness affects not only the individual concerned, but also the whole reputation of the American government. Our organization itself is directly involved: among other facts, we contributed information to the investigation. Conspiracy theories have frequently thrown suspicion on our organization, for example by falsely alleging that Lee Harvey Oswald worked for us. The aim of this dispatch is to provide material countering and discrediting the claims of the conspiracy theorists, so as to inhibit the circulation of such claims in other countries. Background information is supplied in a classified section and in a number of unclassified attachments.

3. Action. We do not recommend that discussion of the assassination question be initiated where it is not already taking place. Where discussion is active [business] addresses are requested:

a. To discuss the publicity problem with [?] and friendly elite contacts (especially politicians and editors), pointing out that the Warren Commission made as thorough an investigation as humanly possible, that the charges of the critics are without serious foundation, and that further speculative discussion only plays into the hands of the opposition. Point out also that parts of the conspiracy talk appear to be deliberately generated by Communist propagandists. Urge them to use their influence to discourage unfounded and irresponsible speculation.

b. To employ propaganda assets to [negate] and refute the attacks of the critics. Book reviews and feature articles are particularly appropriate for this purpose. The unclassified attachments to this guidance should provide useful background material for passing to assets. Our ploy should point out, as applicable, that the critics are (I) wedded to theories adopted before the evidence was in, (II) politically interested, (III) financially interested, (IV) hasty and inaccurate in their research, or (V) infatuated with their own theories. In the course of discussions of the whole phenomenon of criticism, a useful strategy may be to single out Epstein's theory for attack, using the attached Fletcher [?] article and Spectator piece for background. (Although Mark Lane's book is much less convincing that Epstein's and comes off badly where confronted by knowledgeable critics, it is also much more difficult to answer as a whole, as one becomes lost in a morass of unrelated details.)

4. In private to media discussions not directed at any particular writer, *or in attacking publications which may be yet forthcoming,* **the following arguments should be useful:**

a. No significant new evidence has emerged which the Commission did not consider. The assassination is sometimes compared (e.g., by Joachim Joesten and Bertrand Russell) with the Dreyfus case; however, unlike that case, the attack on the Warren Commission have produced no new evidence, no new culprits have been convincingly identified, and there is no agreement among the critics. (A better parallel, though an imperfect one, might be with the Reichstag fire of 1933, which some competent historians (Fritz Tobias, AJ.P. Taylor, D.C. Watt) now believe was set by Vander Lubbe on his own initiative, without acting for either Nazis or Communists; the Nazis tried to pin the blame on the Communists, but the latter have been more successful in convincing the world that the Nazis were to blame.)

b. Critics usually overvalue particular items and ignore others. They tend to place more emphasis on the recollections of individual witnesses (which are less reliable and more divergent—and hence offer more hand-holds for criticism) and less on ballistics, autopsy, and photographic evidence. A close examination of the Commission's records will usually show that the conflicting eyewitness accounts are quoted out of context, or were discarded by the Commission for good and sufficient reason.

    c. Conspiracy on the large scale often suggested would be impossible to conceal in the United States, esp. since informants could expect to receive large royalties, etc. Note that Robert Kennedy, Attorney General at the time and John F. Kennedy's brother, would be the last man to overlook or conceal any conspiracy. And as one reviewer pointed out, Congressman Gerald R. Ford would hardly have held his tongue for the sake of the Democratic administration, and Senator Russell would have had every political interest in exposing any misdeeds on the part of Chief Justice Warren. A conspirator moreover would hardly choose a location for a shooting where so much depended on conditions beyond his control: the route, the speed of the cars, the moving target, the risk that the assassin would be discovered. A group of wealthy conspirators could have arranged much more secure conditions.

d. Critics have often been enticed by a form of intellectual pride: they light on some theory and fall in love with it; they also scoff at the Commission because it did not always answer every question with a flat decision one way or the other. Actually, the make-up of the Commission and its staff was an excellent safeguard against over-commitment to any one theory, or against the illicit transformation of probabilities into certainties.

e. Oswald would not have been any sensible person's choice for a co-conspirator. He was a 'loner,' mixed up, of questionable reliability and an unknown quantity to any professional intelligence service. *[Archivist's note: This claim is demonstrably untrue with the latest file releases. The CIA had an operational interest in Oswald less than a month before the assassination. Source: Oswald and the CIA, John Newman and newly released files from the National Archives.]*

f. As to charges that the Commission's report was a rush job, it emerged three months after the deadline originally set. But to the degree that the Commission tried to speed up its reporting, this was largely due to the pressure of irresponsible speculation already appearing, in some cases coming from the same critics who, refusing to admit their errors, are now putting out new criticisms. g. Such vague accusations as that 'more than ten people have died mysteriously' can always be explained in some natural way e.g.: the individuals concerned have for the most part died of natural causes; the Commission staff questioned 418 witnesses (the FBI interviewed far more people, conducting 25,000 interviews and reinterviews), and in such a large group, a certain number of deaths are to be expected. (When Penn Jones, one of the originators of the 'ten mysterious deaths' line, appeared on television, it emerged that two of the deaths on his list were from heart attacks, one from cancer, one was from a head-on collision on a bridge, and one occurred when a driver drifted into a bridge abutment.)

5. Where possible, counter speculation by encouraging reference to the Commission's

Report itself. Open-minded foreign readers should still be impressed by the care, thoroughness, objectivity and speed with which the Commission worked. **Reviewers of other books might be encouraged to add** to their account the idea **that, checking back with the report itself, they found it far superior to the work of its critics.**

BIBLIOGRAPHY

Books

Ayers, Bradley Earl, *The War That Never Was: An insider's account of CIA covert operations against Cuba,* Indianapolis/New York, Bobbs-Merrill, 1976

Bamford, James, *The Puzzle Palace: Inside the National Security Agency, America's Most Secret Intelligence Organization,* New York, Penguin, 1982

Baker, Robert 'Bobby' Gene, with King, Larry L., *Wheeling and Dealing: Confessions of a Capitol Hill Operator,* New York, W.W. Norton, 1978

Belin, David W., *Final Disclosure: The Full Truth About the Assassination of President Kennedy,* New York, Scribner's, 1988

Belfield, Richard, *Terminate with Extreme Prejudice: Inside the Assassination Game – First-Hand Stories from Hired Killers and Their Paymasters,* London, Constable & Robinson, 2005

Benson, Michael, *Encyclopedia of the JFK Assassination,* New York, Facts on File, 2002

Blakey, G. Robert and Billings, Richard N., *The Plot to Kill the President,* New York, Times Books, 1981

Brown, Madeleine Duncan, *Texas in the Morning: The Love Story of Madeleine Brown and President Lyndon Baines Johnson,* Baltimore, Conservatory Press, 1997

Canfield, Michael and Weberman, Alan, *Coup d'Etat in America: The CIA and the Assassination of John F. Kennedy,* San Francisco, Quick American Archives, rev. edn 1992

Chambers, G. Paul, *Head Shot: The Science Behind the JFK Assassination,* New York, Prometheus Books, 2010

Crenshaw, Charles A., MD, with Shaw, J. Gary, Kizzia, D. Bradley, JD, Aguilar, Gary, JD and Wecht, Cyril, MD, JD, *Trauma Room One: The JFK Medical Coverup Exposed,* New York, Paraview Press, 2001

Curry, Jesse E., *Retired Dallas Police Chief Jesse Curry Reveals His Personal JFK Assassination File,* Dallas, 1969

Davis, John H., *Mafia Kingfish: Carlos Marcello and the Assassination of John F. Kennedy,* New York, McGraw-Hill, 1988

Eddowes, Michael, *The Oswald File,* New York, Clarkson N. Potter, 1977

Epstein, Edward Jay, *The Assassination Chronicles: Inquest, Counterplot and Legend,* New York, Carroll & Graf 1992

Farrell, Joseph P., *LBJ and the Conspiracy to Kill Kennedy: A Coalescence of Interests,* Adventures Unlimited Press, Kempton, IL, 2011

Fetzer, Dr James, PhD, *Assassination Science: Experts Speak Out on the Death of JFK,* Chicago, Open Court Publishing, 1997

Flammonde, Paris, *The Kennedy Conspiracy: An Uncommissioned Report on the Jim Garrison Investigation,* New York, Meredith Press, 1969

Fonzi, Gaeton. *The Last Investigation: A Former Federal Investigator Reveals the Man Behind the Conspiracy to Kill JFK,* New York, Thunder's Mouth Press, 1993

Garrison, Jim, *On the Trail of the Assassins,* New York, Sheridan Square Press, 1988

Giancana, Sam and Giancana, Chuck, *Double Cross: The Explosive, Inside Story of the Mobster Who Controlled America,* New York, Warner Books, 1992

Gibson, Donald, *The Kennedy Assassination Cover-Up Revisited,* New York, Novinka Books, 2005

Goldfarb, Ronald, *Perfect Villains, Imperfect Heroes: Robert F. Kennedy's War Against Organized Crime,* New York, Random House, 1995

Groden, Robert J., *The Search for Lee Harvey Oswald: A Comprehensive Photographic Record,* New York, Penguin Studio Books, 1995

—and Livingstone, Harrison Edward, *High Treason: The Assassination of President Kennedy and the New Evidence of Conspiracy,* New York, Berkley, 1990

Holland, Max, *The Kennedy Assassination Tapes: The White House conversations of Lyndon B. Johnson regarding the assassination, the Warren Commission, and the aftermath,* New York, Knopf, 2004

Hosty, James P., Jr, with Hosty, Thomas, *Assignment: Oswald,* New York, Arcade Publishing, 1995

Hunt, E. Howard, *An American Spy: My Secret History in the CIA, Watergate and Beyond,* Hoboken, NJ, Wiley & Sons, 2007

Joesten, Joachim, *The Dark Side of Lyndon Baines Johnson,* London, Peter Dawney, 1968

Jones, Penn, Jr, *Forgive My Grief: A Critical Assessment of the Warren Commission Report on the Assassination of President John F. Kennedy,* four vols, Midlothian, TX, *Midlothian Mirror,* 1966, 1967, 1969, 1974

Kantor, Seth, *Who Was Jack Ruby?,* New York, Everest House, 1978

La Fontaine, Ray and La Fontaine, Mary, *Oswald Talked: The New Evidence in the JFK Assassination,* Gretna, LA, Pelican Publishing, 1996

Lane, Mark, *Rush to Judgment: A Critique of the Warren Commission's Inquiry into the Murders of President John F. Kennedy, Officer J.D. Tippit and Lee Harvey Oswald* (1966), second edn, New York, Thunder's Mouth Press, 1992

Lifton, David S., *Best Evidence: Disguise and Deception in the Assassination of John F. Kennedy,* New York, Macmillan, 1980

Lynch, Grayston L., *Decision for Disaster: Betrayal at the Bay of Pigs,* Washington, DC and London, Brassey's, 1998

Manchester, William, *The Death of a President,* New York, Harper & Row, 1967

Mangold, Tom, *Cold Warrior: James Jesus Angleton: The CIA's Master Spy Hunter,* New York, Simon & Schuster, 1991

Marchetti, Victor and Marks, John D., *The CIA and the Cult of Intelligence,* New York, Knopf, 1974; paperback edn New York, Dell, 1989

May, Ernest R. and Zelikow, Philip D. (eds), *The Kennedy Tapes: Inside the White House During the Cuban Missile Crisis,* Cambridge, MA, Belknap Press, 1997

McClellan, Barr, *Blood, Money, and Power: How LBJ Killed JFK,* Los Angeles, Hannover House, 2003

Meagher, Sylvia, *Accessories After the Fact: The Warren Commission, the*

Authorities & the Report, New York, Vintage, 1992

—and Owens, Gary, *Master Index to the J.F.K. Assassination Investigations,* Lanham, MD, Scarecrow Press, 1980

Meyers, Dale, *With Malice: Lee Harvey Oswald and the Murder of Officer J.D. Tippit,* Milford, MI, Oak Cliff Press, 1998

Newman, John, *Oswald and the CIA,* New York, Carroll & Graf, 1995

North, Mark, *Act of Treason: The Role of J. Edgar Hoover in the Assassination of President Kennedy,* New York, Carroll & Graf, 1991

Oglesby, Carl, *The JFK Assassination: The Facts and the Theories,* New York, Signet, 1997

Phillips, David Atlee, *Secret Wars Diary: My Adventures in Combat, Espionage Operations and Covert Action,* New York, Stone Trail Press, 1988

Posner, Gerald, *Case Closed: Lee Harvey Oswald and the Assassination of JFK,* New York, Random House, 1993

Phillips, Donald T., *A Deeper, Darker Truth: Tom Wilson's Journey Into the Assassination of JFK,* Marion, IL, DTP/Companion Books, 2009

Ragano, Frank and Raab, Selwyn, *Mob Lawyer: Including the Inside Account of Who Killed Jimmy Hoffa and JFK,* New York, Scribner's, 1994

Roberts, Craig, *Kill Zone: A Sniper looks at Dealey Plaza,* Consolidated Press, 1994

—and Armstrong, John, *JFK: The Dead Witnesses,* Consolidated Press, 1994

Russell, Dick, *The Man Who Knew Too Much: Hired to Kill Oswald and Prevent the Assassination of JFK,* New York, Carroll & Graf, 1992

Russo, Gus, *Live By the Sword: The Secret War Against Castro and the Death of JFK,* Baltimore, Bancroft Press, 1998

Sample, Glen and Collom, Mark, *The Men on the Sixth Floor,* 2nd edn, Garden Grove, CA, Sample Graphics, 1997

Scheim, David E., *Contract on America: The Mafia Murder of President John F. Kennedy,* reprint edn, New York, SPI Books, 1992

Schreiber, G.R., *The Bobby Baker Affair: How to Make Millions in

Washington, Chicago, Henry Regnery, 1964

Scott, Peter Dale, *Deep Politics and the Death of JFK,* Berkeley, CA and London, University of California Press, 1993

Shesol, Jeff, *Mutual Contempt: Lyndon Johnson, Robert Kennedy, and the Feud That Defined a Decade,* New York, W.W. Norton, 1997

Smith, Matthew, *JFK: The Second Plot,* Edinburgh, Mainstream, 1992

Sol Estes, Billie, *Billie Sol Estes: A Texas Legend,* Granbury, TX, BS Productions, 2004

Summers, Anthony, *Conspiracy,* New York, McGraw-Hill, 1980

—, *Official and Confidential: The Secret Life of J. Edgar Hoover,* New York, G.P. Putnam's, 1993

—, *Goddess: The Secret Lives of Marilyn Monroe,* London, Gollancz, 1985

Thompson, Josiah, *Six Seconds In Dallas: A Micro-Study of the Kennedy Assassination,* New York, B. Geis Associates/Random House, 1968

Torbitt, William (pseud.), *Nomenclature of an Assassination Cabal,* Internet published; print edn Santa

Barbara, CA, Prevailing Winds Research, 1964

Valentine, Douglas, *The Strength of the Wolf: The Secret History of America's War on Drugs,* New York and London, Verso Books, 2004

Waldron, Lamar with Hartman, Thom, *Ultimate Sacrifice: John and Robert Kennedy, the Plan for a Coup in Cuba, and the Murder of JFK,* New York, Carroll & Graf, 2005

Weberman, Alan J. and Canfield, Michael, *Coup d'Etat in America: The CIA and the Assassination of John F. Kennedy,* rev. edn, San Francisco, Quick American Archives, 1992

Weisberg, Harold, *Case Open: The Unanswered JFK Assassination Questions,* New York, Carroll & Graf, 1994

—, *Post Mortem: JFK Assassination Cover-Up Smashed!,* Ipswich, MA, The Mary Ferrell Foundation, 2007

—, *Whitewash,* four vols, self-published, 1965–74; new edns, New York, Skyhorse Publishing, 2013: *Whitewash: The Report on the Warren Report;Whitewash II: The FBI–Secret Service Cover-Up; Whitewash III: The Photographic Whitewash of the JFK*

Assassination; Whitewash IV: The Top Secret Warren Commission Transcript of the JFK Assassination

Wrone, David, *The Zapruder Film: Reframing JFK's Assassination,* Lawrence, KS, University Press of Kansas, 2003

Useful articles

As well as the articles mentioned in the sources (see section "A NOTE ON THE SOURCES"), the following may be of interest:

Artwohl, Robert R., 'JFK's Assassination: Conspiracy, Forensic Science, and Common Sense', *JAMA: Journal of the American Medical Association,* 269 (12), 1993, 1540–3

Bickel, Alexander M., 'The Failure of the Warren Report', *Commentary,* October 1966

Epstein, Edward J. 'The Final Chapter in the Assassination Controversy', *New York Times Magazine,* 20 May 1969

Fonzi, Gaeton, 'The Warren Commission, the Truth, and Arlen Specter,' *Greater Philadelphia Magazine,* 1 August 1966

Garrison, Jim, 'The Playboy Interview: Jim Garrison', *Playboy,* October 1967

Holland, Max, 'The Assassination Tapes', *Atlantic Monthly,* June 2004

Jacobs, George and Stadiem, William, 'Sinatra and the Dark Side of Camelot', *Playboy,* June 2003. Jacobs had been Sinatra's valet.

Kempton, Murray, 'Warren Report: Case for the Prosecution', *New Republic,* 10 October 1964

Lane, Mark, 'The Playboy Interview: Mark Lane', *Playboy,* February 1967

Lattimer, John K. and Lattimer, Jon, 'The Kennedy-Connally Single Bullet Theory: A Feasibility Study', *International Surgery,* vol.50, no.6, December 1968

MacDonald, Dwight, 'A Critique of the Warren Report', *Esquire,* March 1965

McLynn, Frank, 'History isn't always a cock up', *New Statesman,* 20 September 1999. This article supports the idea that conspiracies should be scrutinised with academic rigour and not just dismissed.

Meagher, Sylvia, 'The Curious Testimony of Mr Givens', *Texas Observer,* 12 August 1971

Newsweek, 'Special Investigative Report': *The JFK Cover-Up: It's Not What You Think* (various authors), 22 November 1993. The eight most common theories (including the CIA, the Mafia, anti-Castro exiles, Castro, the KGB, and accidental shootings)

Olson, Don and Turner, Ralph F., 'Photographic Evidence and the Assassination of President John F. Kennedy', *Journal of Forensic Sciences,* vol.16, no.4, October 1971

Salandria, Victor J., 'The Impossible Tasks of One Assassination Bullet', *The Minority of One,* March 1966

Turner, William, 'The Garrison Commission on the Assassination of President Kennedy', *Ramparts,* January 1968 Wise, David, 'Secret Evidence on the Kennedy Assassination', *Saturday Evening Post,* 16 April 1968

Reports:

Government reports and documents

Report of the President's Commission on the Assassination of President Kennedy, plus 26 volumes of hearings and exhibits, September 1964, referred to as the 'Warren Commission'

Investigation by New Orleans District Attorney Jim Garrison into the assassination of President Kennedy, including Clay Shaw trial transcripts

Senate Select Committee to Study Governmental Operations with Respect to Intelligence Activities, 1975, known as the 'Church Committee'

House of Representatives Select Committee on Assassinations, investigation of the killings of John F. Kennedy and Martin Luther King, Jr, 95th Congress, 1976, known as 'HSCA'

The United States President's Commission on CIA Activities within the United States, by President Gerald Ford, 1975, known as the 'Rockefeller Commission'

Government documents held at the National Archives and Records Service, College Park, MD

Assassination Records Review Board

CIA Inspector General, 'Inspector General's Survey of the Cuban Operation', October 1961, CIA History Staff files, HS/CSG-2640

Federal Bureau of Investigation, John F. Kennedy Files concerning the President's Commission on the Assassination of President Kennedy

FRONT COVER FLAP

JFK AN AMERICAN COUP D'ETAT
THE TRUTH BEHIND THE KENNEDY ASSASSINATION

Ever since President John F Kennedy was gunned down in Dallas fifty years ago various theories have swirled around what was a key event in American – and world – history. JFK's death affected the Cold War, Vietnam, and the economic and social history of the United States.

Whatever the conclusions of the US official Warren Report – that the President had been assassinated by a lone gunman, Lee Harvey Oswald – many people doubt that to be true. Indeed, President Nixon later admitted on tape that the report was 'a hoax committed on the American people.'

John Hughes-Wilson, a former colonel in British Intelligence, set out in 2007 to go through the millions of words and thousands of pieces of evidence, to put together an intelligence jigsaw of what really happened that dreadful high noon in Dallas in 1963. The result is a dramatic exposure of what really happened and a clear indication that, while some of the pieces of that jigsaw may be missing, the truth is emerging. While the US Federal Archive still keeps a million documents relating to the case under lock and key, he has uncovered enough information available for us now to see the overall picture. It is beyond reasonable doubt that Jack Kennedy was the victim of a plot to remove the President of the United States.

John Hughes-Wilson highlights the facts behind:
- The myth of 'Camelot'
- Jack Kennedy's insatiable sex life
- Why Marilyn Monroe had to be silenced
- How the President was blackmailed by J Edgar Hoover
- LBJ's corrupt and murderous secrets
- How the Kennedys secretly planned a coup in Cuba
- How a hero of the revolution wanted to work for the CIA

- Why Israel and the White House were openly at loggerheadsp
- How the Mafia manipulated politicians and the CIA
- Rogue elements in the CIA
- How the assassination was covered up- and why
- What the KGB discovered

Reading this book no-one can be in any doubt that JFK's life was not at the hands of a lone deranged gunman, but a deadly plot to remove a President who threatened vested interests at home and abroad.

BACK COVER FLAP

COLONEL JOHN HUGHES-WILSON, is one of Britain's leading military historians, and a well-reviewed author and commentator on a wide range of intelligence and military historical subjects. He was selected to be the author of the Imperial War Museum's History of the First World War For 2014. John has been a frequent broadcaster for BBC television and radio and worked alongside Huw Edwards and David Dimbleby providing commentary for events including the Falklands 25th Anniversary and Cenotaph memorial. During his twenty-five years in the Intelligence Corps and as a Special Forces Operations officer John saw active service in the Falkland Islands, Cyprus, Arabia, and Northern Ireland as well as the dangerous jungles of Whitehall and NATO.

Index

A
8F Group, *106, 181, 185, 187, 192*
5412 Group, *23*
Alba, Adrian, *233*
Alderson, Dr Lawrence, *292*
Aldrich, Nelson, *116, 117*
Aléman, José, *174*
Almeida, Juan, *210*
Alpha 66, *85, 177, 201, 223*
Altgens, Ike, *321, 334*
Alyea, Tom, *323*
Andrews, Jim, *354*
Angleton, James, *44, 192, 194, 195, 462, 532, 534, 540, 543, 548*
arms industry, *14, 16, 112, 226*
Arnold, Gordon, *267, 269, 334, 336*
Arvad, Inga, *40*

assassination of JFK,
bullet questions concerning, *299, 301, 302, 304, 306, 459, 469*
CIA officers cheer, *78*
confessions regarding, *515, 517, 548, 549*
as coup d'état, *550, 556*
cover-up concerning, *420, 422, 424, 425, 427, 430, 431, 433, 435, 436, 438, 440, 441, 443, 445, 524, 526*
day of, *255, 257, 259, 260, 262, 264, 265, 267, 269, 270, 271, 274, 275, 278, 280, 536, 538, 540*
deaths following, *44, 471, 473, 474, 477, 478, 480, 482, 484, 486, 487, 489, 491, 528*

films and photographs of, *260, 265, 269, 312, 319, 321, 323, 325, 326, 328, 330, 332, 334, 336*
see also Zapruder, Abe,
Garrison investigation into, see Garrison, Jim,
genuine advance warnings of, *509*
guns and shots questions surrounding, *308, 310, 312, 314, 315, 317, 319, 338, 339, 342, 343*
see also Warren Commission, intelligence precedes, *221*
KGB probe into, *554, 556*
and kidnapping of body, *280, 281, 436*
most Americans support conspiracy in, *502*
and motorcade route, *242, 244*
night before, *250, 252, 254, 255*
planning of, *199, 201, 203, 204, 205*
potential sites for, *203*
principal marksmen for, *538*
Secret Service files disappear after, *231*
three distinct conspiracies in, *530, 546*
and 'three tramps', *278, 280, 540*
weeks and days before, *221, 223, 224, 226, 227, 229, 231, 233, 235, 236, 238, 240, 242, 244, 246, 247, 248*
Assassination Records Review Board, *242, 408, 468, 504*
Atsugi, *365, 366, 368, 374*
Ayers, Capt. Bradley, *179*

B

Baker, Bobby, *50, 129, 136, 138, 140*
Banister, Guy, *231, 240, 391, 393, 400, 493, 497, 532, 534*
Barnes, Tracy, *21*
Barris, George, *64*
Bartlett, Charles, *145*
Baruch, Bernard, *116*
Batista, Fulgencio, *18, 94, 213*
Becker, Ed, *175*
Belin, David, *345, 363*
Belknap, Jerry, *260, 262*
Bellah, Sgt, *343*
Belmont, Alan, *433, 435, 457*
Ben-Gurion, David, *151, 153, 155, 157, 158, 160, 191, 194*
Benavides, Domingo, *350, 356, 477*
'Bishop, Maurice', *223, 224*
Bissell, Richard, *26*
Blakey, Robert, *338*
Bloom, Sam, *224, 242, 257, 417, 513*
Bloomfield, Louis, *188, 191, 192, 194, 224, 248, 497, 517, 532, 543*
Bogard, Al, *482, 484*
Boggs, Thomas Hale, *452, 459, 500, 502*
Bond, Wilma, *323, 334*
Boswell, Dr Thornton, *296*
Bowers, Lee, *259, 274, 484, 486*
Brading, 'Jim' Eugene, *518, 520, 522, 534, 538*
Brennan, Howard, *259, 270*
Bringuier, Carlos, *393, 395, 397*
Bronfmann, Edgar, *191*
Bronfmann, Sam, *188, 224, 248*
Brown & Root, *2, 106, 112*
Brown, George, *252*
Brown, Madeleine, *250, 252, 541, 543*

Bufalino, Russell, and Castro, *171, 174*
Bundy, McGeorge, *26*
Burton, Richard, *62*
Bush, George H.W, *21*
  as CIA asset, *25*
  whereabouts, vagueness of, *280*
Byars, Billie, *103, 106, 187*
Byrd, D. H. 'Dry Hole', *112, 187, 513, 522, 532*

C

Cabell, Gen. Charles, *26, 27, 88, 457*
Cabell, Earle, *252, 457*
Campbell, Judith, see Exner, Judith,
Capone, Al, *8, 94, 179*
Carbajal, Ruben, *549*
Carr, Richard, *259, 260, 425, 459*
Carr, Waggoner, *106, 231, 233*
Carter, Cliff, *130, 133*

Castro, Fidel, *14, 18, 19, 21, 23, 25, 26, 27, 30, 83, 85, 162, 209, 210*
  and Cuban missile crisis, *33*
  and JFK shooting, *287*
  and LHO, see under Cuba,
  plots to kill, *97, 168, 171, 174, 175, 177, 204, 213, 214, 235, 397, 508, 509*
Cellar, *254, 255*
Cellini, Dino, *254*
Central Intelligence Agency (CIA), *77, 78, 79, 82, 83, 85, 87, 88*
  condemned by own words and deeds, *528*
  and Cuba, *19, 21, 23, 25, 26, 27, 30, 35, 77, 78, 82, 83, 85, 87, 88, 166, 168, 171, 174, 213, 214, 223, 391, 395, 397, 406*
  FBI raids camp of, *223*

and harmonisation with FBI line, *461, 462*
and Israel's nuclear plans, *151, 157*
JFK seeks to weaken, *82, 83, 194*
and Mafia, *95, 97, 166, 168, 170, 177, 179*
and Operation 40, *23*
origin of, *77*
tight surveillance by, on LHO, *397*
Centro Mondiale Commerciale (CMC), *188, 191*
Charamie, Rose, *248, 509*
Christchurch Star, *430, 431*
Civello, Joe, *252*
Clark, Ed, *106, 130, 133, 134, 136, 183, 185, 203, 250, 252, 520, 522, 532, 538, 543*
    coordinating role of, *540*
Clemmons, Sgt Jack, *67*
Cold War, *30, 147, 160, 532, 554*
    see also Soviet Union,
Commission, The, *92, 94*
    see also Mafia,
Connally, John, *106, 221, 252, 254, 299*
    JFK–LBJ car row over, *262, 524, 526*
    wounds to, *264, 301, 302, 304, 312, 343*
Cooper, John, *452, 459*
Corson, William, *25*
Costello, Frank, *8*
Craig, Roger, *260, 315, 317, 486, 487*
Crichton, Jack, *21*
Crozier, Ron, *224*
Crump, Raymond, *44*
Cuba, *16, 18, 19, 21, 23, 25, 26, 27, 30, 32, 33, 35, 74, 77, 78, 79, 82, 83, 85, 87, 88, 94, 207, 209, 210, 213, 214, 216, 218*

Bay of Pigs, *19, 21, 23, 25, 26, 27, 30, 78, 82, 88, 207, 508*
  gun-running to, *171*
  and LHO, *389, 391, 393, 395, 397, 422*
  and Mafia, *18, 35, 97, 166, 168, 170, 177, 179*
  missile crisis, *32, 33, 207, 209*
  and Plan Amworld, *35*
  US decides to destabilise, *21*
Cubela, Rolando, *213, 397*
Curry, Chief Jesse, *236, 306, 425*

D

Dallas Morning News, *140, 238, 334, 513*
Dassault, Marcel, *147*
David, Christian, *517*
Davis, Deborah, *48, 50*
Davison, Henry, *117*
Day, Lt, *315, 317, 430*
de Gaulle, Charles, *158, 556*
de Mohrenschildt, George, *383, 385, 389, 489*
del Valle, Eladio, *231, 489, 497*
DeMenil, Jean, *532*
Dickinson, Angie, *39, 40*
Diêm, Ngô Dình, *164, 508*
DiMaggio, Joe, *59*
Dinkin, Eugene, *236, 509*
Dobrynin, Anatoly, *33*
Dougherty, Jim, *57*
Dulles, Allen, *25, 77, 78, 79, 82, 83*
  JFK fires, *83*
  on Warren Commission, *452, 454, 455, 457, 459*
Duran, Silvia, *398*
death of, *489, 497*
  Shaw denies meeting, *498*

E

Edwards, Col. Sheffield, *97*
Eisenhower, Dwight, *14, 16, 79*
Ellis, Sgt, *312, 443*
Escalante, Fabian, *21*
Eshkol, Levi, *157*
Estes, Billy Sol, *129, 134*
Exner, Judith, *39, 44, 46, 60, 62, 170*

F

Fair Play for Cuba Committee, *218, 231, 240, 389, 395, 413*
Federal Bureau of Investigation (FBI),
　CIA training camp raided by, *223*
　entire plot likely known by, *541*
　and Files claim, *315*
　and harmonisation with CIA line, *461, 462*
　investigation taken over by, *290*
　and JFK's affairs, *40, 42, 46, 51, 53, 57, 62*
　and Kennedys' affairs, *66*
　and LBJ, *136*
　see also Johnson, Lyndon B.,
　'lone nut' media plants by, *433*
　and Mafia, *46, 94*
　and Monroe, *57, 62*
　and Nagell, *240, 242*
　stories leaked by, *342*
　warnings passed to, *509, 511, 513*
Federal Reserve, *110, 114, 116, 117, 119, 121, 122, 125*
　establishment of, *117, 119*

Jekyll Island meeting concerning, *116, 117*
JFK's Executive Order concerning, *110, 125*
for-profit entity, *116*

Feinberg, Abraham, *145*
Feldman, Mike, *149*
Ferrie, David, *83, 175, 192, 231, 238, 240, 365, 391, 393, 400, 406, 495, 497, 498, 518, 532, 540*
Files, James, *314, 315, 515, 517, 538, 549*
FitzGerald, Desmond, *213*
Fonzi, Gaeton, *549*
Ford, Gerald, *450, 500*
Franqui, Carlo, *210*
Frazier, Buell, *257*
Friedman, Milton, *119*
Fritz, Capt. Will, *315, 317, 408, 409, 413*
Fruge, Lt Francis, *248*
Fulbright, William F., *147*

G

Gable, Clark, *64*
Garfield, James A., *122*
Garrison, Jim, *88, 240, 330, 495, 497, 498*
Gauntlet, William, *397*
General Dynamics, *112*
Giancana, Sam, *6, 8, 35, 44, 46, 48, 60, 138, 223*
  and Castro, *97, 168, 170, 171, 174*
  killing of, *487*
Gibson, Lois, *278*
Goldwater, Barry, *95*
Gonzalez, Pedro, *238, 240*
Gould, Deborah, *71*
Graham, Katherine, *48, 50*
Graham, Robert, *240*
Grandison, Lionel, *71*

Great Apalachin Mafia Bust, *99*
  see also Mafia,
Greer, Bill, *264, 265, 332, 524*
Groden, Robert, *336*
Guantánamo, *23, 26, 30*
Guevara, Che, *209, 210, 213*

H

Hall, Loran, *406, 518*
Halliburton, *112*
Halpern, Sam, *87*
Hamilton, Capt. James, *70*
Hardee, Julius, *259*
Harrelson, Charles, *278, 515, 538*
Harris, Martin, *203*
Harvey, William, *87, 88, 231, 397, 487, 532, 548*
Hathcock, Sgt, *319*
Hecht, Rudolf, *191, 192*
Hemming, Jerry, *518*
Hicks, Jim, *538*
Hill, Clint, *265, 280*
Hill, Jean, *461, 462*
Hill, Ralph, *138, 140*
Hoffa, Jimmy, *60, 66, 67, 170, 171, 174, 177, 235, 549*
  and Castro, *97, 174*
  and JFK shooting, *287*
  and LHO shooting, *408*
Holland, Sam, *274, 459*
Hollingworth, Gen. James F., *21*
Holt, Chauncey, *278, 280, 522, 538*
Hooker, Joe, *145*
Hoover, J. Edgar, *46, 48*
  condemned by own words and deeds, *528*
  and doctored film, *312, 330*
  entire plot likely known by, *541*
  fails to warn JFK, *175, 177*
  and Freemasons, *457*
  and JFK shooting, *289, 312, 425*

JFK threat known by, *181*
and Kennedys' affairs, *40, 42, 46, 51, 53, 57, 62, 66*
and LBJ, *136, 181, 185, 187*
see also Johnson, Lyndon B.,
'lone nut' media plants by, *433*
and Mafia, *46, 94*
and Monroe, *57, 62*
motives of, *508*
Nagell's warning letter to, *509*
and oil, *106*
presidential commission favoured by, *449*
and RK, *46, 51*
RK hated by, *99*
and Sullivan, *489*
Hosty, Jim, *235, 236, 417, 534*
House Select Committee on Assassinations, *236, 332, 336, 438, 468, 487, 504, 540, 541*
Howard, Tom, *477, 478*
Hughes, Robert, *323, 334*
Hughes, Judge Sarah, *289*
Humble Oil, *106*
Humes, Dr James, *296, 298, 299, 438, 440, 459*
Hunt, E. Howard, *21, 247, 248, 515, 534, 543, 549*
 confession of, *548*
Hunt, Haroldson L., *103, 106, 187, 254, 522, 532*
Hunt, Lamar, *520, 522*
Hunter, Bill, *477, 478*
Hurt, Lt Col., *412, 413*
Hyde, Johnny, *57*

I

Ince, Claire, *140*
International Anti-Communist Brigade, *85*
Israel, *142, 144, 145, 147, 149, 151, 153, 155, 157, 158, 160, 162, 188, 191, 192, 194*

and Arabs, US partiality in conflict between, *145*
'controls the US Senate', *147*
and nuclear weapons, *149, 151, 153, 155, 157, 528*
Truman recognises, *147*
US alliance with, start of, *147, 149*
see also American Israel Public Affairs Committee; Anti-Defamation League; Jewish influence on US; Mossad,

J

JKF's meeting with, *151, 153*
JFK fires, *83*
Jackson, Andrew, *121*
Jackson, J. W., *477*
Jacobs, Arthur, *70*
Jacobs, George, *48*
January, Wayne, *244, 246, 247, 424*
Jefferson, Thomas, *108, 110*
Jenkins, Jim, *298, 299, 306*
Jewish influence on US, *142, 144, 145, 147, 149, 151, 153, 155, 157, 158, 160, 162*
and Senate, *147*
see also American Israel Public Affairs Committee; Anti-Defamation League; Israel,
Johnson, Josefa, *133, 134*
Johnson, Lady Bird, *140, 262*
Johnson, Lyndon B., *127, 129, 130, 133, 134, 136, 138, 140, 181, 183, 185*
on assassination day,

see under assassination of JFK,
ballot-rigging by, *2, 129, 130*
blackmail by, *450, 452*
bribery by, *2, 130*
and Brown, *250, 252*
committee investigates, *140*
condemned by own words and deeds, *528*
and Connally car choice, *262, 524, 526*
entire plot likely known by, *541, 543*
five charges that could ruin, *129*
and Freemasons, *457*
Hoover's relationship with, see under Hoover, J. Edgar,
Jewish interests supported by, *158, 160*
and JFK assassination, *201, 203*
JFK threat known by, *181*
KGB probe accuses, *554, 556*
and Kirkwood, *254*
and LHO shooting, *424*
and Mafia, *95, 177*
and 'magic bullet', *301*
motives of, *508, 528*
murders ordered by, *129*
and oil, *106*
personal fortune of, *183*
seen as Israel's benefactor, *528*
sworn in, *287, 289*
and Vietnam, *112*
Jones, Penn, *486, 491*
JFK's body kidnapped by, *280, 281, 436*

remarkable security blunders by, *522, 524*
warning phoned to, *204*
and Zapruder film, *326*

K

Kellerman, Roy, *280*
Kelman, Dr Jeffrey, *37*
Kennedy, Edward 'Teddy', *12, 97*
Kennedy family, Mafia links of, *8*
Kennedy, Jacqueline, *40, 552*
  on assassination day, see under assassination of JFK,
  and JFK's casket, *294*
  and LBJ swearing-in, *289*
Kennedy, John F.,
  affairs of, *39, 40, 42, 44, 46, 48, 50, 51, 53, 55, 57, 59, 60, 62, 64, 66, 67, 70, 71, 72*
  see also Monroe, Marilyn,
  anti-Semites target, *145*
  assassination of, see assassination of JFK,
  autopsy on, *292, 296, 298, 299, 301, 440*
  autopsy photographs of, *336*
  Ben-Gurion's meeting with, *151, 153*
  and casket, *294, 296*
  coalition against, detailed, *164, 166, 168, 170, 171, 174, 175, 177, 179*
  coalition against, widening, *181, 183, 185, 187, 188, 191, 192, 194, 195*
  death of, *278*

embalming of, *440, 441*
enemies amassed by, *160, 164, 505, 508*
Hoover's scrutiny of, see under Federal Bureau of Investigation; Hoover, J. Edgar,
ill health of, *37, 39*
inauguration of, *2, 4, 39, 40*
JK's press campaign against, *145*
kidnapped body of, *280, 281, 436, 440*
Marcello's threat to kill, *174, 175*
postmortem surgery on, *296, 435, 436, 438, 440, 441, 443*
previous-marriage rumours concerning, *42*
and recreational drugs, *48, 50*
seeker after peace, *160*
votes cast for, *6*
Kennedy, Joseph Jr, *12, 53*
Kennedy, Joseph Sr,
affairs of, *40*
alcohol stockpiled by, *11*
anti-Semitism of, *144, 145*
becomes UK Ambassador, *11*
and Mafia, *6, 8*
and Pantages, *10*
RKO created by, *10*
Kennedy, Regis, *325, 489*
Kennedy, Robert, *12*
coup d'état suspicions of, *550, 552*
and Cuba, *33, 35, 83, 87, 550*
Cuba coup oversight given to, *213*

elite surprised at appointment of, *97*
grief-stricken, *447*
Hoffa assaults, *100*
Hoffa's hatred of, *99, 100, 170, 177*
Hoover's hatred of, *99*
Hoover's scrutiny of,
see under Federal Bureau of Investigation;
Hoover, J. Edgar, and LBJ, *136, 140*
see also Johnson, Lyndon B.,
and LBJ swearing-in, *289*
and Mafia, *46, 48, 99, 100, 171, 550*
Marcello deported by, *175*
and Monroe, see Monroe, Marilyn,
presidential ambitions of, *97, 99*

'Special Group' role of, *85*
Warren believed a fraud by, *502*
KGB, *216, 366, 368, 379, 382, 385*
  assassination probe of, *554, 556*
  see also Soviet Union,
Khrushchev, Nikita, *18, 162, 213, 216, 554*
  and Cuban missile crisis, *32, 33, 35, 207, 209*
Kilduff, Malcolm, *281*
Kilgallen, Dorothy, *480*
Killam, Hank, *474, 477*
Kimmel, Thomas, *548*
Kinser, Doug, *133, 134*
Kirkwood, Pat, *254, 255*
Kissinger, Henry, *108*
Koethe, Jim, *477, 478*

L

La Follette, 'Fighting Bob', *119*

Lane, Mark, *495*
Lansky, Meyer, *8, 18, 92, 94, 95, 144, 168, 188, 191, 194, 254, 404, 406, 517, 532*
Lawford, Peter, *48, 57, 62, 64, 66, 72*
Lawrence, Jack, *484, 538*
Lawson, Winston, *236, 242*
Leary, Timothy, *50, 60, 556*
LeMay, Curtis, *16*
Lemnitzer, Gen. Lyman, *16, 18*
Lewis, David L., *400*
Liebeler, Wesley, *464, 466*
Life, *136, 138, 328, 330, 427, 430, 457, 466, 498, 543*
Lifton, David, *298, 436, 440*
Lilienthal, Alfred, *145*
Lincoln, Abraham, *121, 122, 557*
Lindbergh, C.A., *119*
Ling Temco Vought (LTV), *112*
Lipsey, Lt Richard, *294*
Little Caesar, *92*
Long, Russell, *495*
Lopez, Gilberto, *218*
Lorenz, Marita, *247, 248, 515, 518*
Luce, Henry, *457, 543*
Luciano, Charles 'Lucky', *92, 94, 168*

M

McClellan, Barr, *183, 252*
McCloy, John, *452, 454, 455, 457*
McCone, John, *83, 462, 500*
McFadden, Louis T., *121, 122, 125*
Macmillan, Harold, *53*
McWillie, Lewis, *187, 406, 408*
Mafia, *90, 92, 94, 95, 97, 99, 100, 508*
   arrival of, in US, *90*

and CIA, *95, 97, 166, 168, 170, 177, 179*
and Cuba, *18, 35, 97, 166, 168, 170, 177, 179, 214, 404, 406*
Hoover blackmailed by, *46*
and LHO shooting, *408*
and Monroe, *59, 60*
and oil, *106*
and omertà, *90*
and Phenix City, *197, 199*
presidential election bought by, *6, 46*
and Prohibition, *8, 92*
and Ruby, see Ruby, Jack, Serve U front of, *138*
and Teamsters, *170, 171*
Malcolm, Durie, *42*
Marcello, Carlos, *100, 174, 175, 177, 187, 199, 223, 233, 238, 252, 254, 391, 404, 495*
and Castro, *97, 171, 174*
confession of, *548*
immigration charges against, *255, 257, 259, 260, 262, 264, 265*
and JFK shooting, *287*
'only a tomato salesman', *325, 489*
Marchetti, Victor, *378*
Markham, Helen, *347, 348, 350, 356, 409, 459, 495*
Marrs, Jim, *274*
Marshall, Henry, *134, 136*
Martin, Jack, *493, 495, 497*
Martin, Jim, *477, 478*
Martineau, Maurice, *229*
Masferrer, Rolando, *235*
Masseria, Joe, *92*
Meagher, Sylvia, *466*
Meir, Golda, *149*
Mercer, Julia Ann, *257, 259, 461*

Mertz, Michel,
  see Roux, Michel,
Meyer, Cord, 44, 526, 532, 543, 548
Meyer, Mary, 39, 44, 48, 50, 556
  death of, 44
Miller, Austin, 310
Miller, Murray, 235
Millican, A.J., 269, 270
Milteer, Joseph, 216, 218, 418, 509, 543
Mob,
  see Mafia,
Monroe, Marilyn, 39, 55, 57, 59, 60, 62, 64, 66, 67, 70, 71, 72
  death of, 55, 66, 67, 70, 71, 72
  diary of, 64, 66, 71
  'Happy Birthday, Mr President' sung by, 62
  see also Kennedy, John F.: affairs of,
Monrow, Robert, 231
Moorman, Mary Ann, 321, 334

Morales, David, 168, 179, 213, 489, 518, 548, 549
Mossad, 155, 158, 187, 188, 191, 192, 194, 248, 532, 536
Moyers, Bill, 242, 449
Mullins, Chief, 218
Murchison, Clint, 103, 106, 187, 250, 252, 254, 532

N

Nagell, Richard, 240, 242, 509, 534
Nasser, Gamal Abdel, 147
National Security Council, 23
New York Times, 431, 433
Nichols, H. Louis, 415
Nicoletti, Chuck, 204, 487, 489, 517, 538
Nicoli, Michel, 517
Nix, Orville, 323, 334
Nixon, Richard, 6, 74, 252
  and Cuba, 21, 88
  and Mafia, 95
  on Warren Report, 466

whereabouts, vagueness of, *280*
Norton, Charles, *117*
Novotny, Mariella, *51*
NUMEC, *153*

O

O'Connor, Paul, *296, 298, 306*
Odio, Sylvia, *224*
Office of Naval Intelligence (ONI), *366, 368, 375, 378*
   LHO files destroyed by, *427*
Office of Strategic Services (OSS) (later CIA), *77, 94, 188*
Oil Depletion Allowance, *103, 106*
Operation Amworld, *397*
Operation 40, *21, 23, 85, 201, 247, 518*
Operation Mongoose, *85*
Oswald, Lee Harvey, *78, 192, 221, 223, 226, 227, 229, 231, 233, 235, 281, 282, 285, 363, 365, 366, 368, 371, 372, 374, 375, 376, 378, 379, 382, 383, 385, 387, 389, 391, 393, 395, 397, 398, 400, 402, 420, 422, 424, 425, 427*
   as 'Aleksei Hidell', *240, 308, 310, 361, 387, 413*
   arrest of, *282, 285, 360, 361*
   on assassination day, see under assassination of JFK,
   birth of, *363*
   bound over, *393*
   charged with JFK murder, *292, 413*
   charged with Tippit murder, *292, 412*
   CIA's tight surveillance on, *397*
   and communism, *365, 371, 372*
   court-marshalled, *368, 371*

cover-up concerning, *420, 422, 424, 425, 427, 430, 431, 433, 435*
and Cuba, see under Cuba,
'defection' of, *374, 375, 376, 379, 382*
doctored photograph of, *415*
and guns, see under assassination of JFK; Warren Commission,
'lone nut', *290, 433, 455, 502*
Lopez's similarity to, *218*
many support innocence of, *502*
in Marines, *365, 366, 368, 371, 372*
marriage of, *382*
net closes on, *281, 282*
ONI destroys files on, *427*
overheard conversation concerning, *292*
paraffin tests on, *290, 319, 412*
in police custody, *282, 285, 290, 292, 408, 409, 412, 413, 415, 417, 418*
Ruby shoots, *418*
'sightings' of, *224, 226, 227, 229, 233, 235, 247, 259, 260, 278, 285, 287, 348, 350, 358, 387, 398, 400, 482, 520, 540*
and Tippit shooting, see Tippit, J.D.,
unaware of magnitude of plot, *540*
US return of, *382, 383*
and Warren Commission, see Warren Commission,
Oswald, Marguerite, *415, 461*

Oswald, Marina, *227, 382, 383, 385, 387, 389*

P

Paine, Michael, *227, 229, 389*
Paine, Ruth, *227, 229, 389*
   Pantages, Alexander, *10*
Parker, James, *70, 71*
Parr, Duke, *130*
Partin, Ed, *174*
Paterson, B.M., *350*
Patman, Wright, *114*
Patterson, Albert, *197, 199*
Pawley, Bill, *487*
Permindex, *158, 187, 188, 191, 192, 497, 532, 540*
Perry, Dr, *441*
Phillips, Dave Atlee, *168, 179, 224, 227, 391, 395, 526, 534, 543, 548*
Pitzer, Lt Cdr Bill, *486*
Plan Amworld, *35*
Plumlee, 'Tosh', *285, 540*
Pringle, Eunice, *10*
Profumo affair, *50, 51*
Prohibition, *8, 10, 11, 92*
Prouty, Fletcher, *110, 502*
Prowse, Juliet, *48*

Q

Queen Bee, *366*
Quorum Club, *50, 138*

R

RK hated by, *99, 100, 170*
Rabin, Yitzhak, *287*
Ragano, Frank, *549*
Ramsey, Prof. Norman, *342*
Rankin, Lee, *454*
Rather, Dan, *330*
Rayburn, Sam, *130*
Revill, Lt, *306*
Reynolds, Warren, *350, 477*
Richardson, Sid, *103, 106, 187, 254, 532*
RKO Pictures, JK creates, *10*
Roberts, Delphine, *231*

Roberts, Earlene, *281, 352*
Roberts, Emory, *262*
Roberts, Jack, *183, 185*
Robinson, Edward G., *92*
Robinson, Mike, *290, 292*
Robinson, Thomas, *440, 441*
Rogers, Charles, *278, 280*
Rometsch, Ellen, *39, 50, 51, 62*
Roosevelt, Franklin D., *94*
   Ambassador by, *11, 12*
Rose, Earl, *280, 281*
Rosenbaum, Tibor, *187, 191, 194*
Ross, Robert G., *252*
Rosselli, Johnny, *85, 168, 177, 179, 285*
   and Castro, *97, 171, 174, 214, 216*
   killing of, *487*
Rostow, Eugene, *449*
Rothschild, Mayer Amschel, *108*
Roux, Michel (a.k.a. Mertz; le Souetre), *248, 292, 517, 518*
Rowley, Chief James J., *242, 445*
Ruby, Jack, *171, 187, 192, 216, 223, 252, 398, 400, 402, 404, 406, 408, 409, 413, 415, 417, 418, 474, 477, 520, 522, 536*
   arrests of, *404*
   business meeting of, *238*
   and Charamie, *248*
   dangerous to know, *480*
   death of, *491*
   death sentence on, *491*
   gun-running by, *404, 406*
   interstate calls made by, *235*
   LHO shot by, *418*
   under Marcello's thumb, *548*
   mug shot of, *259*

at Parkland Hospital, *302*
sudden pay-off to, *408*
Willis's photograph of, *334*
Russell, Bertrand, *493*
Russell, Richard, *301, 450, 452, 459*
Russia,
  see Soviet Union,
Russo, Perry, *497, 498*

S

St Louis Post-Dispatch, *441*
Santa Anna, *26, 77, 78*
Santana, Emilio, *534, 538*
Sarti, Lucien, *517, 538*
Schepps, Julius, *224*
Schlesinger, Arthur, *160, 162*
Schweiker, Richard, *379, 466, 468, 504*
Scott, Win, *534*
  Secret Service,
    on assassination day,
      see under assassination of JFK,
    JFK warned by, *95*
Senator, George, *477, 478*
Serve U, *138, 482*
Seymour, William, *398, 400, 534, 538*
Shapiro, Zalman, *153*
Shaw, Clay, *187, 188, 191, 192, 240, 330, 391, 497, 532, 540*
  murder charge against, *88*
  trial of, *438, 487, 497, 498*
Siegel, Bugsy, *8*
Silbert, Agent, *296*
Similas, Norman, *269, 323, 336*
Simmons, James L., *274*
Sinatra, Frank, *48, 59, 64*
Slatzer, Robert, *64, 66*

Smith, Mrs Earl T., *480*
Smith, Matthew, *244, 247*
Snyder, Richard, *374*
Somersett, Willie, *216, 218, 418, 543*
Sorrels, Forest, *242*
Souetre, Jean, *292*
Soviet Union: and Cuban missile crisis, *32, 33, 207, 209*
   see also Cold War,
   and LHO, *365, 366, 368, 374, 375, 376, 378, 379, 382, 383, 385*
   and US Cuba ambitions, *213, 214, 216*
Specter, Arlen, *457, 461*
Spindel, Bernie, *60, 67*
Stalin, Joseph, *166*
   death of, *79*
Starnes, Richard, *79*
Stevenson, Adlai, *221*
Stevenson, Coke, *130*
Stockdale, Grant, *482*
Strong, Benjamin, *117*
Sturgis, Frank, *168, 247, 248, 515*
Sullivan, William, *489*
Swanson, Gloria, *39, 40*

T

Tague, James, *306, 310, 461*
Taylor, Elizabeth, *50, 62*
Taylor, Henry, *42*
Teamsters, *60, 170, 171*
Texas Movie Theatre, *281, 360, 361*
Thomas, Albert, *289*
Thornberry, Judge, *240*
Tippit, J.D., *238, 281, 345, 347, 348, 350, 352, 354, 356, 358, 360, 361, 409, 540, 541*
   LHO charged with murder of, *292, 412*

Tolson, Clyde, *97*
Trafficante, Santos, *6, 18, 100, 174, 231, 404, 406, 487, 532, 549*
   and Castro, *97, 171, 174, 235*
   and Patterson murder, *199*
Trapnell, Garrett, *511*
Truitt, Jim, *50*
Truman, Harry S., *78, 79, 147*

U

Underhill, Gary, *473, 474*
US Steel Corporation, *102*

V

Valee, Thomas, *204*
Vanderlip, Frank, *117*
Varona, Tony, *214, 238, 240*
Veciana, Antonio, *223, 224*
Vietnam War, *110, 112, 162, 226, 227*
Vinson, Robert, *285*

W

Wade, Henry, *306, 413*
Walker, Maj. Gen. Edwin, *387, 389*
Wallace, Mac, *129, 130, 133, 134, 136, 185, 252, 517, 538*
Wallace, Mary André, *133*
Walter, William, *238, 511*
Walthers, Buddy, *306*
Walton, Bob, *549*
Warburg, Paul M., *117*
Warren Commission, *447, 449, 450, 452, 454, 455, 457, 459, 461, 462, 464, 466, 468, 469*
   acknowledged as whitewash, *462*
   conclusions of, *462, 464*
   on LHO, *282*
   lies and inaccuracies in, *466*
   mandate of, *452, 454*
   members of, *450, 452*

omissions by, *454, 466*
Prouty slams, *502*
Select Committee damns, *468*
and selective evidence, *347, 457, 459, 526, 528*
on shots fired, *270, 301, 332, 338, 339, 342, 347*
see also assassination of JFK: guns and shots questions surrounding,
and Tippit shooting,
  see Tippit, J.D.,
Warren, Earl, *447, 449, 450, 491*
Watergate, *88*
Weaver, Jack, *334*
Weiss, Dr Victor, *248*
Weissman, Bernard, *238*
West, Joe, *315*
Westbrook, Capt., *361*
Whaley, Bill, *412, 491*

White, Roscoe, *235, 292, 540, 541, 549*
Wilcott, Jim, *379*
Willis, Philip, *269, 321, 332, 334*
Wilson, Woodrow, *114, 116, 119*

Y
Yarborough, Ralph, *262*

Z
Zangretti, Jack, *474*
Zapata, *25*
Zapruder, Abe, film shot by, *265, 319, 321, 323, 325, 326, 328, 330, 332, 336, 343, 427, 457*
  at Garrison hearing, *498*
  see also assassination of JFK: films and photographs of,

www.ingramcontent.com/pod-product-compliance
Ingram Content Group UK Ltd.
Pitfield, Milton Keynes, MK11 3LW, UK
UKHW021315180426
11947UKWH00015B/1245